Making Jesus Known Today and Tomorrow

Spreading the Gospel in Twenty-First Century Britain

Edited by

Martin Erwin and Stephen McQuoid

First published in 2023 by Counties UK
30 Haynes Road, Westbury, BA13 3HD

25 24 23 22 21 / 5 4 3 2 1

British Library Cataloguing in Publication Data
A catalogue record for this book is available from the British Library.

ISBN 978-1-7391283-1-9

Typeset and cover design by ProjectLuz.com
Printed and bound in Great Britain
for Counties UK
by Bell & Bain, Glasgow

Contents

Contributors

Rupert Abbott cut his teeth in cross-cultural ministry while working in the inner city of Birmingham in the 1980s. He then spent ten years in Muslim communities in northern Pakistan followed by nine years in Buddhist Thailand. Latterly he has served as Missions Director with Echoes International.

Beverley Bedford is a gifted preacher, teacher, trainer and mentor. She grew up in Northern Ireland and at 20 years of age joined the ranks of The Faith Mission in Scotland. Now married and living in North Devon, she has served as a Counties evangelist and as Training Officer with Counties.

Jacquie Bodman gave her life to Jesus, aged 12, after he answered a desperate prayer miraculously. Since then, God has moved mightily in her life in many ways. She joined Counties in 2018 and has had many years of evangelistic experience. She is a pastor's wife and serves as a church deacon.

Tim Cracknell spent 25 years in dairy farming before being called to replant an extinct church in Cinderford, Gloucestershire. 18 years on, Forest and Wye Community Church is thriving there, is replanting in Ross-on-Wye, and has a strong online presence. Tim is married to Katrina, a former schoolteacher.

Gordon Curley and his wife, Penny, are based in Fareham and work full time as evangelists with 'Counties' in Hampshire. They enjoy the challenge of sharing the Christian message with a variety of age-groups and in a variety of situations, e.g., churches, pubs, schools, youth clubs, their home—in fact, wherever an opportunity opens up!

Phil Davies was at university in Cardiff and then served for 19 years with OM. He returned to Swansea, and joined Counties as an evangelist in 2004.

He is one of the leaders in Dunvant Christian Fellowship, Swansea. Phil is married to Sheila, and they have four married children and 10 grandchildren.

Martin Erwin comes from Northern Ireland but has spent the last 30 years in England with Counties. He planted Challenge Community Church in Hereford and in 2016 became CEO of Counties. He is married to Rachel and they have three adult daughters. They fellowship with Queensway Chapel, Melksham.

Allan McKinnon was a cross-cultural missionary for 17 years in Tanzania, East Africa where he was involved in Bible teaching and training local church leaders. Since 2010, he has been on the staff of Tilsley College, Motherwell, now as Principal. He is also church planting in south Glasgow.

Jacqui McKinnon worked as a children's and community nurse and then in mission, caring for children and serving the community at Moshi, Tanzania. Caring and hospitality have always featured in her Christian ministry, including sharing Jesus in the home at a growing church plant in south Glasgow.

Stephen McQuoid has been General Director of GLO Europe since 2010 and before that was Principal of Tilsley College. He is a trustee of Counties. He preaches and teaches in many churches in the UK and abroad, and is a prolific writer. He is married to Debbie and they have three children.

Matt Rich has been in full-time mission work of various forms for more than 30 years and set up the first UK online mission in the year 2000. He is currently both a global online missionary and a pastor of an independent local church in Cumbria.

Neil Summerton was a government official for many years and at the same time a local church leader. For the last 25 years, he has largely devoted himself to extending God's Kingdom, including through writing and editing, and furthering the work of Partnership and the International Brethren Conferences on Mission.

Dave Symons has been a Counties evangelist for 15 years, helping churches and Christians in North and Mid Devon to reach people with the gospel. He works with young people through events and small groups, including in a local sixth form college. He and Katie have two daughters, Eloise and Annabel.

Aderyn Taylor-Roberts has a background in arts curation, education, business marketing, and management. She is a developer of people and ideas and is passionate about breaking down barriers of entry to church, using social media and online platforms. She lives in the Forest of Dean and is a church leader there.

Bob Telford joined Counties as evangelist for Warwickshire, following Bible College and five years' evangelistic work with another Midlands organization. He became a national evangelist with Counties in 1996. He now has an international evangelistic and teaching ministry, while mentoring and training incoming evangelists for Counties and advising churches on revitalization.

Paul Willmott has worked in ministry with children and families since 1995. A Counties Evangelist, he works with primary schools, to help to connect them with local churches, and speaks at church-based outreach events. He is the creator of Twist Online, short puppet videos exploring big faith questions for children.

Introduction

Martin Erwin

In March 2020 when the global pandemic took hold, we all knew that the world had radically, and perhaps irreversibly, changed. This book was conceived then, as together (and often alone) we grappled with the new reality, the new norm, without ever fully understanding what it was, what it would look like, or how it would change us.

Since the worldwide shock of COVID-19, Europe has seen a land war in the Russian invasion of Ukraine, and the cost-of-living crisis which has followed. Politics feels broken with 2022 seeing a merry-go-round of Prime Ministers in the UK, and cynicism reaching new heights (or depths) even for us notoriously cynical 'Brits'.

In this fast-changing landscape, two things have become more evident to many of us who are both observers and participants in these times. The first may on the surface seem negative, while the second is more encouraging. Perhaps both can be seen together, as preparation for what God might do among us in the coming days.

First, the crisis of the decline and closure of many local churches has accelerated. Crises will do that—hasten a trajectory that already seemed baked in. For example, the move from cash to cashless purchasing, and from the High Street to online shopping, are two related demonstrations of such a social acceleration. Both were already happening, but increased exponentially during the pandemic, with a return to pre-pandemic patterns unlikely ever to happen. In the case of local churches, if they were struggling in 2019, they might have lasted another ten years before apparently inevitable closure. But

COVID forced closure of some and accelerated the decline of others, and, like businesses, many of the latter will not recover.

Secondly, there has been a definite upturn of spiritual interest, even a growing hunger and thirst for purpose and meaning in the souls of British people. During the first lockdown 1 in 4 British people accessed online Christian worship and other online Christian material. This number held up consistently from April to August 2020.[1]

While, no doubt, these numbers will have dropped significantly once life got back to 'normal', this metric should not be overlooked quickly. People are thirsty for water that satisfies. When everything that they depended upon to cover or soothe their aching souls, such as entertainment and shopping, were removed, the ache was exposed, and the search for God and community (a community which the church provided in remarkable ways during the pandemic) was unleashed in the heart of a hungry nation.

So, on the one hand, decline was hastened, yet, on the other, at one and the same time, the very hunger for God that we have prayed for became quickly and vitally evident.

Stories that began to emerge during the pandemic, of God at work, saving and changing lives, have continued. Such stories are often told in our own Counties quarterly, *Ignite*. In our own church, where we had seen little fruit and few baptisms over the three years before 2020, we ran online and then in-person Alpha courses. People began turning to Christ, and still are. Counties evangelists were able to help discover and demonstrate how God was at work, and churches that were willing to adapt their methods to overcome the obstacles and grasp the opportunities saw seekers in growing numbers and droplets of blessing begin to dampen previously parched ground!

The publication of this book coincides with the 125th anniversary of the work of Counties, which began in 1899, to further an evangelistic thrust which had been increasingly and spontaneously evident in many places in England and Wales in the previous 40 years following the revival that began in 1859. Counties was begun by representatives of local churches who were committed to sharing the gospel of Jesus with communities around them. Their desire

1. Huge increase in online worship during Covid - New Life Newspaper (newlifepublishing.co.uk)

to make disciples utilised the many gifted evangelists that were to be found among their congregations, and those early Counties evangelists, working as partners with local churches, pursued the great commission with passionate and joyful hearts. In making disciples, the establishment and growth of new churches, planted by local people and grown with love and prayer, was the natural outcome. The difficult post-war decades of the 1920s and 1930s, and the 1950s and 1960s, saw remarkably fruitful mission, much of which was told in our centenary book, *A story to tell*, by Brian Mills.[2] That book rightly and helpfully looked back, in order to give God thanks for all he had done.

Now, we believe, is the right time for a new book on evangelism. The world changes, like shifting sands or leaves blown on an autumnal wind, and culture is constantly moving. How do we navigate this changing landscape, identifying principles, and setting a course that will help us to share the unchanging Good News of Jesus? This book looks forward at what we need to do now and in the future, and at how it can be done. Through stories and examples, and with a mix of the personal experience of each author rooted in biblical wisdom, *Making Jesus known today and tomorrow* seeks to both inspire and equip for this great task.

In our church culture, we often think of faith as something that relates to the past. For example, we ask at baptism, 'Do you believe that Jesus died for your sins and rose again on the third day?', 'Have you trusted him as your Lord and Saviour?'. There, belief and trust are backward looking—to the cross and resurrection of Jesus in history, and to the day of conversion—'yes, I ***HAVE*** trusted Jesus!'

But in the great chapter of faith in Hebrews 11, men and women inspired by what God was yet to do as he had promised, or by what they believed he would do, acted in faith: they left homes and nations behind, moved families, built boats, faced down dictators, founded cities, and looked hungry lions in the eye. All because they believed that God was going to do something amazing, something that he had promised—and they believed his promises. 'Faith is the substance of things hoped for!' (Heb. 11: 1 (KJV)).

---

2. *A Story to Tell: Evangelism in the Twentieth Century*, Carlisle: OM Publishing for Counties, 1999.

This book has been written because we believe that God keeps his promises, and I believe that its readers believe that too!

Two promises in particular have driven the passion for this book.

1. The power and authority of the promise of the great commission

> Then Jesus came to them and said, "All authority in heaven and on earth has been given to me. Therefore go and make disciples of all nations, baptizing them in the name of the Father and of the Son and of the Holy Spirit, and teaching them to obey everything I have commanded you. And surely I am with you always, to the very end of the age." (Mt 28: 18–20)

Jesus gave us our marching orders. As we pursue this primary calling, we discover that his power and authority are evident and that, as Paul reflected, the gospel is the power of God saving all who believe! (Rom. 1: 16)

Many believers lack a sense of the presence and power of God in their lives, but it seems to me that these very things that we crave—his power and presence—are bounded to his commandment. 'Go and make disciples, make that your goal and mission, and you will discover that my power and my presence are very real to you!'

Let us act in light of his command to 'Go,' and his promise to be with us in power to the very end of our mission.

2. The power and authority in the hands of the church

> "I will build my church, and the gates of Hades will not overcome it." (Mt. 16: 18)

We know that the power and authority belong to Jesus: he told us so in the great commission. But closely related is the commission that Christ gives to Peter in Matthew 16, where he promises to build his church, and then gives the keys to Peter. So, ultimately, the Church of Jesus Christ cannot and will not fail! Do we, do you, believe this?

Often our hearts and minds are seared by experience of local church failure: failure of leadership, failure to take the great commission seriously, failure of people we trusted. However, the promise of Jesus is true—his Church can never fail, and indeed, when it sets its heart on raiding hell, saving captives, and bringing them into the kingdom of God, the Church cannot be stopped.

Local church decline and failure, while it has many causes, ultimately boils down to a loss of focus on keeping the main thing the main thing. If we take the great commission seriously, to make disciples; see the Church on earth as a resistance movement with victory a certainty; and set our hearts on charging the gates of hell, then the future is bright! Faith in the promises of God, to keep his word, and action based on his promises, ultimately cannot fail.

The chapters of this book are a demonstration of ways in which we can engage in this task. Perhaps the decline and closure of older fellowships is part of the plan. Christ will fulfil his mission with a coalition of the willing. Are you willing? Will you commit with us to the fulfilment of the great commission? Will you see the local church as a regional raiding party, set up to smash the gates of hell, and rescue and restore lost people, bringing them into the fellowship of his great Church?

If yes, then this book is written for you.

PART 1

Understanding What We Are Trying To Do

Chapter 1

Critiquing the soul of the nation: The many faces of the UK today

Stephen McQuoid

The one thing we can guarantee about life is that nothing remains the same. The world we live in is one where changes occur all the time and, as they do, we need to get accustomed to the world as it is, not as it once was. We might not like the change, indeed it can be confusing and unsettling in equal measure. But change happens, and this is a process that we cannot stop.

I came to the UK in 1978 from Ethiopia where I grew up. Back then, almost no one had a mobile phone and Apple was nothing more than a two-year-old start up. The Iron Curtain was still firmly in place, and Leonid Brezhnev presided over the powerful Soviet Union. James Callaghan was the Prime Minister of the UK, a Mars Bar cost 15 pence, 'Grease' was the best selling movie, and 'Night Fever' by the Bee Gees the bestselling single. The most popular video game was Space Invaders, Argentina were world cup winners, and the first test-tube baby had just been born. Life is utterly different now. However, one of the biggest changes since then is not at first very obvious: that is the spiritual one.

The harsh reality is that the UK has been in decline spiritually for decades. That may not seem apparent to the general public, as 'spirituality' appears still to be a feature of national life. However, often when people talk about spirituality, they are referring to nothing more than a general sense that many people have that the world is more than just the physical and tangible. When we come to more concrete expressions, such as church attendance or formulated theological beliefs, the decline becomes much more apparent.

By a whole range of indicators, we as a nation have been doing much less well than a few generations ago. A great many local churches have grown smaller, and literally thousands have closed their doors since the 1950s. The influence that Christians and Christian values have had on culture in general is also diminishing. Traditional Judeo-Christian ethics are now being widely rejected, especially in the realm of sexuality and reproductive ethics. In the process, the Christian church faces greater pressures on faith now than at any point in our lifetime.

One way of drilling down into this decline is to take a quick look at the National Census for England and Wales which is carried out every decade or so. This is a valuable source of information, as comparisons can be made between, for example, the 2001 census and the one taken in 2011. The results are both interesting and alarming, and have been continued in the 2021 Census.

The UK is historically a Christian country. So it is unsurprising to find that in the 2001 census some 71.7% of the population identified themselves as Christian. Even though that does not necessarily indicate any genuine personal faith, and could include many people who are just cultural Christians, it was nevertheless an impressive figure. However, by the 2011 census that figure had fallen to 59.3% (equating to about 33.2 million people). That was a decline over a 10-year period of some 12.4%. In real terms, it means that about 4.5 million fewer people in the population as a whole considered themselves to be Christian than was the case in at the time of the 2001 census.[1] Again, this is using the term Christian in its broadest possible sense. Evangelical Christians represented only a small proportion of this figure—perhaps two million of the 33.2 million in 2011. In the 2021 census, the figure of 59.3% fell again to 46.2% (a further 13% decline since 2011), while the proportion saying that they had no religion increased to 37.2%.

Another matter requiring reflection is immigration, which has made a significant impact on the UK in recent years. It has contributed significantly to the religious make-up of the UK since 1945. While Christianity in the UK is in

1. These are snapshots of a dynamic changing position. In reality, older people who did consider themselves Christian will have died, to be replaced by younger generations in which smaller proportions say they are Christian. It does not mean that the 4.5 million were all people who decided at some stage in the 10-year interval that they were no longer Christians.

overall decline, over the period covered by the two censuses, around 1 million people who identified as Christians migrated to the UK. The implications of this are clear. While Christianity is declining rapidly, the rate of decline is being slowed down to some extent by immigration. Without these newly-arrived Christians, most of whom are African, the decline would be much worse. Indeed, in some of the large urban areas of the UK, declining churches been brought to life again by immigrants and many new churches have been planted by them and church attendance has actually been growing in London.

Another insight which the 2011 census gave us is the age spectrum of those who call themselves Christian, especially when this is compared with other religious groups. Statistically, some 22% of those who called themselves Christian were pensioners, but when we focus on people who identify as Christians and also attend church regularly, this number rises to 33%. If we compare this to the data on Islam, something significant emerges. Islam is the second largest religion in the UK and, by contrast to the decline in Christianity, Islam has been growing very quickly. Between 2001 and 2011 the number of Muslims in England and Wales grew from 1.2 million to 2.7 million, doubling in number. In 2011, nearly 1 in every 20 people in England and Wales was Muslim. Their age profile is also startling. While Christianity is the religious grouping which is on average oldest, Islam is the youngest. Almost half of all Muslims in England and Wales were under 25 years of age in 2011 and 90% were under 50. In other words, while self-declared Christians were an aging group, Islam was young and vibrant.

Before we get too discouraged, we should note that, while the Christian faith is struggling in the UK and continental Europe, it is thriving in many other places. I have already mentioned that I grew up in Ethiopia, where my parents went as missionaries to share the gospel. The result of years of missionary activity, as well as the advent of communism in the early 1970's through to the 1990s, was a dramatic growth in the church. Today, there are nearly 17 million evangelical Christians in Ethiopia (about the same number as the whole of Europe), out of a population of 107 million. What is true of evangelicalism as a whole is true of individual denominations. When my parents left Ethiopia in 1978, there were three small churches of their denomination (Christian Brethren) in the country. Today, that denominational group has grown to 367 churches, with 65,253 attenders supporting 385 full-time pastors. The same denomination in the UK has experienced dramatic decline over the same time period—the number of congregations has halved since 1960.

Of course, Islam is not the only, nor even the biggest, threat to Christianity in the UK. Of far greater significance is the sheer secularisation of UK culture. Those who claim to have no religion are increasing in number, and by 2021 accounted for well over one-third of the population of England and Wales. Of course, this varies from one part of the country to the next. Some cities are more religious than others, but in some places such as Norwich some 53.5% of the population now claim to be non-religious. Like Islam, the age profile for the non-religious is young. Some 4 out of 10 are under 25 and 80% under 50.

The data mentioned above relate to England and Wales, but the picture in Scotland is not very different. Christian belief in Scotland has also declined, while both other religions, especially Islam, and the non-religious, have grown in number. Even Northern Ireland, traditionally a hotbed of Christianity, has experienced a slight decline, though not to the same extent (by 3.5% in the decade 2001–11, almost all in the Protestant community).

Lots of statistics can have the impact of numbing our minds with information overload. Consequently, we will stop thinking about numbers and data and start to think of what this all means on the ground and in everyday experience. We will do this by mentioning a number of observations that we will all be aware of and that should cause us concern.

Church—an unfamiliar place

First, church has become an unfamiliar place for the majority of the population. Of course, there has always been a section of the population that never went to church and showed no interest in Christianity. This was even true in the nineteenth century, the heyday for Christianity in the United Kingdom. However, it is more a reality than ever now. Not only do most people not go to church, they have no intention of going, even if they were to be invited by a Christian friend. We are now facing the phenomenon of households containing several generations, yet no one in that household has ever been to church. This is not necessarily because they object to Christianity. Indeed, members of the household may have Christian friends whom they respect and admire. It is just that their lives and lifestyles have never included church and so they have never even considered the possibility. Deciding, for example, to attend the local village carol service is no more likely a possibility than taking a package holiday to Pyongyang. It is just not something you do!

The privatisation of faith

Secondly, faith has been privatised throughout most of Western society, including the UK. This is a subtle shift, but one that has a profound impact on the way that we do evangelism. Most people in UK culture would not argue that Christianity if false or dangerous; indeed, they would not even want a conversation about Christianity. They would take the view that faith is a private thing. If you want to have a belief and live by it that is perfectly acceptable. You are even entitled to believe that your belief system is true, or at least true for you. But you must keep it wholly to yourself and not bother others with it. Such beliefs are for the individual, not for society at large. A person can believe what they want, but they are just not entitled to tell others what they should believe and how they should live. It is this privatisation of faith that makes evangelism offensive in our society.

Biblical illiteracy

At the same time that the church became an island and faith became personalised, our culture also started to forget the Word of God. While virtually everyone knows that the Bible is the holy book of Christianity, fewer and fewer people have any commitment to the idea of the authority of Scripture or knowledge of what it contains. Most would still say that the Bible is a source of wisdom and morally helpful material, but this is a far cry from a belief in the inspiration of Scripture. Moreover, Bible knowledge is also starkly lacking, something which can be evidenced by watching TV quiz shows. The contestants may be well educated and with a good general knowledge. However, even the most basic of questions on the content of the Bible will prove a challenge. Despite the positive impact of the Reformation and subsequent spiritual events, we are living at a time in our history when people know almost nothing about the Bible's storyline or the key characters who dominate its pages.

Pluralism rules

Another observable feature of life in the UK today is the rejection of what could be termed Christian exclusivism. Biblical Christians believe that Jesus is not only the unique son of God, but that he is also the only way to find forgiveness, salvation and eternal life. The idea of the uniqueness of Christ stems from, among other things, Jesus' own claim in John 14: 6, to be 'the way, the truth and the life'. We unashamedly claim that Jesus is the only true path to God and the only way to heaven. Of course, we are not the only people who make exclusive claims for their beliefs. Muslims, for example, would believe that they possess the truth and that alternative views are false.

These exclusive notions are alien to many in our pluralistic culture. The vast majority of people, in effect, hold to some form of universalism, though they would not label their beliefs in that way. They would recognise that there are many religious viewpoints, and would even acknowledge that there are some significant differences between faith systems. But they would stop short of believing that one of these could claim to be true and the rest must therefore be false. Instead, they suggest that all faith systems have an element of truth and that there are many commonalities; so we don't have to make a decision about who is right or wrong. As long as people are sincere and act charitably, if there is a God he must look kindly at them. The idea that one group of believers, like Christians, could claim to be correct and everyone else wrong, worse still condemned to hell—such an idea is viewed as repulsive and immoral. Everyone is allowed to be right in their own way, and God will receive them, whatever that may mean. The rise of multiculturalism, particularly in big cities, has contributed to this kind of pluralism.

Rejection of Judeo-Christian ethics

Linked to pluralism is a fairly widespread rejection of the Judeo-Christian worldview with parts of its ethical framework. This is particularly true when it comes to human sexuality and reproductive ethics. Indeed, we have witnessed radical ethical shifts in our culture over the space of just a few decades. Abortion has become so common and accepted that it is barely questioned, this despite the fact that in the UK we terminate somewhere in the region of 200,000 unborn children annually. More that that, anyone who dares to question a woman's right to do whatever she wants with her body is immediately castigated with venom. Homosexuality has likewise come out of the shadows and is not just accepted, it is positively celebrated. More than that, if anyone doesn't celebrate it, even for religious reasons, they are assumed to be intolerant and homophobic. The very idea of stable gender has also been questioned, to the point where a person can choose to be whatever gender they want to be, or none, irrespective of the reality of biology. To question this dogma is to be transphobic.

In this kind of world, Christianity gets a frosty reception, like a new cold war. Biblical Christianity teaches that marriage is between one man and one woman for life, and that sexual promiscuity is a sin. It teaches that male and female are distinct, different, and rooted in the creation order, that life in the womb is invaluable, and that our goal as humans ought to be a quest for holiness because God is holy. All of this is now counter-cultural and demonstrates how far apart the church and culture have grown.

Secularism

A final feature worth observing is that of secularism. There are various definitions of secularism, but in essence it is a commitment to conduct human affairs based on secular, naturalistic considerations. This is a very broad definition, but it encapsulates not only what secularism is but also how it affects daily life. In practice, the influence of secularism in our culture means that, when people do their day-to-day thinking on almost any subject, the spiritual or religious is left out. That does not mean that secularist people do not believe in God and neither does it assume that they lean towards atheism. In that sense, it is not a narrow belief system. Rather it is an attitude to life in which anything to do with the spiritual world is considered to be a special category and not part of the norm of life.

When secularist people suffer, they do not cry out to God, even though they may accept that God exists, because their normal everyday lives are confined to the physical and not the spiritual. When something good happens to them, they do not express thankfulness to God for much the same reason. When they ask themselves deep questions about the purpose of life and the need for meaning and personal fulfilment, they will try and find these things in the physical world, in money, or career, or image, or possessions. They will not seek meaning in a relationship with God, not because they believe he does not exist (of course some secularists are atheist), but because their worldview is limited to the physical and tangible world around them which they see.

And the rest . . .

Of course not everyone fits neatly into the descriptors mentioned above. As I stated earlier, an increasing number of people in our society are Muslim or belong to another major world faith, for example Hinduism. There are also significant though decreasing numbers of people who could best be described as committed Roman Catholics, Orthodox Christians, and Protestants. However, the above descriptions are a good fit for the majority of people in UK society, whatever their particular worldview.

What does this mean for evangelism? This book has been written to encourage readers to share their faith, and it stands to reason that we need to have a sense of what kind of a culture we are sharing the good news of Jesus with. Any series of statements in this regard can only be generalisations at best. However, having been involved in evangelism for many years, I would argue that the following statements are generally true:

People are not in a hurry to hear the good news.

In general, the average man or woman in the street is not waiting anxiously for you to tell them about Jesus' love. This may seem an obvious thing to say, but it needs to be emphasized. Sometimes churches behave as if they expect people to queue up to hear the gospel. They lay on outreach services and then get disappointed when no one shows up. After all, they have a good praise band and a compelling preacher—so what is the problem? Actually the problem is simple. Most people don't care what you believe about Jesus and they are not anxious about their eternal destiny. There is a profound lack of spiritual seeking for all the reasons I have already mentioned.

People often give push-back because of the offence of the gospel.

Some elements of the gospel are unpalatable to most people. It might be that the idea of our human sinfulness and guilt are the issue, or perhaps some of the particular sins that the Bible condemns. For some, the offence may come from the exclusive claims of Jesus or his demand that we repent. For still others, it is the anger of God, or the call to worship and to lay our lives before him. Whatever the offence, we should not be surprised if, in our sharing of the gospel, we find that people can be put off, annoyed or even angered by the content of our message, such is their cultural conditioning.

People often have a reason for not believing.

Even when we get past the initial offence of the gospel, many people will still have genuine reasons for not wanting to make a commitment to Christ. It may be because of an honest intellectual doubt. The constant preaching of the New Atheists or other sceptics may have raised genuine doubts in their minds about the existence of God or perhaps the deity of Jesus. Perhaps belief in miracules or the resurrection of Christ is a point too far for people whose entire thought processes are caught up in the secularist realm. On the other hand, the sticking point might not be intellectual, it could be emotional. They may have experienced personal suffering, or who have witnessed the suffering of others, and concluded that a loving God cannot be real. Whatever the situation, many people can offer some reason for not believing.

People need our patience.

Even beyond the doubts and the resistance there is also a sense of hesitation. We are not living in revival times or even times of heightened spiritual interest. There have been times like that in our nation's history, and there are places in the world today where that sense of spiritual life in a culture is very apparent. But not here and not now. We are a spiritually weary and sceptical culture that is still emerging from a long pandemic, one in which the church has been prevented from reaching out to the wider community. It has been a tough time for the gospel. As we kick start our evangelistic endeavours once more, we need to be aware of the times, to understand and interpret our culture, and recognise how great the challenge of evangelism is in the UK today!

For discussion

1. Think about the observations that were made in this chapter about life in the UK. Which of these do you think are the most significant and why?
2. The chapter finished with four statements about people in UK culture. From your own experience give an example of someone you know who fits one of these statements.

Chapter 2

Reclaiming the heart of the gospel: What it is, and how it transforms lives

Martin Erwin

In 2002, I was invited to a gathering of young evangelists at the King's Park conference centre in Northampton. This two-day get-together was arranged by the Billy Graham Evangelistic Association (BGEA), as part of their launch of the Emerging Evangelists Institute (EEI). EEI has contributed to the development of many evangelists in the UK since then, and Counties trainees make up a significant part of each cohort. In fact, it was in part the brainchild of Roger Chilvers, who for many years has served as a Counties evangelist in Gloucestershire and continues to serve on the British board of the BGEA.

For me, the major draw to that event was that John Stott was to address us on the second day. I had not heard him speak before, but, like many Christians, I have been greatly shaped by his writings and influence in the evangelical world.

Stott opened the Scriptures in Romans chapter 1. With a gentle warmth and typical soft winsomeness, he unpacked the gospel. This was the message that had changed my heart as a child and was the battle cry of my soul as an evangelist. However, as Stott continued to lead us through the glory of Paul's introduction to this letter, I became thrilled by something else. Unbelievably, the great evangelical leader of the twentieth century seemed to be sharing a message that I had studied and preached myself just a few months before. Now I was not only transfixed to be sitting at his feet, but I was also buzzing to discover that I too seemed to have unearthed the exact same points from

Romans 1: 1–17 myself. Quietly, I thought to myself, I may just be the next John Stott!

Afterwards I shared my delight with a friend who had travelled with me to the meeting. He laughed: "Those are the same headings that he uses in his commentary," he chuckled. When I got home, I looked out my notes and sure enough I had studied Romans 1 with John Stott as my guide! Somewhat humbling.

Why do I tell you this story? Well, the truth be told, this chapter is both the result of personal conviction and study, **and** the overflow of much that has been poured into me by others. Parents who loved Jesus and were saved by the gospel; an upbringing in churches in Northern Ireland, so convinced of the gospel and its importance that they named their meeting places, 'Gospel Halls'; friends, mentors, and authors who helped shape my life and my ministry. I cannot claim that you will find lots of new ideas in this chapter. A new perspective on Paul, I leave to others better qualified.

This chapter will revisit the gospel. However, in a book dedicated to 'Evangelism', this chapter will undoubtedly contain shortcomings and gaps. My purpose is not to weigh all the nuanced arguments or examine discussions on perceived differences between Paul's gospel and that preached by the other apostles. Nor will I spend much time here on theological arguments regarding the nature of the gospel of grace as opposed to the gospel of the kingdom. My simple conviction is that the gospel preached by Paul was the outworking of Christ's great commission, and was in step with the apostolic church in Jerusalem. As Paul himself writes in Galatians 1, 'I am astonished that you are so quickly deserting the one who called you to live in the grace of Christ and are turning to a different gospel—which is really no gospel at all.' (Gal. 1: 6 & 7). That view was of course endorsed by the apostles in Acts 15.

Confidence in the gospel

It seems to me that there continues to be a battle for the soul of the gospel, repeated in each generation, a struggle for the heart of the central message of the Church. The evidence of history is undeniable. The cyclical drift towards liberalism (a denial of the gospel in some key regard), or political activism, as demonstrated by the alignment of the gospel with some political party cause, or programme leads the Church of Christ to repeat the sins and mistakes of the past. It seems that knowing or learning from past mistakes from history is still no guarantee that we will not repeat them.

That said, I do passionately believe that the transforming power of the gospel, and the reality of knowing Christ, always leads the Church to social engagement, political involvement, and a desire to see change on multiple levels across nations. However, these things are the **results** of the gospel, not an alternative to it. Too often, the Church has hitched itself to a worthy cause, only to discover that the engine which drives us, the gospel itself, has been jettisoned, and we are careering down the road, being overtaken by an unwieldy trailer that stops us from steering a straight course and, unsurprisingly, will lead to a mighty crash!

Modern examples abound, and I am cautious to mention them as I know that they touch on raw nerves and deeply held convictions. Too often an unhealthy marriage of church and state leads to a weakening of our testimony. The 2020 US election was an example of the unhealthy blending of the temporal and the eternal, as though the USA (or the UK or Europe for that matter) was some earthly expression of the kingdom of God! I saw this all too often growing up in Northern Ireland, where gospel preachers too closely aligned themselves with a political cause. As a result, they robbed themselves of much of their authority to speak freely, without contradiction, from the Scriptures, and automatically excluded themselves from being heard by half their potential audience. The trailer overtakes the car and drives us off the road into the nearest convenient ditch!

Standing in a court with kings and governors as his audience and judges, Paul declared 'So then, King Agrippa, I was not disobedient to the vision from heaven.' (Acts 26: 19 (NLT)). That vision was of Jesus, his authority, and his commission to take this message to the nations. That is our calling too.

So, what is this gospel?

Well, without apology, let us return to Romans 1 and, with due deference to John Stott[1] , look at the six key aspects that Paul unfolds for us there. (The

1. *The Message of Romans: God's good news for the world* (Leicester: Inter-Varsity Press), 1994.

content and headings are my own, but I cannot deny the shaping of others upon it).

As with much of Paul's writings in Scripture, the sweetest spot is often when he is at his most autobiographical. Although Romans 1 is not his testimony, as told elsewhere, the convictions expressed reflect his experience. That God saved him, 'the chief of sinners,' (1 Tim. 1: 15) was never far from his mind as he pioneered this message westward to Europe. From verses 1 through to 17, Paul takes us on a remarkable tour of the majestic sweep of the gospel. Having never been to Rome but intending to get there soon, Paul wants the growing group of Jesus' followers in the Empire's capital to be sure of the message that they have believed. He wants them to be sure that the foundations on which they are building their faith, with all the cost of eviction from synagogues and ejection from Rome, is factually reliable, historically accurate, and eternally true.

The six areas that he explores in Romans 1 resonate throughout his letter. They are:

The source of the gospel
The pedigree of the gospel
The subject of the gospel
The object of the gospel
The power of the gospel
The goal of the gospel

The source of the gospel—it's from God

In recent years, the concept of 'fake news' has really taken off. Used by some to decry news sources that they do not like, it has brought to public attention the reality that the source of the news is vitally important. In our highly politicised age, there is really no such thing as complete objectivity. When I tell a story, it will have a subtext. For example, does it make me look good? How will my hearers spot this (if so, perhaps I will adapt it)? Who do I want to impress? What cause do I believe in or wish to promote? News sources are compromised and conflicted by these realities, and so editorial spin is always a threat or reality.

Imagine that you are told that you have been invited to a Royal Garden Party at Buckingham Palace. Who is telling you? How can you be sure it is true? Usually such an invitation should come on Palace headed-paper, with all the accompanying evidence that it is authentic. Only then might you believe it. The source of the news, of the invitation, is vital if its validity and veracity are to be accepted. So numerous are scam emails and phone calls that the UK Government has set up a website to report false numbers and email addresses. Cleverly, each scam email address or website is remarkably similar to the original that it seeks to imitate, sucking in many unsuspecting victims, often stealing life savings and bringing devastation in their wake.

Paul's very first words to the believers in Rome underpin his absolute certainty that the gospel is reliable. Paul, a servant of Christ Jesus, called to be an apostle and set apart for the gospel of God (Rom. 1: 1). This 'good news', for that is what the gospel is, is good in the first place because it is from God. 'The gospel **of** God,' writes Paul. As the Living Bible puts it, Paul has been 'sent out to preach God's Good News.'

The point? This news is the best news, the greatest story ever told, because its source is heaven itself, and the author is God. Such a truth is fundamental to everything that flows from this message. It can and does change lives ***because*** it is from God! So amazing and simple is this message, that you could not make it up!

Fundamentally, there is nothing I can do to save myself, to get right with God, to re-establish relations with him, and bring about full reconciliation with God and restoration of what humanity has lost. Individually and culturally, we all fall short of God's glory (Rom. 3: 23), and there is no way back—at least no route made by human hands, intellect, or guile.

So, Paul expands on this source. Not only is this news ***from*** God, but its glorious victory has also been delivered ***by*** God. He is not simply the author of the news, he is the news! We shall look at this shortly when we think about the subject of the gospel, but for now let us satisfy ourselves with Paul's introduction of the theme of love at the heart of this message—'To all in Rome who are loved by God', he goes on (Rom. 1: 7).

John, the disciple of Jesus, writes in his first letter 'Whoever does not love does not know God, because God is love. This is how God showed his love among us: he sent his one and only Son into the world that we might live through him.' (1 Jn. 4: 8 & 9) God is Love. The source of this good news is the very heart of God, and God is Love! This is stunning as a statement, both then in a world of performance-driven religion, and today into a world of broken dreams and failure. God is Love, and his very heart is the source of this global gospel! Paul expands his theme further as he writes, 'But God demonstrates his own love for us in this: while we were still sinners, Christ died for us.' (Rom. 5: 8) Humanly, there was no way back … 'But God'!

At the very heart of our gospel is this conviction: we did not make this up! This is not simply another in the pantheon of world religions, cults, and philosophies. It is not a clever idea, or something that can be dismissed with an 'I'm-glad-it-works-for-you', post-modernistic shrug. No—this message is of ultimate, eternal significance, because the creator God, the maker of heaven and earth, designed it, demonstrated it, delivered it, and now declares it. It is his gospel. It is the gospel of God, and it is about his love for the human race, for his creation, and is the only hope for all who are lost.

I wrote a very simple little tract a few years ago, to help train others to know and share the gospel. We call it 'The Loved Tract.' It begins with a simple statement 'God loved the world so much.' If we are to be effective in our evangelism, we must know and believe that the good news that we share is from God, and that it is about the declaration of his love for humanity, the demonstration of his love through Christ, and the delivery of that great news through evangelism—the gospel shared through word and action.

The pedigree of the gospel—it's in the Bible

Having declared that God is the source of this good news, Paul goes on to establish what antique dealers call *provenance*. This concept is vital in establishing the origins or history of a piece of art, literature, or a concept or viewpoint. In Romans 1, he writes, 'Paul, a servant of Christ Jesus, called to be an apostle and set apart for the gospel of God— *the gospel he promised beforehand through his prophets in the Holy Scriptures*'. (Rom. 1: 1 & 2)

One of the arguments that could have been aimed at the message emanating outward from first-century Jerusalem to the furthest reaches of the Roman Empire, was that this was new, and anything new was regarded as suspicious.

This was true particularly for the Jews, who were always the first audience that the apostle and his team sought to reach. When Paul and Barnabas set out on their first missionary journey, they began their work in the local synagogue where men and women gathered to hear the Scriptures read and explained. 'At Salamis,' we read, 'they proclaimed the word of God in the Jewish synagogues.' (Acts 13: 5) Again, in Acts 14: 1, Luke records, 'At Iconium Paul and Barnabas went as usual into the Jewish synagogue.'

There are a couple of important reasons why this is worth mentioning. Paul went to the synagogues first because they were full of people who read and believed the Scriptures, our Old Testament, and, secondly, the Old Testament Scriptures are full of the gospel. "You see," says Paul, "not only are we not making this message up, it is from God, but furthermore, as the scrolls are unfurled in every synagogue in the empire, this story unfolds before your eyes. This good news was promised, expected, foretold, anticipated, and it is this message, with this provenance, that we proclaim!"

This is vitally important for us too. While most in our nation no longer accept the authority or provenance attested to by the Bible, that was also true for Paul. His approach with non-Jewish or God-fearing Greeks certainly had a different starting point, as demonstrated by his debates in the Areopagus in Athens, or his discussions in the lecture hall of Tyrannus in Ephesus. However, one of those early believers from the first missionary journey was Timothy, an uncircumcised Greek with a Jewish mother. It was the influence of his mother and grandmother that would prepare him for faith in Christ, as they schooled him in the Scriptures, and so Paul could write confidently in later years, 'But as for you, continue in what you have learned and have become convinced of, because you know those from whom you learned it, and how from infancy you have known the Holy Scriptures, which are able to make you wise for salvation through faith in Christ Jesus. All Scripture is God-breathed and is useful for teaching, rebuking, correcting and training in righteousness, so that the servant of God may be thoroughly equipped for every good work.' (2 Tim. 3: 14–17) Indeed, in a verse reminiscent of Paul's visits to those first century Mediterranean synagogues, the writer of Psalm 119 declares: 'The unfolding of your words gives light; it gives understanding to the simple.' (Ps. 119: 130)

Our approach to those who do not accept the pedigree or provenance of Scripture must be varied and appropriate to the circumstances, the audience, or the hearer. However, we must be convinced of the heritage and historicity of this message. Our convictions about the power of the entrance of God's Word will be borne out by the impact and effect that it has on those whose hearts are exposed to it. Truly, unfolding God's word with care, compassion and conviction will bring light.

I wrote these words in Christmas week 2020. A new Covid-19 strain had forced Britain into a tighter set of restrictions: Christmas would be lonely for millions, and France had closed its ports. Fruit and veg might soon be off the menu! That morning, I visited the osteopath about an ongoing back complaint. This was my fifth or sixth visit in the previous five months. These visits had allowed me to share a little of my story, my faith, always gently and in response to an opening.

Three weeks before, the osteopath asked me, "As a Christian, how do you feel about the commercialisation of Christmas? I cannot find any peace or meaning in it." I sent up an arrow prayer, and then asked her if she had access to a Bible. I encouraged her to find a quiet place and open the Gospel of Matthew and that of Luke. "Read the first two or three chapters of each and if you pray," I said, "Ask God to help you understand the truth at the heart of the Christmas story. It is about a person, Jesus, not a religion, and certainly not all about the tinsel and wrapping which so often robs us of the simple story unfolding at the centre of that first Christmas. The peace which he came to bring is available to you."

At the following visit, as I was having my neck and shoulder pulverised by a machine called 'Shock Wave,' the osteopath said, "I want to thank you for the conversation we had last month. I did what you said, I read those Scriptures and have thought about them since then on my journeys to and from work. As I read them, it was as though a door opened in my chest, and lots of butterflies flew out. I have experienced a peace that I have not had since my parents died when I was a child, and I can see the meaning and purpose of Christmas for the first time since childhood."

I was stunned. Staring at the blank wall in front of me, I held back the tears and sent up another silent prayer. "Thank you, God! The unfolding of your words truly gives light!"

The subject of the gospel—it's all about Jesus

Paul has not even completed a thought, a sentence, as he writes to the believers in Rome, before blurting out the central theme of the whole message: '[I have been] set apart for the gospel of God—the gospel he promised beforehand through his prophets in the Holy Scriptures regarding his Son' (Rom. 1: 2 & 3) and continuing in verse 9, he declares that his mission can be defined simply as 'preaching the gospel of his Son.' This is the message, the subject, the theme.

One of the most beautiful incidents in the days after the resurrection of Christ happened only hours after the empty tomb was discovered. The story draws together both the provenance of the message, and its majestic, central theme.

Cleopas and his companion are walking to Emmaus, a village about seven miles from Jerusalem. With no headphones to distract or mobile phones to blankly stare at, they fill their two-hour walk with conversation. Their subject, "What on earth just happened?" These two followers of Jesus were stunned by the suddenness and brutality of his death. The promised Messiah, hanging abandoned and deserted on a Roman cross, it seems, would not fulfil his promise. When he was buried in a borrowed tomb, their hopes and those of hundreds more, lay buried with him. A weekend of desolate contemplation was followed by the dreaded trudge home where the haunting thoughts full of "if only's" and "what if's" echoed with their footsteps.

Soon, and surprisingly, a stranger joined them on the road. "What are you talking about?", he asks with interest. Apparently, their conversation was animated and interesting enough to draw the attention of a fellow walker. Surprised that anyone leaving Jerusalem could have missed the commotion of this unique Passover weekend, they unpack the story—the bits they know, and the accounts brought by some, of angelic messengers, and the confirmation by some disciples of the now empty tomb.

Of course, the stranger is Christ, and the next few verses are central to understanding his mission, and a fuller understanding of the Old Testament in light of it. Luke records, 'He said to them, "How foolish you are, and how slow to believe all that the prophets have spoken! Did not the Messiah have to suffer these things and then enter his glory?" And beginning with Moses and all the Prophets, he explained to them what was said in all the Scriptures concerning himself.' (Lk. 24: 25–27)

This, he tells them, **IS** the story of the Scriptures. The coming of Christ, his suffering, his death, and resurrection. This is the message of Moses, from Genesis through to the prophets. This, perhaps, above all others, would have been the message that I would most like to have heard from the lips of Jesus himself. But we do not need to hear it! We have it, preserved for us—the Scriptures, God-breathed, and in our own language. And what do they say? What is their message? What is the core subject of this gospel? 'And beginning with Moses and all the Prophets, he explained to them what was said in all the Scriptures concerning himself.'

It is all about Jesus! Our message is not a mantra, a method, or a meditation. It is not a matter of rules to follow or laws to keep. Rather, our message is a person, and his name is Jesus. This is the very heart of the gospel. Often rejected as simplistic by those who want 'deeper' teaching, who desire to unpack end-time secrets, or create systematic schemes, there is a great danger that we will over-complicate what God has made so plain.

> For God so loved the world that he gave his one and only Son, that whoever believes in him shall not perish but have eternal life. For God did not send his Son into the world to condemn the world, but to save the world through him. (Jn. 3: 16 & 17)

Some years ago I listened to a podcast in which the preacher and writer, Tim Keller, shared a conversation that he had with his wife after a sermon that he had delivered. (Preachers will know that it may be a fatal error to ask those closest to you for honest feedback on your preaching.)"Well," said his wife, "it was OK." Believe me when I say that such a compliment is incredibly damaging to the ego (and therefore, probably no bad thing!) "What do you mean, 'OK,'" he asked. "What is the difference between 'OK' and 'Great?" As Keller tells the story, a period of stony silence followed as they drove to the restaurant for their lunch date. When they arrived, Kathy sat up straight and delivered the coup de gras, which in reality, may prove something of a 'eureka' moment for the rest of us."It was good," she said, "because you gave me information, something to think about, something to do. I enjoyed it. It was good. However, it is 'great' when you tell me about Jesus, when you preach to my heart about him, it moves me to the core of my being. When you preach about Jesus, that is great!"

In a lecture that Keller gave entitled 'How to preach the Gospel every time,' he quoted Charles Spurgeon on preaching Christ: 'I often hear sermons that are very learned . . . but there is not a word about Christ in those sermons. I say, "They have taken away my Lord and I do not know where they have laid him."'[2] Spurgeon went on to tell the story of a Welsh preacher who heard a young preacher give a sermon with no Christ in it. The older man pointed this out to him, and explained that every text has some road to Christ, just as every town, village or hamlet has a road to London. And so, from every text in Scripture, there is a road to the metropolis of the Scriptures, which is Christ.

Keller noted, 'Every text has a major point, a main street in the village. This is the main point in the original context that the author was trying to get across. But the fact is that there is a road out of town that leads to London.'[3]

In regard to preaching, this thought is picked up and developed further by Phil Davies in chapter 10 of this book. However, the reality for all of us who want to share the gospel is this—it centres around Christ, it is his story, and the story of how God made a way back to himself through his Son and his death for us.

Paul picks this up in multiple and various ways in his New Testament letters. For example, Paul writes to the struggling church in Corinth,

> Now, brothers and sisters, I want to remind you of the gospel I preached to you, which you received and on which you have taken your stand. By this gospel you are saved, if you hold

2. C.H. Spurgeon, *The New Park Street Pulpit*, 'Christ Precious to Believers', Sermon 242, March 13, 1859, reprinted online at https://info1.sermon-online.com/english/CharlesHaddonSpurgeon/1_Peter_2_7_Christ_Precious_To_Believers_18590313/pdf ., p. 4.

3. Keller, Six Ways to Preach Christ | nik lingle

> firmly to the word I preached to you. Otherwise, you have believed in vain. For what I received I passed on to you as of first importance: that Christ died for our sins according to the Scriptures, that he was buried, that he was raised on the third day according to the Scriptures . . . (1 Cor. 15: 1–4)

The gospel is all about Christ, our lostness, and God's great rescue plan. Social action without the gospel will improve life for many, and the Church of Christ is right to engage in loving people through action, bringing better education, medical care, and improving environmental conditions. But unhitched from the gospel, these efforts will lack spiritual impact, and fail to bring genuine transformational change.

In a reflective, perhaps impulsive phrase, as Paul reflects on his calling in the letter to the Christians in Galatia, he writes, 'I have been crucified with Christ and I no longer live, but Christ lives in me. The life I now live in the body, *I live by faith in the Son of God, who loved me and gave himself for me.*' (Gal. 2: 20). It was knowing that he was loved, knowing the one who loved him, and in laying down his life for that one, Jesus, that Paul discovered his central purpose. And he assures us that in full surrender to the Saviour, there we will find ours too.

Frederick Whitfield captures this thought perfectly in his hymn:

> There is a name I love to hear,
> I love to speak its worth;
> It sounds like music in my ear,
> The sweetest name on earth
>
> *O, how I love the Saviour's name,*
> *O, how I love the Saviour's name,*
> *O, how I love the Saviour's name,*
> *The sweetest name on earth.*
>
> It tells me of a Saviour's love,
> Who died to set me free;
> It tells me of His precious blood,
> The sinner's perfect plea.

It tells of One Whose loving heart
Can feel my deepest woe;
Who in my sorrow bears a part
That none can bear below.

It bids my trembling heart rejoice,
It dries each rising tear;
It tells me in a "still, small voice"
To trust and never fear.

Jesus, the name I love so well,
The name I love to hear!
No saint on earth its worth can tell,
No heart conceive how dear!

The gospel is all about Jesus, and his centrality in its retelling is fundamental to the success of our evangelism.

The object of the gospel—it's for everybody

A theological earthquake was needed to move the early Church from the comfort of preaching only to Jewish people, and force them into the wider world, so that they would take this good news to all people. A variety of events occurred, as God moved the pieces and touched the hearts of people so that the champagne bottle containing the gospel might be shaken, and the cork unpopped.

Think about the events that unfolded in a short period of time to bring this about:

> At Pentecost, devout Jews and God-fearing Gentiles from the known world filled Jerusalem, thousands heard the gospel, repented, and believed in Jesus Christ as Saviour and Lord. Many took this message back with them to their home areas
>
> A mixture of famine and persecution forced many of the believers out of the city, and beyond Judean borders

Philip sees a revival-scale response among the Samaritan people, viewed as 'mongrels' at best by devout Jews

The Ethiopian Eunuch trusts Christ and takes the gospel to Africa

Through dreams, visions and circumstances, God leads Peter into the house of a Roman soldier, and while Peter is speaking about 'Israel's' hope, the Holy Spirit is poured out on a houseful of Gentiles

The greatest opponent of the church and its message, Saul of Tarsus, is converted by a direct and exceptional act of divine intervention, and commissioned to take the gospel to the Gentile world

Barnabas introduces Saul (Paul) to the apostles, and then later calls him to help reach and disciple the burgeoning multi-cultural church in Antioch

God calls Paul and Barnabas to take the gospel to the Mediterranean world

And so, Paul declares to the believers in Rome, 'Through him and for his name's sake, we received grace and apostleship to call people from among all the Gentiles to the obedience that comes from faith.' (Rom. 1: 5)

From time to time, I become disturbed by extreme or unbalanced outworkings of strongly-held doctrinal viewpoints. Sometimes, it is the political narrowness that comes from temporal applications of spiritual truths, as discussed earlier in this chapter. Sometimes, my frustration is with the promotion of a narrow vision of the breadth and depth of God's love, and of the unlimited and universal reach of the gospel message. Not only does Paul declare that he is taking the gospel to the non-Jewish world, but he sees the great commission as having no cultural or racial limits. Jesus told his followers to go into ALL the world, and to make disciples of ALL peoples, without limit and without exception (Mt. 28: 16–18).

The gospel is for the whole world, and its reach knows no bounds. I find Peter's explanation for the delay of the final judgement to be deeply moving: he writes, 'The Lord is not slow in keeping his promise, as some understand slowness. He is patient with you, not wanting anyone to perish, but everyone to come to repentance.' (2 Pet. 3: 9) The reason that God holds back from wrapping things up, at least as expressed here, is so that everyone might have the opportunity to come to repentance. And please note, that is God's heart. He **does not want** anyone to perish. He, the God of all things, **wants** everyone to come to repentance!

I love the gospel, and its reach (reflecting the heart of God whose message it is) motivates me to take the good news with me wherever I go, sharing it as I go, seeking to make disciples of all people. This message is for everybody.

The power of the gospel—it saves sinners

That the gospel is for everyone is intrinsically linked to the possibility that it can transform anyone! Lee Marsland (known locally as 'Mars'), a Counties evangelist in Oldham, tells the story of his coming to Christ. Feeling a failure as a person and a parent, and having struggled with drugs and a self-destructive culture, Lee made his way on a miserable night, to a local motorway bridge which was still under construction. His intention was to throw himself off it and end it all. Hanging over the parapet, Lee heard a voice say, 'God loves you, Mars.' These were words spoken to him by a friend who had become a Christian and had shared the gospel with him. 'God loves you, Mars,' the voice repeated. Pulling himself back from the abyss, Lee made his way to see his friend. God saved him, and his life has been transformed.

Lee's story is a demonstration, a testimony of Paul's words in Romans 1: 16. 'For I am not ashamed of the gospel, because it is the power of God that brings salvation to everyone who believes: first to the Jew, then to the Gentile.'

Note Paul's emphasis, beginning with his personal conviction—'I am not ashamed . . .' I believe that a limiting factor in the impact of the gospel in our time, and the countries and regions of the UK, is that too many of us are at least a little ashamed of the gospel. In a diverse world, with vying messages, faiths and atheistic materialism seemingly underpinning our educational culture, are we just a little embarrassed about this message?

Ways in which the gospel can be embarrassing

Its description of people

The message defines people as sinners! That is an uncomfortable word. Growing up in the Gospel Halls in Bangor, Northern Ireland, it was a common way for the preacher to address his hearers at the Gospel Meeting, "Sinner friend in the meeting tonight!" Let us not confuse uncomfortable cultural approaches to sharing the good news, with discomfort about the actual content and nature of the message. Personally, these days, I could never address a congregation with those words, but the concept that all are sinners in need of God's grace, extended through the gospel, is right at the heart of our message.

A couple of years ago, I took part at a conference at which Christians were exploring ways to express God's love through social action and acts of compassion. I am fully sold on this as a valid and necessary expression of the love of God to all people. However, one of the speakers, the CEO of a Christian charity, spoke with passion challenging us that we needed to stop thinking of people as 'lost.' I thought that I may have misheard, or at least misunderstood, but the charge was repeated. This time with greater conviction, 'we need to stop thinking of people as lost.'

I have addressed this earlier in the chapter, but by definition the good news, that Jesus came to declare and to die for, is for those who need it. Recognising lostness, sin, brokenness in my own life is a prerequisite to coming to faith in Christ. Jesus, addressing the accusations of the Pharisees that he hung out with sinners, responds by saying, 'It is not the healthy who need a doctor, but the sick. I have not come to call the righteous, but sinners.' (Mk. 2: 17) His words were surely not an endorsement of their righteousness, but rather a challenge that those who find help, healing and hope in Christ are those who first recognise their need of a Saviour from sin!

Again, Paul brings this argument to a head when he states bluntly in Romans 3: 23 that 'all have sinned and fall short of the glory of God.'

Without Christ, people are lost. This is uncomfortable for us, but the gospel is clear: those without God are without hope. (Eph. 2: 12)

We should note the startling challenge of William Booth, founder of the Salvation Army:

> "Not called!", did you say? "Not heard the call," I think you should say. Put your ear down to the Bible and hear Him bid you go and pull sinners out of the fire of sin. Put your ear down to the burdened, agonized heart of humanity, and listen to its pitiful wail for help. Go stand by the gates of hell and hear the damned entreat you to go to their father's house and bid their brothers and sisters and servants and masters not to come there. Then look Christ in the face—whose mercy you have professed to obey—and tell Him whether you will join heart and soul and body and circumstances in the march to publish His mercy to the world.

Its declaration of exclusivity

Paul's declaration in Romans 1: 16 also forces us to confront any embarrassment or shame that we may feel about the exclusive claims of this message. Contained in the gospel, in fact, the gospel itself, is the power of God to save!

In Mark 4: 26, 27 Jesus gave this illustration, 'This is what the kingdom of God is like. A man scatters seed on the ground. Night and day, whether he sleeps or gets up, the seed sprouts and grows, though he does not know how.'

The farmer scatters the seed, says Jesus, and goes to bed; he does nothing for a season, but after a while shoots start to appear, a stalk, and then the grain. The farmer may have sown the seed, but the power lay within the seed itself. This kingdom application is at the heart of what Paul is saying about the gospel. In Romans, Paul compares his message with both the lawlessness within the human heart and the law as given to Israel. Sin destroys us and the law cannot save us. Only the gospel of God has the power to change sinners, wash away their sin, and give them a new heart.

Jesus said, 'I am the way, the truth and the life, no-one comes to the Father except through me.' (Jn. 14: 6). Peter is clear in his defence of the apostolic preaching in Jerusalem, when charged by the Jewish leaders to desist from speaking in the name of Jesus, 'Salvation is found in no one else, for there is no other name under heaven given to mankind by which we must be saved.' (Acts 4: 12).

This is the only message which brings hope of salvation, bringing people back to God. Where there was no way, God made a way. This too is an uncomfortable truth in a world that seeks comfort, appeasement and tolerance. But the gospel is the most wonderful, inclusive message ever known.

> There's a way back to God from the dark paths of sin;
> There's a door that is open and you may go in:
> At Calvary's cross is where you begin,
> When you come as a sinner to Jesus.

Its demand for a response

The gospel is the power of God to save everyone ***who believes***. I posted a review on Amazon of the book, *The Shack*, a number of years ago. There were many things about the book that I loved, and some that I found a little troubling. I mentioned in my response that it seemed to hint towards universalism—the notion that all people will ultimately be saved, whatever their response in life may have been to the gospel. Rob Bell proposes this more forcefully in his book, *Love Wins*. But that does not appear to be the clear view of Scripture. Death and hell will give up their inhabitants at the last judgement, only for them to be cast into the 'lake of fire.'

These issues are troubling for comfortable people in a western nation. However, the gospel demands a response. 'God commands all people everywhere to repent,' Paul tells the intelligentsia of ancient Athens! (Acts 17: 30). "What should we do?" pleads the crowd on hearing Peter's Pentecostal message. 'Repent and be baptised,' he responds. (Acts 2: 37, 38)

There is a clear message, and, because it is simple, it should not be confused or presented as simplistic.

I mentioned earlier about the little tract that we have produced to help Christians express and explain the gospel to their friends or to people they meet. We call it 'The Loved Tract.' It is an attempt to help teach and train believers in a simple way to share this good news, but without allowing us to skip or fluff the more unseemly, culturally challenging parts. If you would like to have copies of it or would like to train your church in this tool, please get in touch with us at Counties.

Paul says that the power of this message is unleashed in the lives of everyone who believes. Put another way, there is a simple **A-B-C**.

> There is something to **A**dmit to God—'I am a sinner, lost without Jesus.'
> There is something to **B**elieve—'Christ died for me, taking my sin and offering me new life.'
> There is something to **C**onfess—'Christ is risen from the dead, is Lord of all, and I confess Christ as Lord of my life.'

This public confession is vital and can so easily be missed. Telling others that I am a follower of Jesus, and publicly owning his Lordship through baptism, are fundamental to the process of truly accepting this message.

If you are struggling with cultural embarrassment regarding the gospel, ask God to help you, giving you assurance and renewed confidence in this wonderful good news. Pray daily for opportunities—including personally demanding oppportunities—to explain the gospel to others.

The goal of the gospel—changing lives

Paul writes 'For in the gospel a righteousness from God is revealed, a righteousness that is by faith from first to last, just as it is written: "The righteous will live by faith."' (Rom. 1: 17).

The need for righteousness is evident in our world. The absence of mercy or justice, of grace or compassion, continue to mark us as fallen people—unrighteous. This condition is fatal, but does not have to be final! Paul tells us that God is revealing a way that people can be made righteous—that is, can be put back into good standing with him, and have power to live a life worth living, filled with the good fruit that he alone can give. 'I have come to give you life in all its fulness,' declares Jesus (Jn. 10: 10). Everything missing, all that is needed, can be found through faith in Christ.

In his song, *You alone can rescue*, Matt Redman writes

> Who, oh Lord, could save themselves,
> Their own sin could heal?
> Our shame was deeper than the sea,
> Your love is deeper still.

You alone can rescue, You alone can save.
You alone can lift us from the grave.
You came down to find us, led us out of death.
To You alone belongs the highest praise

God's people are changed people. Far from perfect, and wrestling with the enemy daily, nevertheless, as Paul declares in Romans 8: 37–39,

> No, in all these things we are more than conquerors through him who loved us. For I am convinced that neither death nor life, neither angels nor demons, neither the present nor the future, nor any powers, neither height nor depth, nor anything else in all creation, will be able to separate us from the love of God that is in Christ Jesus our Lord.

Changed lives, hope where there seems only hopelessness, peace when all around is turmoil, the ability to forgive when others are driven by hate, and love flowing from Christ through the hands and feet of his church, this is the power of the gospel. This is the message that we are called to affirm, to share and to preach. It is from God, on every page of Scripture, all about Jesus, for everyone, and has the power to change the lives of everyone who believes. What a gospel, what good news. May God use this book to encourage, inspire and equip you to share the gospel with others.

We have a Gospel to proclaim,
Good news for all throughout the earth;
The Gospel of a Saviour's name:
We sing his glory, tell his worth.
(Edward J. Burns)

For discussion

1. How central do you think gospel proclamation is in the life of your church? Explain why you think this.
2. In your own words define what you understand by the gospel.
3. Many evangelicals shy away from openly sharing the gospel with others. Why is this and what can be done about it?

Chapter 3

What is conversion?

Stephen McQuoid

The word 'Christian' is one of the most misused in everyday speech. That is principally because it means very different things to different people. For many in Britain today, the word 'Christian' is no more than a cultural label. They do not have a personal belief in Jesus and neither do they attend church. Being a Christian is merely an expression of their inherited culture. The descriptor distinguishes them from others who might be Muslim, atheist or agnostic. For others, the word 'Christian' signifies a definite belief system, though it might not be the same as that espoused by evangelical Christians. Someone who is Roman Catholic, or even Orthodox, would fit into this category. For evangelicals, however, to describe someone as 'a Christian' has very specific connotations and at the heart of it is the idea of conversion.

In order to properly understand what the biblical doctrine of conversion is, we first need to grasp the life from which we are converted. That involves understanding the damage caused by sin. If the word 'Christian' is misused, so too is the word 'sin'. In essence, the Bible sees sin as anything within us that is contrary to the character of God. In that sense, sin is much more than just some of the bad things that we might do, for example, sexual sins or theft. It is more subtle and pervasive than that. Anything in our character which does not point to or glorify God is sin.

It also needs to be stated that sin affects every part of our being. This is important because, once we grasp this reality, we begin to understand what an all-encompassing experience conversion is. Sin affects our will (Jn. 8: 34), making us slaves to sin. However hard we try to be good or virtuous, sin always gets the upper hand, so that we sin whether we want to or not. It also affects our mind (Gen. 6: 5). Actually, it can be argued that this is where sin often begins. We allow our minds to become polluted; we dwell on things we should not, and eventually we act on our thoughts. Sin also has an effect on our emotions. Rather than being horrified and repelled by sin, we love it. Its grip on our lives grows as we willingly surrender to it (Rom. 1: 24; 1 Tim. 6: 9). We can also hear the impact of sin in our speech as we say things that we should not, but we have so little control over our tongues that we cannot help it (2 Tim. 3: 3; Jas. 3: 5–10). It also affects our behavior and we end up doing things that we know to be wrong, but we do them anyway (Gal. 5: 19; Rom. 1: 28).

It is never easy coming to terms with the fact that we are desperately sinful and, of course, that sometimes makes evangelism challenging because people don't want to face up to the reality of the ugliness of human sin. However, unless we know what sin is and how much of an offence it is to God, we will never want to confess our sin and find forgiveness. Recognizing the power of sin is also important in discipleship. To follow Jesus is to say no to sin. Indeed, conversion is the starting point, where we turn our backs on the past and follow Jesus into the future. This will only work if we are aware of sin's power and the areas of our lives where we struggle. We need to determine to consciously live our lives resisting sin's grip.

Back to basics

Before we look at the actual moment of conversion, we need to think first of the journey that we make to get to the point of conversion. In Romans 10: 14, Paul made a pertinent point about evangelism stating, 'How, then, can they call on the one they have not believed in? And how can they believe in the one of whom they have not heard? And how can they hear without someone preaching to them?' His point was that, in order for someone to experience true conversion, they need someone to guide them and introduce them to the truth. Conversion is not just some vague religious experience: it is a specific commitment we make to God, based on our grasp of the truths that are revealed in Jesus Christ. Without grasping those truths, it is not possible to make that conscious decision to repent of our sin and trust Jesus. Given the importance of this journey towards conversion, it is worth tracing the steps that we take towards it, to enable us properly to understand the process.

On the journey

Anyone who is a true Christian will have made this journey that leads to conversion. But the starting point of the journey is different for everyone, and these differences can be significant.

Many Christians have grown up in homes where their parents not only told them about God and his love from a very young age, but also lived consistent Christian lives in front of their children. This is a privileged position to be in, and it is unsurprising that many such people make their own commitment to Christ when they are very young.

Others, however, have had a very different upbringing and therefore they had a different starting point. I will illustrate this by introducing three people who are Christians now, but whose upbringing meant that they had to travel a long way before they were able to convert to Christianity.

First, there is Asif, a Birmingham-born son of Pakistani immigrants. He came from a pious and traditional family who brought him up to be a hard-working and honourable individual. His father took him to the Mosque where he learned about the Islamic faith and he became personally very devout. He knew some Christians from his workplace, but believed their faith to be false and a corruption of the truth. His long journey to the point of his conversion involved many conversations over years with one particular friend, a journey in which he discovered who Jesus really was and eventually broke free from the constraints of Islam.

James, on the other hand, grew up in a prosperous home where both his parents were well-paid professionals, but with no religious background. His father, a chemistry professor, was also a committed atheist. The many conversations James had with his father during his teenage years convinced him that atheists occupied the intellectual high ground, and his university years studying physics confirmed his own atheism. James knew very few Christians personally, and inwardly he would sneer with derision when anyone even hinted that they believed in the existence of God. For James, the journey to the point of his conversion took many years and sustained contact with a couple of Christian teachers in the school where he taught physics. Also a Christian neighbour who demonstrated extreme patience and grace in the face of James' persistent criticism of the Christian faith.

Sarah grew up in a nominal Catholic family. She was occasionally taken to chapel, but was then allowed to do what she liked once she reached high school age. She choose not to go and lacked any kind of belief. She married young and had a daughter whom she adored. Having lapsed totally, she had little desire to bring her daughter up as a Catholic. Suddenly disaster happened. Her daughter got leukaemia and, after several years of suffering, died. The trauma of all of this put such a strain on Sarah and her husband that their marriage fell apart and they divorced. Sarah was very hurt and angry and blamed God for everything. Her journey to the point of her conversion was a painful one, full of tears and helped by a deeply empathetic Christian friend whom Sarah got to know through a mutual friend.

Each of these stories reminds us that some people will have a long and arduous journey to travel before they come to the point of being able to make that decision for Christ. There is no particular formula that assists in that journey, and evangelism requires patience, grace, persistence and courage. We are also highly dependent on the Holy Spirit, not just to give us wisdom and the words to communicate the gospel, but also to speak into the life and situation of the person that we are witnessing to. After all, being born again is a spiritual event and the Holy Spirit gives the spiritual life necessary for spiritual decision-making. This is why evangelists should be people of prayer. They work with (and for) the Holy Spirit as they share the good news about Jesus.

Paul's point in Romans 10: 14, however, is that the job of the evangelist is of vital importance as they share this good news. Before a person comes to the point where they are ready to take that step and be converted, they need to know certain things. They do not need to know much, but the basics are important. They need to understand they are accountable to God and have sinned, that Jesus died to pay the price for sin, and that trusting in him brings forgiveness. They also need to have faith, not only in the essential truth statements of Christianity, but also faith to believe that, if they take this step towards conversion, it will make a difference to life now and for eternity. They also need to have a willingness to surrender. After all, being a Christian is not merely a matter of accepting some doctrinal truths: a Christian is someone willing to give their lives to Christ and follow him. All of this needs to be in place before conversion can happen and given how far from God many people are, this journey can take a lot of time and effort.

What is conversion?

Now that we have done the ground work, what do we actually mean by conversion? For many people becoming a Christian was a long drawn-out process. Nevertheless, however long this process, there was still a defining moment, or moments, when the decision was taken to surrender to Christ. In that sense, we don't drift into faith: it is a conscious and deliberate thing. That does not mean that there is some formulaic prayer that we need to utter, or even that any words are uttered. But the person must both want to be a Christian and consciously commit their life to this.

I have already mentioned the issue of knowledge. The person who is becoming a Christian must know they have offended God because of their personal sin and that Jesus' death and resurrection can not only deal with their sin, but also give them new life. This knowledge cannot just be theoretical; after all, even demons are aware of these as matters of mere fact (Jas. 2: 9). There has to be the practical recognition that accepting these facts needs to be accompanied by a willingness to accept that these truths really must make a difference in our lives when we willingly embrace them for ourselves. In other words, Jesus is not just a character from history: he is a living person who can be involved in my life now and can totally transform the person that I am. It is a bit like the difference between a person who looks at an armchair and theoretically acknowledges that the chair would be capable of bearing his weight but does not trouble to sit in it, and another person who looks at the same chair and declares he is tired and so sits down and totally relaxes in the comfort of the armchair. It is this living belief that leads to conversion (Jn. 3: 16). This living faith does not need to be verbally expressed at the moment of conversion, though that is often what does happen, but the person does need consciously to express their commitment to that faith in some deliberate way and certainly needs to express it in the heart to God (Rom. 10: 9 ; Jn. 1: 12).

This faith needs also to be accompanied by repentance. We need the forgiveness that Jesus offers precisely because our lives are an offence to God. Consequently, there is no point in making some kind of tokenistic commitment to Christ, but not actually changing the way we live. In Romans 6: 1–3, Paul talks about our dying to sin. Repentance is essentially a complete change in the direction of our lives. Before our conversion, we followed our own desires (and sin) and were unconcerned about what God thought about our behaviour. To repent is to stop following our own direction and follow Christ instead. This should result in a very radical change of life which also leads to a profound transformation in our daily behaviour.

It is important to make the point that repentance is not some matter-of-fact altering of our direction. A person who is repenting is not just saying, "I'll give it a go and see if life gets any better." Repentance is a 'heart thing', as well as a 'head thing'. In 2 Corinthians 7: 9 & 10, Paul says,'your sorrow led you to repentance. For you became sorrowful as God intended and so were not harmed in any way by us. Godly sorrow brings repentance that leads to salvation and leaves no regret, but worldly sorrow brings death.' (NIV) It is clear from these verses that repentance involves a genuine sorrow and regret for the lives we have lived and the offence it has caused God. It is a recognition that my life cannot continue in the same way, but rather I need to address the sins in my life and endeavour to live as Jesus did, a life characterised by holiness and obedience to God's will.

Repentance is also a joy! While sin can give temporary pleasure, it is also very destructive. I have frequently met people who recognise what damage it does to their lives and relationships, as well as to other people. My own experience was like that. I was totally fed up with my old life and I felt enormously guilty. The prospect of being completely forgiven and having a fresh start was like drinking from a beautifully cold mountain stream on a hot day when you are parched. I felt utterly refreshed! Just as Jesus said in Matthew 11: 28 & 29, "Come to me, all you who are weary and burdened, and I will give you rest. Take my yoke upon you and learn from me, for I am gentle and humble in heart, and you will find rest for your souls. For my yoke is easy and my burden is light." It is a real thing! Not everyone has an emotional conversion, but they still know that life is now different.

Conversion is a beginning not an end

It is important to recognise that the point of conversion is not the end of the line: rather it is the start of a new adventure. This is important for evangelists to understand. While we celebrate a person becoming a Christian, the hard work continues because we now need to help them understand what it means to follow Jesus. This is no easy pathway because while each new convert begins a new life, their old nature is still with them. They may not be slaves to sin any more (Rom. 6: 6), but their old attitudes and desires are still there and it will be a constant battle for the rest of their lives here on earth (Rom. 7: 22–24). Christians still succumb to temptation and fall, and this has to be resisted constantly. In that sense, the Christian's life is a continual commitment to faith and repentance.

Conversion and changing society

Conversion is a personal thing, but the results of conversion potentially affect the whole of society. There is a great deal of discussion among politicians, social scientists, sociologists and law enforcers as to how to change society for the better and give a new sense of direction. There are many things that policy-makers can do to make a difference. But society is ultimately made up of individuals, and how they behave will inevitably impact society at large.

Society can be changed through conversion, one person at a time. This has been evidenced throughout history and is apparent today. There are many accounts of marriages that were salvaged, and families saved because a husband or wife was converted and experienced such a change of behaviour that they went from damaging family life to healing and affirming it. Employers who were ruthless and often dishonest were transformed because of their conversion and became different people in the workplace. The gospel has a powerful social dimension. In the early nineteenth century, slavery was abolished in the British Empire and at the heart of the abolitionist movement were Christians, some of whom were even slave-owners or traders before they became Christians. Today, some of the most troubled communities in the country are experiencing a transformation as people with a history of drug abuse and crime are being converted and experiencing the transformative power of the gospel.

Not every conversion is dramatic, yet a real change takes place as new Christians begin to follow Jesus and live according to biblical values rather than their own. There is a real sense in which the only sure way in which to genuinely change a community or even a whole society for the good is to have transformation from within as one person after another begins to deny themselves and follow Jesus. In that sense, conversion has a real impact on everyone.

Conclusion

Conversion is central to conversion! The job of the evangelist is to share the good news with people who are not Christians and encourage them to make a clear decision to follow Jesus. The doorway into the Christian life is through repentance and faith, without which a person cannot be a Christian. While people's experience of conversion may vary greatly, the conscious decision to rely on Jesus's work on the cross in faith, and the determination to change and follow him though repentance are both central features. Evangelists need to keep that in mind as they share the gospel. Moreover conversion is just the beginning. It is the start of a life of discipleship which will continue for the rest of life and that is also something that the evangelist needs to prepare people for.

For discussion

1. In a single sentence, how would you explain to a non-Christian friend what conversion is?
2. What should the visible results of conversion be? What role does discipleship have in achieving this?

Chapter 4

Has church become irrelevant in twenty-first century Britain?

Tim Cracknell

For those of us who love the church and regularly give large amounts of time and energy to the life of our local church, the question of relevance seems a crazy question. Of course the church is relevant, and if you are like me, you believe it to be more needed now than ever. However, we live in a fast-paced world that worships the gods of materialism, science, and popularity. It is a world in which credibility is gained by receiving the endorsement of the in-crowd or being an A-list person, and without this credibility you are considered a misfit on the road to nowhere. To add to the mix, the Judaeo-Christian values which have provided the framework for British life for the last couple of centuries are rapidly being replaced by a new set of values—ones that teach that, now we have advanced as a society, we don't need these old-fashioned restrictive values. Enlightenment has given us a new freedom to express ourselves and we can cast aside the "rules and regulations" of previous unenlightened generations and embrace the new era. We can satisfy our hedonistic desires to our hearts' content, so long as it doesn't hurt anyone else or, at least, doesn't hurt them too much!

Against that backdrop, the church is often characterised in the media as uncool, out of touch, old-fashioned, not relevant, and increasingly the butt of jokes. Church attendances are in sharp decline and, everywhere we go, we see redundant church buildings turned into everything from flats to mosques. Many observers are starting to pen the obituary for the church in the UK, and it raises the unthinkable question: could it be that the church has actually become irrelevant and those of us who attend them have not even noticed?

This is a painful question for us believers to ask, but a necessary one. Essentially, it highlights the importance of being relevant. If the ambivalent, secular world around us doesn't see the church as having any relevance, have we lost our way? Has something gone wrong? In the book of Acts, ordinary people didn't need to be convinced that the church was relevant. They were queuing up to join. They were wanting their widows to be fed and cared for, their sick to be made better, and Holy Spirit power to transform their lives. How come the watching world in the twenty-first century sees us as just another club to join, which they approach with a 'take-it-or-leave-it' attitude? Yes, we have the welfare state, the NHS and all that goes with it, but has that replaced God and the church?

The daily news headlines tell us that the world is a very unhappy and troubled place. If ever it needed a Saviour, it is now. War, famine, poverty, and family feuds are rife. Even in the affluent West, depression, misery, hopelessness, and unsolvable problems abound, despite all the benefits of modern medicine, science, and every kind of therapy. Perhaps the world does need a demonstration of Holy Spirit power after all and the healing touch of the Saviour, but how is it going to access them if no one is taking any notice of God's chosen tool to convey his message of hope? In the Bible, we see that Jesus only had one plan by which to bring the gospel and nurture spiritual life in the world, and that was through the church. But we must admit that in the western world in recent times, the plan does not seem to be working that well. The church is a delivery agent constituted of broken people like you and me, who are at best a spiritual work in progress, and I for one often mess up!

Let us step back for a moment and remind ourselves of Jesus' words to Peter when he commissioned him: 'Now I say to you that you are Peter (which means 'rock'), and upon this rock I will build my church, and all the powers of hell will not conquer it.' (Mt. 16: 18 (NLT)) The picture here is of a church moving forward like an unstoppable, irresistible army, conquering all before it because it is empowered by Jesus himself. Jesus then commissioned his disciples, as recorded in Matthew 28, to take this glorious, life-giving, hope-filled, joy-producing, life-changing good news of 'salvation through no other name' into all the world. And that is what they did. The book of Acts describes the excitement, the tension, and the challenges of following Jesus' command, complete with all its highs and lows. But the church was on the move, going from Jerusalem, to Judea, to the ends of the earth, empowered by the Holy Spirit as he worked in the hearts and lives of godly, passionate women and men.

This stirs a question in our minds: why did the church explode in so much gospel action and growth? It was birthed in prayer and Holy Spirit power, but why did a sceptical world sit up and take notice? This question points us to the question of relevance. History is littered with powerful men and women who have made a mark on their times, but after their death only a few die-hard fans take any notice. Why was Jesus different? How come at a time when news travelled at a snail's pace and there was no internet or 24/7 rolling news broadcasts, that the news of Jesus spread like wildfire across the world? Several observations in Scripture tell us why.

When John the Baptist was at a low ebb in prison, he sent some of his disciples to double-check whether Jesus really was the Messiah. Jesus replied, 'Go back to John and tell him what you have heard and seen—the lame walk, the lepers are cured, the deaf hear, the dead are raised to life, and the Good News is being preached to the poor.' (Mt. 11: 4–5 (NLT)) It is interesting that Jesus himself highlighted that you could believe in him as the Messiah because he was relevant to ordinary people. Their lives were being changed as miraculous healings were taking place and the gospel was being preached. In Acts 4: 13–14, we see a similar effect, but this time through his disciples: 'The members of the council were amazed when they saw the boldness of Peter and John, for they could see that they were ordinary men with no special training in the Scriptures. They also recognised them as men who had been with Jesus. But since they could see the man who had been healed standing right there among them, there was nothing the council could say.' (NLT) We must remind ourselves that these council members were highly sceptical about Jesus' disciples. They wanted them put away, but they could not deny that the impact of the disciples' actions was real and relevant to the lives of people they were in contact with. Begrudgingly, they were also impressed by the transformation in these disciples' lives: unlike them, the disciples were 'ordinary men', who had been changed by spending time in Jesus' presence. This is a pattern continued throughout the early church. Signs and wonders (see Acts 5: 12–16), resulting from hearts overflowing with compassion for ordinary people, were changing lives, and interest was spreading quicker than a virus because it was relevant to their lives. They saw someone who could make a difference in their lives and it got their attention. On the back of it, the gospel was preached and 'each day the Lord added to their fellowship those who were being saved.' (Acts 2: 47)

Down through history, missionary endeavours have recognised the importance of relevance. Hospitals and schools across the unevangelised world often owe their start-up to pioneer missionaries full of compassion for the people they are seeking to reach, compassion displayed in grace-filled actions. This, combined with communicating the timeless truth of the gospel in a culturally relevant way, was pioneered by the legendary missionary Hudson Taylor in China, and paved the way for the gospel to fall on more fertile ground because it was seen by the indigenous population as relevant to where they were.

Those of us who were brought up in Christian families and in the church have many blessings to be thankful for, but it can blind us to the situation in our communities and the country at large. We need to recognise that we live in a post-Christian culture. The world has changed around us and continues to change at a dramatic pace, and therefore we need to learn to recapture the missionary mindset if we are going to display the relevance of the gospel to our neighbourhoods and see the tide of spiritual decline arrested. I believe that it starts when we understand the importance of relevance to our culture. Therefore, we must become students of our culture as well as of the Bible. The church in Acts understood that, but do we? Or have we drifted into a comfortable malaise in which, in all honesty, we like what we have too much to be willing to become a missionary where we are and to allow the Holy Spirit to enable us to win some for Christ?

Sadly, too many church leaders are unwilling to grasp this nettle and to lead from the front, in order to bring in the change required to make their churches relevant again to their lost communities. They are nervous of upsetting the vocal person who complains about any change brought into the church. The challenge that I always give myself, and anyone else who would care to listen, when I start to be drawn that way is this: "When I am unwilling to take the unselfish steps that bring change, and make the gospel relevant to my community, I am in effect saying to the lost around me, you can go to hell!" And surely none of us want that to happen on our watch.

This said, I am like everyone else as a church leader—I struggle with change and have a strong dislike for making myself unpopular with my congregation. The temptation to let things drift along, and not to upset the apple cart, is persuasive for me! What are the biggest mistakes I have made by avoiding change which would make us more relevant to our community? Here are my top eight.

1. When I stop adding value to my local community

"People don't care how much you know until they know how much you care", Theodore Roosevelt famously said at the beginning of the twentieth century, but his words still ring true today. Unless our communities know that we really, genuinely care about them, they will never stop to listen to our life-giving message. We then become irrelevant, viewed as some kind of elitist country club that only a few will ever be interested in. Conversely, how will they know we care? When they can see that we make a tangible difference to their lives in the areas that matter to them. In their everyday lives, when we roll up our sleeves and help tidy up the streets, serve the disadvantaged, bring relief to the poor, encourage our schools, feed the hungry, and a hundred and one other practical ways in our communities.

When we launched the church in Cinderford, we agonised over what name to give it. We finally landed on Forest Community Church. 'Forest', because we are based in the very picturesque heart of the Forest of Dean. 'Church', because, in this traditional area, if people want to explore issues around faith, they want to come to a church. 'Community', because we realised that if we were to rise above the plethora of churches in the region that were dying fast, we needed to be seen to be relevant and the best way to do this was by positioning ourselves at the heart of the community. I wish that I could take credit for this name, because it was a master-stroke of genius. Since that time, everyone else in the town seems to have got in on the act. We have a community fire service, community hospital, community doctor's surgery, community policing, and the list goes on. People value community and I have had groups call me up and say they would like our church to have a stand at open days, for example, because we are the community church. No other church gets an invitation as, sadly, many do not see them as part of the community.

I love it when, after we have revamped a children's play area or painted up classrooms at a school, non-Christian people come to me and say, "It's great that you do all this good work as well as the religious stuff!" You see, they value the "good stuff" we do when we serve our community, because it is relevant to them and makes a difference to their lives. They are impressed that we do it without expecting anything in return and, as yet, don't understand that the "religious stuff" is even better. They just see religion as a set of outdated rituals for those sad people who need a crutch to lean on. But, as we get alongside them and serve with generous hearts, they start to have their blind eyes opened. Doesn't it sound like Jesus when he was ministering to people's needs?—as in the case of the demon-possessed man of Mark 5 from whom Jesus cast out demons and who then became an evangelist, proclaiming in his area 'the great things Jesus had done for him'.

However, I all too easily to get sucked into the politics and demands of church life, and the business of adding value to our community gets forgotten more often than I would like to admit. The question that I keep asking myself in order to help keep my focus is this: would our community notice if our church closed? The sad fact is that during the COVID pandemic many churches have closed, and they have not been missed! Shame on us! No wonder many people see Christianity as irrelevant. People noticed when Jesus was not about and often went looking for him, as his presence in his community made a difference to the lives of ordinary people. If our community does not notice us when we are absent, we are in trouble.

2. When I allow pastoral pressures and internal church "stuff" to move my focus away from serving our community

Life is busy! Crazily busy if you are an elder, pastor, church leader, and especially if you have a day job and a family to care for too. There are times when something has to give.

I can remember many years ago now when Katrina and I went away for the most wonderful holiday on the Norfolk Broads. It was fun, a relaxing, slow paced, perfect, refreshing holiday after a busy time in ministry. It was shared with great company. And then we came home. Oh my goodness! All our church plans for involvement in the community for the next six months went out the window because a succession of major pastoral issues confronted us as we moved back into church life, and I mean major ones. Wilful immorality amongst our church members, major bust-ups, marriage break-ups, and the list went on. After a couple of days, we were ready for another holiday! We began to understand what Moses felt like when he came down from the mountain to be confronted by Aaron's having made the golden calf. Church leadership is not for the faint-hearted, and is certainly not glamourous. Yet, the hardest part of all is keeping the vision on track. You can call yourself a 'community church', but do you do what it says on the label? If I'm honest, we fail to live up to our labelling far too often.

The easiest way in which the devil can distract us from our calling and effectiveness as churches is by stirring up a load of pastoral problems or by just making us plain busy with urgent pastoral business. As I write this, I have four funerals to take in the next couple of weeks. They are all extra to my normal schedule, but somehow I have to find a way of fitting in the visits to grieving relatives, communication with the undertakers, and planning and preparation of four services and messages. The unique nature of church life has a habit of making it hard to keep our focus: important, legitimate, and urgent pastoral demands so easily take over, and serving our community in a tangible way is the first thing to get pushed down the priority list.

3. When our advertising, branding and building decor conveys that we are outdated, out of touch, and boring

About a year into the launch of our church, I was in the church building trying to decide what to do, when I'm convinced I was visited by an angel! The backstory was that we had inherited a dilapidated old Gospel Hall that was constructed of asbestos, with little in the way of foundations, and, for good measure, built over an old mine shaft! You get the picture? It needed a lot of work. We had re-roofed the building, got rid of the asbestos, and renovated some of the rear part of the building which had not been used for several decades. The rest had been repainted and my heart told me that we should do a major refurbishment on it too, but we had no money. We had used every penny already, so I was resigning myself to accept that we couldn't do any more with the building, and we just had to press on with reaching new people with what we had.

It was at that moment that the church doors burst open and a young lady came in, announcing herself as a journalist from the local newspaper. She was looking for a story and asked what I was doing. I shared the vision of the church to reach out to those who don't come to church in the most enthusiastic way I knew how. She then stopped me, took one disdainful look around the room, our best room, and said, "Well you have a long way to go" and left! If she was not a messenger from God, I don't know what she was.

The next week we got an army of church volunteers in and ripped out the floor, and started the next phase of modernising the building despite having no money. And guess what? When we needed money, the Lord provided all we needed. As Christians who are taught to be good stewards of our resources, we tend to put up with material things that others would not. Therefore, we accept it if our church advertising, branding and building décor is outdated and old-fashioned. After all, we know the unchanging message never goes out of date, right? The problem is that, as Canadian communication expert Marshall McLuhan discovered in 1964, "The medium is the message." In other words, if you are using a building that has the décor of 50 years ago, and doesn't look very cared for, the overarching message that we are sending to our listeners is, " are out of touch with reality, we are old fashioned, we belong to an earlier generation and therefore our message is not relevant."

An important move that I made to help change the image of the church was to screen the football World Cup Live on the big screen in the church building. We sent out a press release and the papers loved it. Apparently, we were the only place in Gloucestershire that was showing the World Cup on a big screen. BBC Radio Gloucester picked it up, and I did a live interview just before the kick off of the England v. Sweden game! Funnily enough, very few people came, BUT the big thing was that this out-of-date, old-fashioned Gospel Hall, which was renowned for its small number of quaint elderly people, got the biggest headlines in town and the locals started to ask what was happening. Could it be that this church was starting to become relevant? It was all part of a process of changing people's expectations of what a community church was all about. Later, during that World Cup campaign, a family came to watch, whose father was an influential builder in town. When we wanted a new carpark laid a few years later, he provided a man and an earth-moving machine for a week to lay the carpark, free of charge. He appreciated that, even if he didn't share our faith, we were adding value to our community and were relevant.

This is vital to understand. The medium IS the message in today's generation. So if we want to get heard, we have to take notice of how we convey our message. The ongoing battle is that fashions change constantly and that means we are always having to make subtle tweaks to our branding in order to keep ourselves relevant. We had a lovely church logo, but after eight years it needed updating. All the older people in the church didn't like the change. I didn't like the change. But it was necessary if we were going to continue to stay relevant to today's generation. We must not sit and rest on our laurels, just because we changed something several years ago. Change is here to stay if we want to remain relevant in our culture, and that presents a massive challenge to church leaders, myself included.

4. When I spend all my time with Christians

I was brought up in a Christian home, I spent 25 years working in a Christian family business, and now I work in a church business. I'm surrounded by Christians. It's my comfort zone and I love it. However, it's not good for me to be constantly with Christians. If I am going to be relevant to my community and in my preaching, I need to understand how the non-churched around me think. I need to sit with them and build meaningful relationships with people who are not like me, in order to reach out to those around me. Playing sport at the local community centre, or golf, or joining a local society or group, are all helpful ways of overcoming this. I have to confess that this is an issue I really struggle with, and one thing I do as often as possible is to build relationships with people around the church building where I'm based. I often get invited in for a cuppa as they see me as a friend, and it all helps me to stay relevant.

5. When my sermons become littered with Christian jargon

Evangelical jargon and yesteryear language are the death of communicating to the non-churched. I sometimes get invited to advise churches on how to move their church forward if they feel they are stuck. One church invited me along to one of their Sunday services. I was not going to speak: I was just visiting and observing. They were the loveliest people you could wish to meet, and ran weekday evangelistic events with sometimes hundreds coming along. Sometimes, some of these visitors would join a Sunday service. Why would they not want to join? However, the church lamented that they never had anyone come back a second time! That's strange, I thought to myself as I waited for the service to begin after a very warm and friendly welcome: I wonder what is putting people off from coming back? The meeting was about three minutes old when I could see what their problem was. Although I had been brought up in a similar kind of church, and I understood every word they spoke before the service, it was as if they changed gear and language when on the platform. Add into the mix that, when the sermon started, lots of complicated theological words flowed out: my mind was reeling and I didn't have a clue what they were trying to say! So I was not surprised that their unchurched visitors, whom they had worked so hard to bring along, failed to return. If I lived in that area, I would have been unlikely to make a repeat visit. They were speaking a different language to twenty-first century Britain, and no one had told them. Their visitors who loved the preservice friendly atmosphere would have gone away thinking, 'nice people but not relevant to my situation.'

When you see this as a visitor to another church, it is easy to identify and call it out. However, I know that I am prone to get lazy, and drift into evangelical jargon-speak myself, all too often. At those moments, I find that it is conversations with new Christians, or not-yet Christians, that pull me up sharp and and give me the chance to get back on track.

6. When my sermons lack practical application

Sermons that lack practical application stink of irrelevance. They are just a process of conveying knowledge. The Apostle Paul warns us of the dangers of knowledge without action which 'puffs up' (1 Cor. 8: 1) and James implores us, 'don't just listen to God's Word. You must do what it says. Otherwise, you are only fooling yourselves.' (1: 22 (NLT)) When we hear God's Word, it is intended to be like looking at a mirror in the morning. We see our out-of-place hair and unshaven look, and move into action. When God's Word is taught, we should also be compelled, and Holy Spirit empowered, to move into action. It grieves me that, at times, we manage to turn the living, dynamic, and transformative Word of God into the driest of history lessons, devoid of life and robbed of power.

In my own experience, my preaching went up several gears when I changed my approach and sought to add a verb into every point. My messages stopped being pointless, and lives began to be impacted. I started to see a response, and often I would have a line of people wanting to have follow-up conversations about the message and how it had impacted them, in contrast to the usual, "that was a nice message", at the door. But, like everyone, I am prone to getting lazy, as unpacking the application involves more work. It is so much easier to say, "I'm sure the Holy Spirit will apply the message to your life" and finish there, than to apply the message. However, the Holy Spirit wants us as preachers to listen to his voice and help our audience, who may not have the knowledge we have, to move into action.

If we are serious about being relevant, we must season our messages with practical application that engages our audience in a meaningful way. After all, Jesus' preaching in the Gospels was full of application. He didn't simply say that you should pray: in the sermon on the mount, he told them how to pray.We should do the same. That's why his listeners hung on every word and 'listened to him with great delight.' (Mk. 12: 37). Every time I take short cuts and in my preaching don't help people to unpack the "how to" of the passage, I am only doing half the job and leave my congregation short-changed. It's vital if I want to show that the message is relevant and want to be faithful to God's Word.

7. When I bow to pressure to conform the church music to yesteryear Christian style

Oh boy! If you want to stir up trouble in church, start changing the music. You are guaranteed to fan the flames to an inferno! I can see why. When we first come to faith in Christ, usually there is a song and music style that goes with our experience as a new believer. The very sound of the melody stirs our heart and emotions, becoming integral to our experience as Christ followers. Such is the power of music. We see it everywhere, whether it is pop concerts or football matches. Crowds sing and people's emotions are moved. The problem is that styles change.

One of the best ways to discover what music style people in an area like is to listen to the radio stations they listen to. In the Forest of Dean, we discovered that 66% of people listened to BBC Radio 2 and Heart FM. These two stations have music with a beat to it and interestingly hardly any organ music. Guess what? In the Forest of Dean, nearly every church has an organ! One of the first funerals I took was a man in his sixties who was typical of the area. His one request for his funeral was that the organ should NOT be used. He could not stand organ music! Yet most churches in our area still have not understood that by making the organ the instrument of choice, and pandering to a family who donated the organ years ago, or to the one vocal person who is passionate about organ recitals, they are driving away the next generation in droves.

I have invested more time with our church musicians than in any other area of church, to help navigate the complexities of this subject. It is too important to ignore. Music style connects us to a generation and it takes unselfish people to grow a church. We have a choice: be selfish, have the music we like and enjoy, or allow the next generation to have a fair crack of the whip and bring in a new style, and see a new generation come to faith in Christ. Every time I relax on this and pander to a certain section of the church who are resistant to changing the music, we lose the chance to reach a new generation for Jesus. It's too important to ignore, but it will stir up a hornets' nest.

8. When I start to lose an emotional connection with my community

I believe a church should reflect the demography of the area in which it is situated. They are our target audience. We have defined what Mr. and Mrs. Average Forest of Dean look like, and they are different from people living in Gloucester or Cheltenham or Bristol or London. Foresters, as they like to be known, are older, more traditional, less ethnically diverse, one of lowest income groups in the county, and mainly employed in manufacturing. You get the drift. Our aim is that the church looks like the area in these regards.

There is a pitfall for me which I easily step into. While I tick some of the boxes that define Mr. and Mrs. Average Forest of Dean, I don't tick them all. It is easy for me to ignore those who are not like me, and focus instead on the "nice", "easy-to-get-on-with" people who are like me. I have to make a conscious effort to keep myself emotionally connected to the community, but it is easy to let this slip, out of convenience. I try to counter this by the following:

a. *Prayer walking around the towns and villages that make up the Forest of Dean*—As I pray when people are going off to work in the morning, I get a feel for the homes they come from, the family units, and the pressures on their lives, and I start to feel a connection with them.

b. *Use the local shops and get to know the shop keepers*—Usually, when I am in town people recognise me and chat.

c. *My hairdresser is the one in the centre of town*—not necessarily the best one, but the one most people go to. We have great chats there, which keep me connected and known.

d. *My wheels*—When replacing my car, I look at what is popular in the area and get one similar, so that I identify with the community. At present, it is a modest, 11-year-old Vauxhall Corsa.

e. *Clothing*—I dress casually, like most people do, so as not to put a barrier between myself and others.

f. *Build strategic relationships*—I make it my business to meet up for a coffee with our local MP, headteacher, chair of town council, and other movers and shakers in the community, to learn from them the concerns in the area and to make them aware of our community work. It means that we are, in the main, seen as an asset to our community. When we were seeking planning permission for a project, and having some difficulties, I was able to phone up one of the movers and shakers about our problems, and his reassuring response was, "We don't want to lose what the church brings to our community. I will help you on this." That came about because I had spent years oiling the key relationships in the community. But it is easy to drop my guard on this.

* * * * * * *

You may think of other reasons why our churches are viewed as irrelevant. The important thing here is to acknowledge that we live in a culture that is constantly changing. While the timeless message of the gospel never changes, we must communicate it in a way that is understood. This is what makes churches relevant. We have the only message of life-giving hope in town. It is sacrilege to wrap it up in the time warp of yesteryear's cultural expressions that reduce our audience to thinking that our message is not for them. Because everyone needs Jesus.

For discussion

1. What are the main causes of churches declining or closing in your area?
2. Go through Tim's list of church changes: list in order of priority which ones you would like to apply to your church and why.

Part 2

How We Can Make Jesus Known in the UK Today

Chapter 5

The evangelist in the twenty-first century

Martin Erwin

I have long loved and used the quotation from J. L. Ewen: 'As long as there are millions destitute of the Word of God and knowledge of Jesus Christ, it will be impossible for me to devote time and energy to those who have both.' I believe the clarity and content of such a statement should shape our thinking in life and about what we are and do as churches.

The thought is often repeated by evangelists more colloquially as, 'I would rather spend my time with those who don't know Christ than attend yet another meeting of Christians.' Given the frailty of the human condition, this kind of thinking exposes a number of potential strengths and weaknesses in both the evangelist and the local church. It may also lead to severing of the relationship between the local church and the evangelist—one of the key gifts that Christ has given to build his Church.

First, notice the passion of the evangelist for lost people: 'Let's go after the "one" rather than waste yet more time with the "ninety-nine".' This mantra, though perhaps not always held or expressed in such crude terms, is still close to the thinking of many evangelists. It has biblical merit and precedent, and should constantly be heard by church leaders. But it also exposes a common flaw in how evangelists view the priority that churches give to evangelism—one that will find an equal and opposite reaction in many churches.

Secondly, such a view if strongly held and expressed by evangelists will lead to frustration in church leaders and members. Pastors will say, 'I have to care for the flock and the evangelist is "unmanageable" in my church.' As a result, pastors, elders, and leaders disengage from the evangelist, perhaps supporting their work through prayerful interest and some funds, but with little meaningful relationship and involvement of the evangelist in the particular fellowship.

Thirdly, this in turn creates a sense of isolation in the evangelist—"I just get on with the work; my church isn't very interested." After all, if the church is not interested, then it becomes a hindrance to, rather than a spur or partner in meaningful mission.

In time, the outcome of such thinking will lead to a separation of the church from effective, sustainable evangelism. Sadly, that is the case in many local churches. The logic expressed above is not the only possible reason for the phenomenon, but is one of many reasons. In this chapter, we will seek to reimagine the role of the evangelist as defined in Scripture and expressed in the twenty-first century church.

The evangelist in Scripture

The apostle Paul, writing to the Christians in Ephesus, explained to them how God would build, strengthen and establish the Church:

> So Christ himself gave the apostles, the prophets, the evangelists, the pastors and teachers, to equip his people for works of service, so that the body of Christ may be built up until we all reach unity in the faith and in the knowledge of the Son of God and become mature, attaining to the whole measure of the fullness of Christ. (Eph. 4: 11–13)

This is one of only three places where the word 'evangelist' is used in the Bible. The other two are Acts 21: 8 where Philip is termed, 'the evangelist', and in 2 Timothy 4: 5 where Paul encourages his son in the faith to 'do the work of an evangelist'.

Not only does the world need evangelists, but, as we shall explore in this chapter, the Church needs evangelists now more than ever! In order for that dream and desire to become a reality, we need to challenge a number of misconceptions about the evangelist, and their role, in the greater scheme of God's unfolding plan. False, inaccurate, and out-of-date historical definitions of the evangelist still dominate in the thinking of many church leaders. This in turn leads to culturally irrelevant, outdated and ineffective way of working that undermine God's mission for the world, rather than strengthening or sustaining it. It is time to revisit the Scriptures and reflect on the role and calling of the evangelist in the life of our churches today.

The 'gospeller.'

The word, 'evangel', is the New Testament Greek word for glad tidings, or good news, usually translated as 'gospel.' But in translating the noun, the 'gospeller' or bringer of the good news is termed an 'evangelist.'

There is a danger that we presume that everyone in our churches understands what the gospel is, and are committed to it. A Counties evangelist said to me a number of years ago, "The problem is that we have many churches that call themselves evangelical, but they are simply not evangelising!" Sadly, too many churches are setting aside a 'mission' or 'evangelism' budget but spending it purely on social enterprise. The gospel of Jesus Christ, and in particular, the work of evangelism requires both our presence—bringing the love of Jesus through our actions, loving our neighbours—and, indispensably, a demand for clear proclamation: 'But how can they call on him to save them unless they believe in him? And how can they believe in him if they have never heard about him? And how can they hear about him unless someone tells them?' (Rom. 10: 14 (NLT))

Counties mission statement was 'Making Jesus known across the UK.' However we, like many others, are facing challenges about the nature of the work of the evangelist, and the relationship between the evangelist and the local church. So, from mid-2022, we have amended our mission statement to 'Making Jesus known across the UK: inspiring and equipping local churches'.

Also, we need to rediscover a confidence in the gospel. While I have covered this earlier, let us remind ourselves that it is the power of God to save everyone who believes (Rom. 1: 16). Through the power of his death and resurrection, Jesus is still in the business of saving people, from themselves, from sin, and from death and hell.

The problem of historic definitions of the word 'Evangelist.'

An early twentieth-century Bible encyclopaedia relates a common view of Ephesians 4: 11, one based both on Philip the Evangelist (Acts 21), and reflecting British and North American experience of the evangelist from the era in which the definition was written.

> But *Ephesians* 4: 11 teaches that one particular order of the ministry, distinguished from every other, is singled out by the Head of the church for this work in a distinctive sense. All may possess the gift of an evangelist in a measure, and be obligated to exercise its privilege and duty, but some are specially endued with it. "He gave some to be apostles; and some, prophets; and some, evangelists; and some, pastors and teachers." It will be seen that as an order in the ministry, the evangelist precedes that of the pastor and teacher, a fact which harmonizes with the character of the work each is still recognized as doing. The evangelist has no fixed place of residence, but moves about in different localities, preaching the gospel to those ignorant of it before. As these are converted and united to Jesus Christ by faith, the work of the pastor and teacher begins, to instruct them further in the things of Christ and build them up in the faith.[1]

There are two assumptions from the definition that I would like to gently challenge, while recognising the value, learning and significance of such works from a past generation.

> *Assumption #1:*
> When people are converted to Christ, the evangelist steps aside, and the pastor and teacher takes over.

1. *International Standard Bible Encyclopedia*, 1915

> *Assumption #2:*
> The evangelist is an itinerant, travelling preacher, with no fixed place of residence.

This is borne out by another similar and influential document from the end of the nineteenth century.

> Evangelist—Judging from the case of Philip, evangelists had neither the authority of an apostle, nor the gift of prophecy, nor the responsibility of pastoral supervision over a portion of the flock. They were itinerant preachers, having it as their special function to carry the gospel to places where it was previously unknown."[2]

The role of the itinerant evangelist is important. I believe it is a biblical model, and one that has served the church well in many generations and cultures, and still has a role to play. However, that does not seem to be the primary role of the evangelist in Ephesians 4.

One other challenge is a much more modern one—that of the perception of evangelists, both in the church and in the world. Some tele-evangelists, and high-profile prosperity preachers, along with the accompanying media coverage, have damaged the term, evangelist. It is a good word, a God word, an honourable word, and we will need to reclaim and redeem it from the hucksters and charlatans who have used their platforms for personal gain, gold or glory, and have robbed the church of a precious and essential ministry for our time.

As the church of Christ meets the challenges of secularism here in the UK, with so many people now living who have never heard the gospel, and many local churches struggling to reach and connect with their communities, there has never been a greater need to re-evaluate the importance and the role of the evangelist. The pandemic, and the shrunken nature of the post-pandemic church only serves to magnify the need to re-examine the calling, nature, and role of the evangelist today. We must recalibrate our thinking in the local church so that we can fully harness the building blocks that God has made available to us to reach this generation for Christ.

---

2. M.G. Easton M.A., D.D., *Illustrated Bible Dictionary*, (London, [3]1897).

The ultimate purpose of the gifts

We need to look briefly at the verses immediately before and after Ephesians 4: 11. Verse 10 asserts both the present and ultimate status of Christ: 'the same one who descended is the one who ascended higher than all the heavens, so that he might fill the entire universe with himself.' (NLT). Verses 12 and 13 underline his present purpose for the Church, through the gifts that he has given it: '. . . so that the body of Christ may be built up until we all reach unity in the faith and in the knowledge of the Son of God and become mature, attaining to the whole measure of the fullness of Christ.'

From these verses and in the context of the whole letter of Ephesians, we can establish the following.

The purpose of the gifts is growth

The term 'Church growth' has become an unnecessarily divisive couplet in some circles. The Church Growth Movement spawned in the United States in the last quarter of the twentieth century brought many helpful challenges to a declining Church in the West. Donald McGavran, a third-generation missionary to India, was seminal to this movement. He wrote, 'It is God's will that women and men become disciples of Jesus Christ and responsible members of Christ's church.'[3] Who could argue with such a statement?

The Ephesians 4 passage is often, or perhaps usually, taught in the context of personal growth, or maturity for disciples or churches. There is no doubt that maturity is at least in part in view, as is clear from verses 12 and 13 just quoted.

However, both experience and Scripture demonstrate to us that it is possible for believers to get fat and slow on an inward focussed, introverted, and stodgy diet. 'Solid' Bible teaching is often the mark sought after in local church life, and it is one among three or four elements that Christians relocating look for in a church that they might join, along with good worship, children's and youth ministry and a warm welcome. Is it possible that at worst this simply translates into looking for somewhere where I can be comfortable—that won't challenge my strongly held beliefs, will provide childcare for my kids, and allow me to relax, enjoy good music and build a new network of like-minded friends.

---

3. Paul E. Engle, Elmer L. Towns, & Gary McIntosh, *Evaluating the Church Growth Movement, 5 Views*. (Grand Rapids MI: Zondervan, 2004).

The Church Growth Movement, at best, sought to challenge a mindset that had led to lethargy and decline in the church in the West. It has been criticised because it took sociological analysis and conclusions in addition to Scripture, as well as allegedly being only about seeking numbers and success.

While some of the criticisms have merit, the movement helped to highlight a serious blind spot that was developing. The Church Growth approach is both a matter of breadth and depth. Breadth without depth leads to shallow churches with a broad reach, but with a serious deficit in discipleship foundations that can sustain the believer and the local church over the long run. However, depth without breadth leads to insular churches that can become nothing more than little monastic communities, isolated from the world and making disciples who are disengaged from it.

The goal of church growth is that Christ 'might fill the entire universe with himself.' (Eph. 4: 10 (NLT)) This glorious vision of the purpose of growth—to bring Christ where he is unknown, and so see a world (and the universe) filled with Jesus, will surely change our mindset, if we let it.[4]

The ground for growth is unity (Eph. 4: 1–6)

In his book, *Natural Church Development*, Christian Schwarz explores the idea that churches grow stronger and larger when they are healthy. The Apostle Paul makes such a claim seem reasonable from the early verses of Ephesians 4. This section, which leads to the key gifts necessary for building the church, highlights that the essential foundation is unity.

> Always be humble and gentle. Be patient with each other, making allowance for each other's faults because of your love. Make every effort to keep yourselves united in the Spirit, binding yourselves together with peace. For there is one body and one Spirit, just as you have been called to one

4. On this point, for further reading, see Christian A. Schwarz, *Natural Church Development: A Guide to Eight Essential Qualities of Healthy Churches* (ChurchSmart Resources, 1996); Rick Warren, *The Purpose Driven Church: Growth without Compromising your Message and Mission* (Grand Rapids MI: Zondervan, [2]2011); Andy Stanley, *Deep and Wide: Creating Churches that Unchurched People Love to Attend* (Grand Rapids MI: Zondervan, 2016); & Jonathan Lamb, *Growing Healthy Churches: Urgent Biblical Priorities for Local Congregations* (Tiverton: Partnership, 2022)

> glorious hope for the future. There is one Lord, one faith, one baptism, one God and Father of all, who is over all, in all, and living through all. (Eph. 4: 2–6 (NLT)

This unity is grounded in the one gospel that we all preach and proclaim, and is sustained by both the hope that we have in Christ and the love that we maintain for one another. Growing churches must be healthy, but a key component of health is an ongoing demonstration and declaration of the gospel to the world.

How often has your faith been strengthened, energised, or renewed by engagement in mission—sharing the gospel with a friend or neighbour, answering the questions of a genuine searcher, seeing people come to faith in an Alpha Course or Christianity Explored, or being exposed to overseas mission for a few weeks. I believe that every believer should:

> learn how to share their own story of faith in Christ
> be equipped with a simple approach to sharing the gospel with a friend
> join a mission team at home or abroad on a regular basis.

This unity that we have been gloriously granted is much easier to sustain through the passion and experience of sharing the good news, rather than a potentially more limited exhortation or Bible study on 'unity.'

The old mantra seems still to hold true. According to a new visual produced by www.wyzowl.com only 10% of people remember what they hear, and only 20% of people remember what they read. But 80% of people remember what they see and do. More than just that, they also learned that people process visuals 60,000 times faster than text; and that 93% of communication is non-verbal!

Unity is best maintained by practising it, rather than talking about it.

The gifts for growth (Eph. 4: 7–12, especially verse 11)

> So Christ himself gave the apostles, the prophets, the evangelists, the pastors and teachers, to equip his people for works of service, so that the body of Christ may be built up until we

> all reach unity in the faith and in the knowledge of the Son of God and become mature, attaining to the whole measure of the fullness of Christ. (Eph. 4: 11–13 (NIV))

God's plan is, through the Church, to fill the universe with Christ, for his glory and name to spread throughout the cosmos, and to complete the task of the universal mission of the gospel. This is a grand vision presented to us by the apostle Paul. Let me state it again. God's great plan is that through the gospel and by his chosen instrument, the Church, he intends that the universe might be filled with Christ. These are why the gifts listed in Ephesians 4: 11 exist.

Historically, many of us grew up in a cessationist world, where some of the more dramatic or dynamic gifts such as speaking in tongues or prophetic utterances were seen to have ceased at the conclusion of the 'apostolic' age (at the death of the last of the twelve apostles, John), having been superseded by the completion of the canon of Scripture. Many evangelicals still hold such a position, and the intention of this chapter is not to promote a particular view on that wider issue. However, one victim of a narrow application of cessationism or, indeed, dispensationalism, was a broader and (I would suggest) healthier application of the five-fold ministries listed in Ephesians 4: 11 and 12. There Paul writes that Christ gave apostles, prophets, evangelists, pastors, and teachers to 'equip his people for works of service, so that the body of Christ might be built up.'

Syphoning off two (apostle and prophet) as no longer applicable and promoting three as alone contemporary and relevant is a view worth re-examining. Much hangs on our definition and understanding of the gifts of 'apostle' and 'prophet' in the context of the church. Accepting all five as essential to the growth and health of the church in every age is explored by Alan Hirsch[5] and is worth some reflection.

There is no doubt however, that the western church has promoted an unhealthy and unbalanced 'Pastor-led' model of local church, and exalted the 'Teacher' to a quasi-cultic superman status, and has at the same time ignored, relegated, or worse (for peace of mind) neglected, the role of the 'evangelist.'

---

5. In *Forgotten Ways: Reactivating Apostolic Movements* (Grand Rapids MI: Brazos, 2016).

Is it any wonder therefore that churches in our nation are growing thin on the ground, while some are growing fat through over-indulged theological appetites, which fill the mind with knowledge but don't move the heart or motivate the feet to engage in the mission of Christ.

So, where are the evangelists?

A meeting of evangelistic ministry leaders took place in Birmingham in November 2016. The title of that consultation came from the opening chapter of Roger Carswell's book, *And Some Evangelists*,[6] which is entitled, 'Where have all the evangelists gone?' That meeting was sparked by a key question: How do we raise the profile of the evangelist and raise up champions for evangelism in the local church?

At the meetiong, there was shared recognition of a number of challenges.

Challenges for local churches

The challenge for local churches is to re-evaluate the mindset underlying paid ministry appointments.

I have no issue with paid or supported roles within local churches, or indeed with the Open Brethren's practice of supporting teachers, preachers and evangelists who 'lived by faith' and served a range of local churches regionally or nationally (sometimes enjoying respect and authority which was quasi-apostolic).

Mission is still often perceived as an activity which is carried out 'overseas,' and sadly, we don't recognise that, in the UK today, we are in a 'missionary' situation which requires a missionary mindset. As a result, many local churches planning to appoint a full-time worker look for a pastor/Bible teacher, never an evangelist. The outcome of this mindset is often appointments which create strong preaching points, and the churches concerned tend to grow on the backs of others that are dying (by attracting to themselves those who are already Christians). Subsequent ministry appointments focus on children, youth, and community activity (that is, narrower, focussed roles within the church). In consequence, we lose sight of the strategic 'Big Picture' of how local churches are to engage and reach our culture and communities today.

6. Fearn, Ross-shire: Christian Focus, 2014.

Furthermore, evangelists are perceived as being out of date, and based on a historical view of 'the good "ole" days' when the evangelist was a travelling itinerant 'missioner.'

However, a straightforward reading of Ephesians 4: 11 suggests that we recognise the need for the evangelist to be church-based, with a close relationship with the local church and playing their part in a team of leaders and equippers who engage the hearts and mind of the church to take the gospel into all the world and so grow the body of Christ.

This gives rise to a number of **questions** which local churches in particular should ask themselves.

> Are there attitudes that we have held from which we need to repent?
> How can we rethink the model of church appointments and paid roles?
> What role have you created for an evangelist?
> How can you create better communication and fellowship with evangelists in your church or region?
> What roles might best be served by inter-church appointments, or the recognition of gifts that are missing in our local fellowship, but present in our region or movement?
> What simple structures or safeguards could we introduce to integrate these essential gifts more fruitfully across networks and regions?

Challenges for Bible colleges

The nature of Bible college training has too often simply turned-out pastors and teachers. Roger Carswell writes, 'I am concerned that would-be evangelists are being redirected from their natural gifting and calling.'[7] So those coming with a sense of gift and calling for something other than the pastor-teacher role are 'squeezed' into a one-size-fits-all model by both the process and the opportunities offered by churches.

---

7. Roger Carswell, *And Some Evangelists: Growing Your Church Through Discovering and Developing Evangelists* (Fearn, Ross-shire: Christian Focus, ²2014), p. 17.

Added to that, 'apologetics' is taught and represented as university-level thought. So our ability to engage with working class and benefits-dependent communities is underdeveloped. Again, this leads local churches to follow a social work and community engagement model, but this lacks the intellectual rigour to challenge the thinking and life-choices of those engaged. This reduces evangelism to mere social work. We haven't done the heavy lifting necessary to equip ourselves to share the gospel at a level and in a way that people can grasp.

A fellow worker once said to me, "I don't know how we reach that particular kind of men, other than to turn up with a crate of beer and a handful of porn! How do we break into their mindset with the gospel?"

The **questions** here are:

> Are there attitudes that we have held from which we need to repent?
> What steps can Bible colleges take to address the historic imbalance towards producing pastor-teachers and train more evangelists?
> What models are being explored or written about to challenge the status quo thinking?
> Can Bible colleges adapt their curricula to consider apologetics and evangelistic methods that will be effective in working class and benefits-dependent communities?
> How can local churches and evangelistic agencies serve Bible colleges better to help shape the outcomes and ministry roles being made available to their graduates?

Challenges for evangelists

Having been defined as 'itinerant' for so long, many evangelists continue in isolation, without pastoral support, so that they feel misunderstood and disconnected from local churches. Others continue to look for 'decisions' that, without local church engagement, discipleship and greater theological 'heavy lifting,' bear little long-term fruit. Still others resort to children's, youth, and schools work, because 'that's what evangelists do!' (though, of course, I do believe that all these categories are legitimate ways of evangelising).

However, many evangelists have created or magnified the problem to such a degree that they make themselves almost impossible to work or engage with. Many evangelists love being classified as mavericks and sadly live up to their reputation. However, Ephesians 4 seems to present something that is more akin to a team rather than an order or sequencing of roles. The evangelist must redouble his or her efforts to engage with the local church, to reach out to leaders and elders and to offer themselves with both humility and a degree of boldness, asking, 'can I help you?' The strong Pastor-led local church without the input and engagement of the evangelist may discover that, ultimately, the ship sails in ever-decreasing circles rather than going forward breaking waves with direction, purpose and mission in her heart!

Many evangelists too have lived with an outdated, outmoded understanding of their gifting and calling. When I discuss with evangelists the implication of the description of their role in Ephesians, some believe that it is not describing them. Some see themselves purely as 'seed-sowers' or 'reapers' pursuing a ministry of solitude and even, to a degree, separation. But if they are to equip churches in the way the text envisages, they must constantly engage with them.

The **questions** for evangelists are:

> Are there attitudes that we have held from which we need to repent?
> As an evangelist, have I been too comfortable living a quasi-separate life from the local church, and, if so, what dangers exist in maintaining such a position?
> As an evangelist, am I willing to learn from and submit to local church leadership and pastoral care?
> In what ways can I renew, or begin, the process of local church engagement with the intention of equipping God's people for this work?
> How might I reshape my application of my gift to support and equip the church for works of service?

So how do we move forward?

The goal of mission and ministry is to point to Jesus

A friend who is a full-time Bible teacher told me 'my personal mission statement is to bring Christians to Christ.' That simple reminder helps us focus on the goal of ALL ministry—bringing people to Jesus. We need to recognise that there is intended to be greater synergy between other church-focused ministries and the work of the evangelist. Genuine deep theology is, in many ways, simple theology: 'It's all about Jesus'.

This should lead us to consider how our churches might reflect more culturally appropriate ways to meet and present Christ.

Invite evangelists to engage at a deeper level with our church and leadership

It will help if local churches are prepared to ask, 'How can we equip our fellowship to do the work of the evangelist where we are?' and 'How can we engage better with the community where God has called us?' These questions should supplement questions about personal growth, not replace them, but perhaps the imbalance requires a drastic and dramatic rebalancing. I believe that the COVID-19 pandemic has created a need for us to address such questions. If not now, when?

Pray that God would send out workers

In Luke 10: 2, Jesus reminds us, 'The harvest is plentiful, but the workers are few. Ask the Lord of the harvest, therefore, to send out workers into his harvest field.' That prayer is answered in the immediate sending of the disciples themselves. This leads me to encourage local churches to three specific actions.

Look for evangelists among our congregation

The answer to the need for evangelists will be met by God who 'gives gifts' to the church. There can be no doubt that evangelists exist, gifted by God, in our fellowships. They may be leading your children's work, youth work or ladies' outreach. Have you ever wondered, 'how can we make every ministry as successful or fruitful as "that one"?' Well, maybe 'that one' is led not by a children's or ladies' worker, but by an evangelist. Perhaps you can invite that person's input into a wider discussion of the work of the church, and, as their gift is recognised and released, many will be equipped and you will discover that healthy churches do indeed grow!

Encourage and seek training for your evangelists

With our friends and partners, Counties has been stepping up in the provision of training opportunities for local churches in the area of evangelism. Will you partner with us? Mentioned in this book is the work of Neighbourhood Chaplains. This programme simply seeks to build a gospel focus into your community engagement and social enterprise, and training and equipping people for that. How many in your fellowship can confidently share the gospel and lead someone to Christ? Neighbourhood Chaplains helps sow and grow ideas in community engagement, and equips team members across the church in knowing and sharing the good news with a greater degree of confidence.

We also have a one-year Evangelists Training Programme (ETP). The ETP is not just for those who may become full-time evangelists, but equips evangelists in and among local churches. The goal is not to produce Counties Evangelists, but for Counties to partner with local churches to produce effective evangelists who can serve and equip where God has called and placed them. Of course, from this group, God may raise up those with a wider itinerant, regional or national ministry, but that is not the goal of the programme.

Young people looking for a gap-year in evangelism and mission will be blessed and equipped on TEAM (Training in Evangelism and Mission). Our TEAM programme works with local churches and evangelists to raise the aspirations and opportunities for fruitful mission, both during the year, and we trust far beyond.

Other groups are training evangelists too. Why not seek to connect with an evangelistic ministry to explore the possibility of training and equipping for your local church?

Appoint evangelists to our leadership teams

If your church is facing the challenge of decline and closure, perhaps the greatest need is not for a pastor or teacher, though that may bring blessing and even growth, though maybe only on the back of other declining and closing churches. It may be that we have come to a time when we should follow what seems to me to be the implication of Ephesians 4: 11. That is, to pray for, train and appoint evangelists to help lead us into the harvest fields, and model, train and equip us to reach a new generation for Christ. Better still, perhaps it is time to recognise the need for evangelists in the senior leadership teams within our local churches, to work alongside each of the other essential gifts 'so that the body of Christ may be built up until we all reach unity in the faith and in the knowledge of the Son of God and become mature, attaining to the whole measure of the fullness of Christ.' (Eph. 4: 12 & 13)

What next?

Contact Counties for support, training or help in your local church or region. Partner with us to 'Make Jesus known across the UK today.'

Contact office@countiesuk.org

For discussion

1. How would you define an evangelist, and what are the most important qualities that an evangelist should possess?
2. What can your church do to raise up new evangelists?

Chapter 6

Evangelism and the local church

Gordon Curley

In a broadcast sermon,[1] Chuck Swindoll preached from Acts 2: 41–47 under the title, 'The W.I.F.E. every Church should marry'. He proposed the following acrostic from the passage, as it described the first church in Jerusalem:

Worship
Instruction
Fellowship
Evangelism

That acrostic lodged itself in my memory and I want to use it in this chapter to frame my thoughts about evangelism and the local church.

Swindoll says that, by using these four words as a guide, 'we will be able to determine the major objectives of any local assembly that comes into existence. These objectives are cross-cultural, cross-denominational, and true, in spite of the ministry style or size. They are the specific avenues, through which we are to carry out the purpose of glorifying God.'[2]

The cradle of the newly-born Church was still rocking, but we see in Acts 2 what church should be about and how evangelism fits into it.

1. Insight for Living Canada: The Bible-teaching Ministry of Charles R. Swindoll (www.insightforliving.ca).
2. Chuck Swindoll, *The Church: Purpose, Profile, Priorities*, Insight for Living Bible Study Guide (New York, 1988).

Preparing the local church for evangelism

When I am invited to work alongside a local church for a time to try to build up their evangelistic outreach, my first question to the Leadership Team is always the same: "Why do you want to evangelise?". The response is usually the same: "To win people to Christ and to see the church grow numerically."

The next question that I tend to ask is: "What do you think will be involved?" This is often where people get stuck, and I find the following illustration sometimes helps to clarify their thoughts. New parents, returning home from the hospital with their first baby, soon realise, if they did not already, that their home is never going to be the same again. The home environment must adjust around the baby; to meet its needs and for it to thrive, preparations must be made. The spiritual parallel to that illustration is that for a new spiritual life to thrive, we need to prepare the 'home' for its arrival and make the necessary adjustments.

Challenge: Can we provide the love, nourishment, and stimulation that new Christians will need in order to thrive?

In Acts 2: 41–47, God uses the fledgling church in Jerusalem to demonstrate the framework that needs to be part of every healthy local church. That framework can help us assess whether our own fellowship is ready to look after spiritual 'new-borns'. Let's look at the four key elements of the framework, using Swindoll's acrostic.

Worship (vv. 42 & 46–47)

We are told that the early church was a 'worshipping community'. We see that worship expressed in three simple ways: 'the breaking of bread [communion] and . . . prayer', and 'praising God'. We are told that they 'devoted themselves' to these things: these Christians were single-minded and committed in their worship; it was a lifestyle they chose to embrace and as a result they experienced God in a fresh and dynamic way: 'Everyone was filled with awe at the many wonders and signs performed by the apostles.' (v. 43)

To reflect on: How can we encourage collective worship that is 'genuine'? Styles of worship will vary from local church to local church, and we all have our own personal preferences with respect to how we express ourselves in worship. We should aim to make our worship to God something from the heart, as we aspire to worship 'in spirit and in truth.' (Jn. 4: 24)

Instruction (v. 42a)

We are told that the early church was a 'learning congregation': 'They devoted themselves to the apostles' teaching.' This is first on the list because the apostles' teaching was their spiritual food, and without food we don't survive. Physically, we find that a good diet helps to maintain our strength and fitness, and promotes a healthy immune system. Similarly, our church's teaching programme needs to be planned out carefully, to ensure we have a balanced spiritual diet, one that develops our spiritual strength and fitness, and protects us from attack, as well as appealing to our spiritual tastebuds.

To reflect on: When we listen to the Word of God, are our souls being fed, and at the same time are our hearts and wills being challenged and encouraged?

Fellowship (vv. 44–45)

We are told that the early church was a 'caring flock': Ruth Fowke writes, 'The Church must be above all a caring community. It must accept people as Christ Himself accepts them, which is just as they happen to be.'[3] Church should be more than a place where we come to worship and learn, and then leave. It should also provide opportunities for us to grow closer to one another. This early-Church family showed genuine care for each other, meeting together regularly (v. 46) and meeting each other's practical needs (v. 45).

To reflect on: Do we genuinely want to help people draw closer to God, or do we just want to fill up more seats in our church buildings? True fellowship requires time and effort and, frequently, sacrifice. We must never forget that the church is made up of individuals, and, if it is to be a caring church, then its members must be caring people. As we read verses 43–47, we see that the quality of fellowship being experienced drew people into the church and to salvation itself.

---

3. Ruth Fowke, *Coping with Crises* (London: Hodder and Stoughton, 1968).

Evangelism (v. 47b)

We are told that the church is an 'out-reaching body of people': 'And the Lord added to their number daily those who were being saved.'

Here is something from the book of Acts that we as twenty-first century Christians appear to have forgotten or even reversed. The church that is gathered is worshipping, and the church that is dispersed is evangelising! These people did not come to church to win the lost. They came to church to worship, to learn, to have fellowship and then . . . they dispersed to evangelise. They first experienced a right relationship with God and then with each other, and the side effect of this was that people were 'added to their number daily'. They were added because these people involved God in their everyday lives, and they evangelised. We see that illustrated many times in the book of Acts: here are just a few examples:

meeting needs (Acts 3: 6)
speaking God's word with courage and performing signs and wonders (Acts 4: 29)
preaching in public and in homes (Acts 5: 42)
daily delivery of food to the poor (Acts 6: 1)
being led by God's Spirit to seeking individuals (Acts 8: 26)
reaching out to all kinds of people (Acts 10: 1, 2)
sending out teams of workers (Acts 13: 2, 3)
encouragement (Acts 14: 23)
keeping the right attitude (Acts 16: 25)
studying God's word (Acts 17: 11, 12)
speaking with love and without fear (Acts 18: 9)
sharing their own story with others (Acts 24: 1–25: 19)

I am not in any way against using our buildings for evangelism, but it seems to me that New Testament evangelism was never limited to where the church met. In fact, it occurred there least of all. The place where the church met was primarily the place where the 'saints' met and not the 'sinners'. The Christians were empowered by good worship, good teaching, and good fellowship, and then they went back to their homes, jobs, and neighbourhoods to evangelise.

To reflect on: As church members, are we prepared to witness for Christ outside the four walls of our meeting place? Can we draw any ideas from the examples given in the book of Acts?

Preparing the individual Christian for evangelism

Having prepared our 'nest' for the new-born Christian, we need to consider how we reach out to those around us and encourage our congregation to get involved.

It will be useful to use Chuck Swindoll's acrostic again, with appropriate changes, to explore how to prepare the individual Christian in our churches to evangelise.

> **W**itness.
> **I**nformation.
> **F**riendship.
> **E**ngagement.

Witness

Sometimes we forget the impact that 'a life lived for Christ' can have. Thinking about this, I am reminded of the event in Mark's Gospel when Jesus meets a man who was naked, out of control, self-harming, in desperate mental anguish, and also terrifying the people of the nearby villages. When Jesus freed him from the demons that possessed him, the testimony of the surprised villagers was that he was 'dressed and in his right mind' (Mk. 5: 15). As we expose our lives and lifestyle to scrutiny by people around us, we hope that they will see that, despite the everyday problems we have, we too are 'dressed and in our right mind'.

Years ago, I came across a quotation from David Winter (in the 1950s and 1960s an editor of *Crusade* magazine, and later a BBC religious broadcaster). His words ring true:

> Eloquent speeches, visual aids, films, seminars and discussion groups are, after all, no substitute for the daily, unspectacular witness of the rank-and-file Christian. If that witness

> is consistent and open, then no improvement in tactics or strategy will better it as a means of winning people for Christ. If it is not, then no evangelistic programme, no matter how ambitious or sophisticated, will make the slightest impact. That is a lesson we have been slow to learn.

Sometimes we 'undersell' the impact of a life lived for Christ, and perhaps we need to stress its importance to our church fellowships more often. I am reminded of the words of Lyman Beecher (Presbyterian minister in the USA, 1775–1863), who often said that the reason he was blessed to see so many converted under his ministry was that he had 'so many pulpit reflectors, who lived out and diffused everywhere the gospel.'

Challenge: How has the sermon you preached or heard on Sunday been reflected in your life this week?

Information

As we reach out to our friends, neighbours, and community, we need to be clear about what we are sharing; what exactly is the good news; and also we need to have briefed ourselves on the common objections to it.

Some Christians only emphasise one aspect of the gospel, e.g., 'God loves you', but fail to mention other vital aspects of the message, such as sin and the need for repentance. Local evangelism will be more effective if congregations are trained to know and share the whole gospel message. And many may be unaware of the need to tailor the expression of the gospel to suit the age, experiences, and level of understanding of the individual enquirer, and will need guidance in this respect.

It is often useful to have a tract or booklet to go through with the enquirer, such as *Journey into Life* by Norman Warren, *Why Jesus* by Nicky Gumbel, or *The Missing Piece* by Mike Hencher. Any of these will help us to cover the essential elements of the gospel in a relevant and engaging way. There are useful Apps, DVDs, and CDs that can be used in the same way, such as,

'Discovering—Real Questions'[4] assembled by Roger Carswell and 'Essentials—The heart of the Christian faith' by Lee McMunn.

I would suggest that training and discussion about the gospel, and how to communicate it, are vital. But at the very least you need to provide good resources.

Knowing how to approach common questions is an important part of equipping Christians to evangelise. Questions like: Why does God allow suffering?, Can you trust the Bible?, and How do you know God exists? are important for those with some Christian experience. Those in the younger, post-Christian generation can be expected to ask, Is there purpose in my pain?, Can science explain everything?, Hasn't science invalidated Christianity?, How can we have harmony in a world with conflicting truth claims? or Doesn't everyone have their own subjective truth which can be different from that of others?

A little bit of preparation will help us give an informed and reasoned response to questions raised (1 Pet. 3: 15). However, please remember to emphasise to your fellowship that there is no problem with saying, "I don't know, let me find out and get back to you". Just keep in mind that you never know if an opportunity will present itself to talk with that person again, so it is better to be prepared if possible.

Challenge: Do you have any evangelism training in your church's teaching programme, or do you need to take steps to build some in? Should you start by encouraging the fellowship to find ways to be more welcoming to visitors to church services, events, and activities? What makes them feel welcome? Could you move on to holding an evangelism training seminar?

Friendship

Many people are drawn to Christ because they have experienced the love and care of a Christian, and friendship may have opened the way for conversations about Christian faith. The best evangelism is always through real relationships and real conversations in which all parties feel that they are accepted and can talk openly with each other. More and more in our society, people are wary

4. In which, in three minutes each, academics and Bible scholars answer 42 questions about faith.

of making any sort of commitment to a group or regular activity or even to a friendship. We have found that, in some cases, it can take years of steady, reliable, loving friendship before we have earned the right to speak about our faith and we are trusted not to 'take advantage' in any way.

This is something in which you can encourage your congregation, reminding them of some of the instances in the New Testament where people just talked to others about faith in their everyday lives:

The influence of a testimony. (Jn. 4: 29 & Col. 1: 4)
The influence of a friend. (Jn. 1: 45, 46)
The influence of a godly mother. (2 Tim. 1: 5; 3: 14–17)

Challenge: Encourage everyone in the church to think about the non-Christians whom they might speak to on a regular basis: are they at the 'trusted-to-share' point in any of those friendships? Remind them not to push too fast, but to be praying that the Holy Spirit will be directing all interactions and moving those relationships in the right direction.

Engagement

This is purposely the final word in my second acrostic. I believe that witness, information, and friendship are the foundations for evangelism, and it is only once these three are firmly established as church culture that successful engagement through specific evangelistic events and activities really begins to occur. We will look at these opportunities in more detail in the next section.

Challenge: Ask your congregation if they feel prepared for personal evangelism and in what ways they would appreciate more training or support?

How it all fits together

I hope that you have now given some thought to preparing the church to receive new converts and to preparing members to see evangelism as a way of life. Now we can move on to activities and events that can support all your enthusiastic and/or nervous and/or fearful evangelists in building the friendships that we have talked about, and in providing 'edge-enquirers' with the opportunities to make connections and ask questions. Before you start anything, or even begin to review your current activities, you need to pray together and to develop a praying dependence on God as part of everything the church organises. THIS IS ESSENTIAL. It may help to keep in mind E. M. Bound's words, paraphrased as 'Before we talk to people about God, we need to talk to God about people.'

As to the practical shaping of your church's evangelistic programme: it will be useful to have an overview of all that your church is engaged in, and to spend time considering how it all fits together. I recommend a big piece of paper or a white board, and a spider-diagram! Then ask yourselves some questions.

> What is the range of needs you are covering (children and teenagers, those with disabilities, young families, the elderly, single people, retired people, care homes, young professionals, men, women, and so on)?
>
> Are you providing any progression for those who show a deeper interest? What can you invite them to that can facilitate further discovery? For example, when
>
> > a child at your kid's club begins to ask questions about the stories they are hearing
> >
> > a mum at toddler group wants to know more about dedicating their child in your church and what it might mean
> >
> > an elderly man asks for prayer after a senior citizens tea
> >
> > a teenager engages you in discussions about the Christian view of suffering after a youth group epilogue.
>
> Are you spreading yourselves too thin as a church and not able to provide the depth of interaction required to really engage with individual lives? Every church family has its limitations. Are you trying to do too much? Do you need to focus your energy in an area where you have already got good connections and possibly expertise?
>
> Do you need to delegate responsibility more, so that the burden of organising and preparing is spread out among the congregation? Do you need to amalgamate some groups or

activities? Is there someone who coordinates church activities? Does at least one person have a comprehensive picture of the evangelism the church is involved in?

Answering these questions should help you decide whether there are any gaps in what you are providing, and also whether there are any dead-end activities which lead nowhere and have no connection to anything else that you are doing. You will not be able to cover every age- or need-group in your community, nor will you be able to provide a full, individual programme to allow your church to interact with every individual it encounters. But it is valuable for everyone to have an idea of what is in place and what they can direct people towards.

I suggest that there are some main areas of evangelistic activity that we regularly engage in as churches and that can be investigated if you are looking to build an evangelistic programme. These include: Regular outreach events; Food based events; and Specific evangelistic events and activities. Let me give some examples of each of these.

Regular outreach events

These could be

1. Parent and toddler groups, children's clubs, youth clubs;
2. Lunch clubs, senior citizens teas;
3. Outreach events designed to attract men, e.g., quiz nights, curry nights, each including a short gospel talk.

Such events are opportunities to build up long-term contacts. For example, we have seen children who as babies were brought along to our toddler group then come regularly to children's clubs, and then move into youth groups. What a great opportunity to input into the first fifteen years of these children's lives! Parents of these children are often appreciative of what we do for them, and parents come along to specific events linked to these activities, e.g., a carol service at Christmas, an Easter Sunday celebration, or a harvest meal. These are great opportunities to be creative and make these times more than just a meeting! For example, Harvest: why not have a meal or concert to celebrate God's goodness? How about a 'ready-steady-cook' evening on portable camping stoves? A harvest or winter craft evening? Is there a Food Bank nearby that you can link with and for which you can organise a special collection? How about a community litter purge in the local park?

Having regular activities helps the church to work strategically, consistently, and on multiple levels, to present the gospel, and really invest in families' and individuals' lives.

Food based events

Coffee Mornings

These can be just social gatherings where friendships are made and invitations to other events are given out, or they can be more evangelistic with a short gospel talk. An important principle for any event with a gospel talk is to make sure those who attend know that this will happen: any publicity or oral invitation must mention that there will be a Christian element included. Being clear upfront in this way will avoid potential embarrassment and avoids misleading people by advertising one thing and giving them something else.

Meals

These can be a summer BBQ and a harvest or church family meal. Most people enjoy relaxed conversation over good food, and they are an effective way to attract visitors.

Alpha and Christianity Explored

These are probably the most popular small group resources for the instructional type of evangelistic event. The courses are designed to be 'consumer friendly', and are informal and relaxed. They start off with a group meal and then move on to a short talk about Christianity, whether in recorded or live form, followed by a chance to ask questions and discuss answers. The courses usually run for 6–10 weeks, allowing friendships and confidence to build up and enabling a relaxed learning environment.

Direct evangelistic events and activities:

1. Door-to-door conversation

These are best done with a specific aim, e.g., by offering a copy of John's Gospel for people to read, doing a survey on what people think about Jesus, introducing the activities of the church or giving people the opportunity to give prayer requests or identify practical needs that the church can pray about or get actively involved in. (See the chapter on Neighbourhood Chaplains for more discussion of the latter kind of engagement with the local community.)

2. Literature distribution

This can be the *Good News* evangelistic newspaper or other suitable tracts. These should be high-quality, professionally produced resources, so as not to reinforce any negative misconceptions that Christianity is old-fashioned. Check out the following websites for suitable materials: Christian Publishing and Outreach (www.cpo.org.uk) and 10ofthose.com (www.10of those.com) or your local Christian bookshop.

3. Big events

Examples are music concerts, testimony nights, and lectures on specific questions.

4. Missions

These entail a short, focussed period when there is a concentrated effort to encourage church members to invite friends, colleagues, and family to a variety of specifically designed evangelistic events. These might include craft or quiz nights, family rambles, competitions, curry nights, or bake sales.You could invite a team of students from a Christian college to work with you, or put together a team of volunteers from local churches and work collaboratively on some 'bridge building' events. The Counties resources, Life Expo and GSUS LIVE, are great ways for churches to pool their resources and work together.

5. Holiday clubs

Home-grown, or using published resources, these can be a highlight or culmination of regular children's and schools work during a half-term or Easter or summer breaks. They can last for a whole week, or just a couple of days, for just an hour or from dawn to dusk!

6. One-to-one Bible studies

There are many good sources for one-to-one Bible studies. 'The Word One to One' helps you introduce your friends to Jesus in his Word by presenting the Bible in an accessible, shareable, and easy-to-use format. These are available from 10ofthose (www.10ofthose.com) or your local Christian bookshop.These are best organised in the home on a friendship basis, but a coordinated effort by the church to run a number in parallel, so that instigators can support each other, would be beneficial.

7. Online interactions during times of restriction . . . and beyond?

Many of the above possibilities can be moved online with a little imagination and technical know-how. We have found that sometimes people are more comfortable interacting from the security of their own homes and that the reach of such activities can be extensive.

And finally

What an amazing opportunity we were given during the pandemic to take a step back and prayerfully evaluate what we do as a church together and how we structure our evangelism. Your church can be used by God to lead people to faith in Jesus Christ. It does not happen by accident though. It takes a mix of personal evangelism, personal church invitations, excellent church hospitality practices, and faithful and engaging proclamation of the Word of God. It also takes prayer, perseverance, and a whole lot of patience.

For discussion

1. Note some of the different types of evangelism mentioned in this chapter. Which of these would be the most useful in your context?
2. Think about the people you have in your church and their skills and gifting. Which of these types of evangelism would they be most suited for and why?
3. Take time to share your conclusions with each of those people.

Chapter 7

Evangelistic missions—yesterday's evangelism?

Bob Telford

The way it was

The annual evangelistic mission, taking the form of a week or a fortnight of 'special' meetings and events at which the gospel would be preached, was at one time an almost defining characteristic of independent evangelical churches. Each year, plans would be drawn up, an evangelist would be engaged, money would be raised, publicity would be printed and distributed, and, more often than not, extra prayer meetings would be scheduled. Unsurprisingly, God sometimes blessed the efforts of his people, and during a mission a few unsure or faltering believers would be helped to get a firmer grasp on Christ, and some unbelievers would be brought to faith. Going further back, a hundred years or more ago, churches grew or new local churches were planted as a result of such missions. But not usually in more recent times.

It must be admitted that, with the passage of time, increasingly there has been very little to be seen by way of tangible results from the annual evangelistic mission. When that has been so, church members have taken comfort in the fact, that some 'good seed had been sown' and they assured themselves that they had faithfully discharged their responsibilities to preach the gospel, for the time being at least.

For many years, reports from churches about their missions were printed in one or another Christian periodical. Such reports sometimes read, "The Gospel was faithfully preached, the singing was bright, and the Saints were encouraged." I can only be pleased that the gospel was "faithfully preached" and, if there had to be singing during the mission, I'm glad it was "bright". Similarly, I wouldn't want the saints to be anything but "encouraged". However, the aim of the believers in arranging a mission had, presumably, not been to stage an enjoyable choral exercise for God's people or merely to gather around and appreciate a doctrinally sound sermon! The goal of the mission was to win people for Christ and in more recent decades most reports from 'missioning' churches have included tragically few mentions of people actually getting saved. After the mission, the life and programme of the church returned to normal, and some members, very probably, breathed a sigh of relief that the disruption and hard work occasioned by 'the mission' was over for another year at least!

The way things have changed

Missions of the sort described have 'dropped off the radar' of most fellowships today. From the 1970s on, fewer churches have persisted in holding missions. A number of developments and factors may have contributed to missions falling out of favour, including:

> The growing tendency to see conversion as a process.
> The belief that sustained relationships are the 'bridge' over which the gospel *has to* travel.
> The elevation of worship over witness, which has led to an emphasis on celebration, rather than proclamation, at services and events.
> The decline in the number of good evangelistic preachers, and downgrading of the prominence and importance of preaching.
> The rise of Alpha, and similar hospitality based and interactive courses, which probably came, for many churches, to replace the evangelistic missions of the previous decades.

Some of these developments have brought something very good into the life of churches. The recognition that conversion is a *process* as well as a crisis, the reminder of the importance of relationships, and the development of Alpha have been good things! There is indeed a process associated with conversion.

Relationships *really do* matter. Preaching *is not* the only way to communicate the gospel—it is not even always the best way. There may actually be something attractive or intriguing to non-Christians about Christians enjoying contemporary sung worship. The Alpha Course has indeed been used powerfully by God.

However, the fact is that none of these developments in thinking and practice are inherently at odds with mission evangelism. The process of conversion needs to be brought to a point of crisis. A mission event can do that. The danger of being too heavily invested in the idea of process is that we can lose sight of the need to call on people to have a moment of crisis. Have we become so scared of jeopardising the process that we now deliberately shy away from calling on people to make up their minds? It would be ironic if this were true. It was our hope that people would make a decision to follow Jesus (have a crisis) that drove us to help them embark on the process in the first place!

Good relationships with unsaved people go a long way to inclining people to respond positively to invitations from their believing friends. The influence and effectivess of the believer who wants to bring their friend to hear the gospel will largely stand or fall on the quality of the relationship between them.

There is a general unease in society today about people who sound too sure of themselves, or their beliefs, and who are too assertive. This unease has possibly crept into Christian thinking. Some believers have become uneasy about confident and candid gospel preaching. Further, the plethora of bad preachers, i.e., those who are muddled, dull, and generally inept, has damaged people's perception of the importance of preaching and dented their confidence in it as a legitimate and God-ordained method of communication in spreading the gospel and building up the church.

A local church mission is of short duration and, for that reason, efforts can be made by the organising group to secure the services of people with a track record of being appealing to non-Christians, courteous, adaptable, clear and compelling. Mission organisers must recognise that preaching in the context of an evangelistic mission, at a variety of carefully-targeted events, is a heavily nuanced 'business'. Some preachers are good, for example, at proclaiming the gospel in the market place or at a Sunday service, but they flounder and embarrass themselves, and everyone else, if they take on the role of, say, an (evangelistic) after-dinner speaker. *The right speaker, however, with the right manner, tone, and message, can with God's help still be extraordinarily effective.*

The prioritising of worship over gospel proclamation, and the belief that people should be brought to faith in the context of events which were strong on worship and subjective testimony, but weak on the objective realities of sin, the atonement, and the need for repentance and faith, needs to be carefully examined rather than just assumed to be the right approach. Worship, praise and thanksgiving should be part of the DNA of local church life, and some singing may well be in order at some evangelistic events, but, if we are really trying to reach people with little or no church background, we will do well not to try to immerse them in an activity which is properly the province and the expression of those who already have an affection for Christ. Generally speaking, unbelievers neither want to worship God, nor are they able to do so, unregenerate as they are. In addition, we live in a time when most people's connection with church is tenuous at best. We must question whether it is really a good idea to try to immerse unchurched people in activities which so heavily reflect the music, culture, and beliefs of the church. Personally, I think that meetings which are *dominated* by contemporary congregational praise have little or no place in an evangelistic mission or evangelism more generally. *To rule out completely however, any element of corporate worship or thanksgiving at a gospel event would be a reaction too far in the other direction.*

The popularity of Alpha is something for which I thank God. Its systematic, hospitality-based, presentation of the truth has been blessed to countless people. Indeed, an Alpha course could be seen as being a mission event stretched out over several months. It is good to note that proclamation is still a key feature of the Alpha course. But in Alpha, unlike in an evangelistic mission, the gospel focus is brief and a great deal of teaching is given on subjects which are not only not central to the gospel, but which can and sometimes do blur the message and overlay it with extraneous, and frankly, less important material which has more to do with laying foundations in those who have become Christians.

A mission should be part of an integrated and ongoing programme of outreach and, as part of that ongoing programme, Alpha can play an important part as preparation for or follow up to a mission. Many people who have had a good experience in an Alpha group are likely to be keen to attend appropriate mission events, and many who register an interest in the faith, or who turn to Christ during the mission, can be helped by attendance at an Alpha course, once the mission has concluded.

Let's thank God for the diversity of approaches and methods that he has given to the Church. Let's recognise that many of these approaches and methods are not mutually exclusive! Building good relationships, running Alpha courses, utilising the performance arts, preaching, hospitality, imaginative multi-media presentations, and so much else, can all be made to work in a complementary manner. The local church mission can and should still have a place alongside other approaches in our attempts to, in John Wesley's wonderful phrase, "Offer Christ to the people"

The way it can be

> A mission, in the life of a local church, can be likened to the crew in a boat race quickening their rate of stroke. It only makes sense for them to do this if they have been rowing purposefully up until that point and if they intend to continue rowing purposefully once the burst of speed is over.[1]

The key words here are 'rowing purposefully'. Missions historically have probably failed to be as fruitful as they might have been because they have not been part of an ongoing evangelistic programme. Two weeks of frenetic activity and sudden friendliness on the part of a church that has for years been perceived by outsiders as being detached and uncaring will not reverse the disinclination of local people to attend! A local church that keeps a low profile in a community and does not engage in any meaningful way with people throughout the year should not expect the community to respond positively to invitations to 'come along to a meeting'. If a mission is to be, in part at least, a 'reaping' time, then it follows that there has to have been some 'sowing' prior to the mission.

The obvious corollary of this simple fact is that struggling churches with small and aging congregations, and no significant 'presence' in their local area,

1. Gavin Reed, *Good News to Share*.

cannot expect to stage and carry through a 'successful' mission. Having an evangelistic mission is not the way to restore the numbers and prospects of a struggling church. Such a church would do better to consult with local pastors and leaders of more vigorous churches in the area and with one or more of the several agencies which can offer advice and support.

Secure the backing of the church

A local church mission needs the 'buy in' of a significant percentage of the membership of the church. When a mission is the enthusiasm of a limited cadre of congregation, and not supported by the majority, it will not work. A good, multi-faceted mission will require the enthusiasm, energy, input and support of a lot of people. If church members feel that the mission has been imposed on them by the leadership, or a small faction within the church, then their commitment to the outreach maybe shallow, their giving grudging, their attendance patchy, and their efforts to reach people sporadic and half-hearted.

Have a goal!

Decide what you are trying to do—Gavin Reid helpfully identified a church as being comprised of a 'Flock' and a 'Fringe'. The 'flock' are believers; the 'fringe' are the families of believers, occasional attenders, the parents of the young people and children who participate in various church clubs and other activities. Churches must decide whether the aim of the mission is to reach the 'fringe' or to make a gospel connection with the wider community.

The wisest, and more easily achieved course of action, will probably be to reach the fringe, i.e., those with whom the local church already has a connection of sorts. When someone on the 'fringe' is won to Christ, they will become, we may hope, part of the 'flock'. When that happens, their families and friends, until then part of the wider community, become the church's new fringe. By reaching 'fringe' people, a church will inevitably make evangelistic inroads into the community. The prior questions are, do we have a fringe, how big is it, and who are they? If there is not much of a fringe, perhaps a mission should be delayed while efforts are made to develop a fringe, or the mission should aim to make connection with the wider community.

Plan well ahead

Long-range planning gives time for consultation within the church. It gives time for consideration, prayer, constructive criticism, and amendment of initial thinking. When people adopt a course of action which has been proposed to them, and examined and adopted by them, rather than one which has been imposed on them, their 'buy in' will be sincere and their support will be substantial.

Get the timing right!

A bit of thought, and a quick look through a diary, will help the church to decide on the optimum time to have a mission. Major holiday times, significant sporting fixtures, term and holiday times, all need to be considered when planning a mission. Clashes with events which will keep most people at home in front of the television are best avoided.

An evangelist accepted an invitation from a church in a coastal resort town, to lead a Beach Mission for the children of holiday makers. Everything was prepared and in place, and the team were assembled and ready to go to the beach. Their puzzlement as to why the beach was devoid of children on the first morning of the mission was resolved when they discovered that the chosen week was not a school-holiday week—an important fact that should not have been overlooked when plans were being made!

Have targeted events

Events aimed at everyone can too easily fail to connect with anyone. Let's take the example of the popular 'all-age service'. Intended to offer something for people of all ages, such a service can too easily fail to really reach anybody. For a long time, the received wisdom about reaching adults was that they could be reached through their children. Despite the evidence of much experience and a bit of common sense, the idea still persists today and may, subconsciously at least, influence the 'all-age service' approach. Some people will concede that reaching parents through presenting truth to children no longer works. I suspect that it is not a case of such an approach no longer working, so much as the fact that it never did!

There have, of course, been some glorious exceptions to this rule, but it can be stated as being generally true, that people are best reached in their peer groups. Do we want to reach fathers? Then we must have something which they feel comfortable about participating in, and can, connect with and respond to. Don't expect 'dad' to be converted because he has been coerced by his wife into coming to an 'all age service', and made to endure the congregational singing of saccharine lyrics possibly accompanied by (to him) silly actions!

Many men will fix a rictus smile on their faces and join in with children's songs with apparent enjoyment when exhorted to do so by the worship leader: "don't be shy". But often their embarrassment, and desire to be a hundred miles away from there, is easily read from their body language! Inwardly, some of them are resolving that it will be a very long time before they submit to such an experience again. An unbelieving man who is made to, variously, clap his hands, wave his arms, stoop down, stand up, or turn around and exchange a cheery smile or handshake with the person to his left, while all the time mouthing words which he doesn't believe, about a God whom he doesn't know, is unlikely to be positively impressed.

Once the singing is over, dad's problems in an 'all age service' are not necessarily over. He then has to listen to a presentation of a parable told by an adult in tones and manner which the speaker fondly imagines are suitable for children from 12months to 12 years of age. The danger for dad in this whole experience is that he could be reinforced in his suspicion that all this 'Jesus stuff' is maybe ok for children and women, but has nothing to offer him.

The fact is that men, women, young people, and children, each 'hear' things differently from each other. We need to reach people in the context of appropriately themed and presented activities. Rational adults need to hear the gospel rationally presented in an adult way. **All-age event planners should be aware that fathers enjoy watching their children enjoying themselves, and will go out of their way to ensure that they can, but that they do not necessarily want to be treated like children or made to do childish things themselves.**

Careful targeting of activities and ensuring that 'form follows function', i.e., that the programme is shaped and styled in a way that is suitable for our target audience, will enable people to engage with the gospel at a level that is appropriate to the particular group.

Have a varied programme

Planning a few carefully targeted events will generally be better than scheduling an extra meeting each evening for a fortnight and packing each day with activities which require the presence of the believers.

At each event, be careful to let function dictate form. If we are clear that the event on a particular day is for a particular age-range or gender, then the form of the event should be constructed around what is appropriate for the people whom we are trying to reach. Believers must be helped to understand the aim and nature of each activity. This will help them to invite appropriate people to the event. They also need to know what to expect in terms of gospel presentation.

I was invited by a church to speak at an outreach skittles evening in a pub. On the Sunday when the congregation were reminded of the upcoming event, one person approached me and said, "I'm bringing a non-Christian with me to the skittles. You will preach the gospel, won't you?" The very next person to speak to me came up and said, "I'm bringing a non-Christian with me to the skittles evening. You won't preach the gospel, will you?" The details of the evening and what people ought to expect had not been made clear to the church, and I found myself in a difficult situation vis-a-vis people's expectations! Programme activities can be based on things and themes which interest and appeal to different groups of people. We need to be sensible, not to say, imaginative.

A leadership team invited me to speak at the mission that they were planning. I asked them what their thinking was regarding the fortnight's programme. It transpired that they were intending to have services each weeknight evening at which the gospel would be preached. "How many unbelievers", I queried, "currently attended their Gospel Services on Sunday?" Apparently none did! I challenged them to consider where, in that depressing fact, they found the mandate to multiply the number of Gospel Meetings! If people are already 'voting with their feet' about what your church is doing, then simply doing more of the same is unlikely to improve the take-up.

Over the years I have spoken at mission events based around:

Golf
Cricket
Short-mat bowls
Antique valuations
Birds of prey and gundog demonstrations
'Walks down memory lane'
Cookery demonstrations
Lectures
Testimonies
Concerts
Choral evenings
Mime
Meals
Dramatic presentations
Quizzes
Movie nights
Death by chocolate
Bible exhibitions
Clay pigeon shoots

and an illustrated history of the local sewage treatment works!

Any pastime or area of interest which is wholesome can be contrived to base an event around. At some events, the speaker will present a brief and clear message, but not press his hearers for a response, other than to take literature or 'have a chat' at the end of the programme. Other events, possibly ones based on testimony, choral music, lectures and Sunday services should, of course, be regarded as opportunities for presenting the message with a particular urgency and with a view to encouraging a response.

All the publicity and invitations for each aspect of the mission programme should make it plain that the event will include the guest speaker saying a few words about his faith. We must be completely honest with people about this. The apostle Paul declared that 'We have renounced secret and shameful ways;

we do not use deception, . . .' (2 Cor. 4: 2) Candour and openness should characterise everything that we do for Christ.

Fail to prepare and you prepare to fail

Most church leaders should be too busy to plan a mission! Mission planning needs the involvement of church leaders, but, ideally, the work of planning and preparation should rest on not solely the leaders but on others in the fellowship as well.

The priority of church leaders should be, 'the ministry of the word and prayer' (Acts 6: 4), coupled with setting direction and pace for the church: the good shepherd goes ahead of the flock, they hear his voice and follow him (John 10: 1–18). Planning a mission is time consuming and difficult. Wise leaders will want to draw others alongside to help with this task.Thorough planning of every aspect of the mission, and keeping the fellowship apprised of developments every step of the way, are a must! The aim of the mission, prayerful preparation, timing, programme, publicity, speakers, finance, training, and the rest should all be carefully and prayerfully arranged.

Prepare for results

Leaders, mission planners and church members should have biblical optimism about the mission. One of the most important parables that Jesus told, with regard to evangelism anyway, was the Parable of the Sower or Seed (Mt. 13: 3–23; Mk. 4: 1–20; Lk. 8: 5–15). The parable makes it plain that not everyone who hears the gospel will believe it. It teaches clearly that not everyone who, on hearing it, claims to believe it will be sincere and follow through on their initial decision. It also teaches us that a percentage of those who hear *can be* expected to believe and to go on to be consistent and fruitful followers of Christ. This is grounds for us to approach evangelism with confidence and with Scripture-fuelled expectation!

I was talking to church leaders about their mission planning and I asked what preparations were being made for the nurture and establishment of new converts. Their response was that they intended to wait and see if "anyone got saved" before planning anything further! That will simply not do. Such a lack of faith and expectancy saws away at the evangelistic nerve, and the suspicion that no-one will be saved becomes a self-fulfilling prophecy.

Better together?

Perhaps a church that is thinking of having a mission might consider whether or not the effectiveness of the mission could be enhanced, and its influence felt more widely, if they were to make common cause with another church in the area? Greater resources, a wider 'fringe', and higher public profile for the mission can be significant advantages. It is also true, however, that larger and more representative committees can become unwieldy and that it must be expected that some of those who respond may never become part of one of the collaborating churches.

I was invited to lead a mission arranged by two churches. One was a Brethren assembly and the other was the local Anglican parish church. They were keen that all the events of the mission should happen in a large marquee or community centre. Knowing that both churches had good facilities, I asked why they were keen to base the mission somewhere other than in their own premises? Their answer revealed a deep unease, on one side at least, about new converts joining the 'other' church! It was a revealing response. Their attitude told me that they were not ready for a joint mission, if indeed they were ready to have a mission at all. I encouraged them to come to a point where what really mattered to them was not which 'net' the 'fish' ended up in, but that they were *in the net*!

If it is decided by a church to focus the mission exclusively on their own church then, at the very least other local congregations should be made aware of what is being planned and their prayerful support should be solicited.

"Evangelists aren't big headed—they just know best!"

An evangelist told me that once. We both chuckled, but I hope that neither of us believed it! I've tried to show that there can still be a place for a mission in the life of a local church. My experience of leading missions at home and abroad stretches over five decades, and, drawing on that experience, I've tried to identify some of the pitfalls and the priorities in planning and carrying through a mission. But long experience does not confer infallibility. Nor does it demand agreement. My experience entitles me to expect nothing more than that readers will take what I have said seriously, and be stirred to think carefully about how a mission might become a valuable part of the ongoing programme of their church.

For discussion

1. When was the last time your church had an evangelistic mission, and why?
2. If you were required to organise an evangelistic mission in your church within the next six months, describe what you think it could look like.

Chapter 8

Is church planting effective evangelism?

Tim Cracknell

Towards the end of the pandemic, I was shopping and the young shop assistant told me that she had never been to church in her life but she was watching our church service online every week. She was trying to be brave and join us one Sunday. She followed it up by saying that she liked our church because it was "not too preachy!"

Let's be clear, we do preach the gospel. We do call for repentance and invite people to commit their lives in faith to Christ. But something about the tone and way in which we conduct our services and sermons didn't feel as though we were preaching at her like other online services that she had watched as she began this spiritual journey. This young lady found it easier to connect with us because, for her, we were more in tune with her culture, and therefore able to speak in a way that she found began to draw her in rather than alienating her. We don't know how her story will unfold but, as you can imagine, I soon visited that shop again!

At the same time, I am under no illusion that our church has everything right and that other churches are wrong. Sometimes it feels as though we get more wrong than right, but in every area one will find a multitude of sub-cultures and that is one of the reasons we need lots of different churches reaching out to each culture. Church plants are much more able to break down the cultural barriers when it comes to evangelism and this conversation is one example.

Many are asking, do we need more churches to be planted when we have so many church buildings out there that are only partially filled? Surely, they are trying their hardest to do evangelism, and common sense would say that there is limited demand for the gospel and church these days. Therefore, by planting new churches we are only going to make matters worse for struggling churches by taking some of the potential new converts away from established churches into new and possibly equally struggling churches. Why would a church plant be any more effective at evangelism than more established and better resourced churches? After all, if we have a heart for the church, we should roll our sleeves up, get stuck in and help the struggling churches rather than create what may be seen as competition that causes the struggling churches to flounder even more? That would have been my view 20 years ago before I explored this question in more detail.

When you delve back into the history of many of the gospel movements in the UK especially the old Gospel Halls, you often find around 200 years ago a small group of likeminded people who were evangelistically focused on bringing the gospel to an area. Researching the Forest of Dean in Gloucestershire where I live, I have found that the same is true for Baptists, Methodists, and Congregationalists. They would often focus on one town or village until a small number of converts were gathering in a house. When the church was firmly planted, they would then go further afield, taking the gospel on foot into other towns and villages nearby, preaching in the open air, in tents and public spaces. These would then lead to new small fellowships becoming established and when they outgrew houses, they would build a small church or chapel so the work of evangelism could continue to take root.

An example of this was when my great grandfather teamed up with several others in the early 1900's to share the gospel in a hamlet called Four Oaks (in Gloucestershire) each Sunday afternoon. Usually, a small group would gather in the village each week but one day they got soaked because of heavy rainfall. As a result my enterprising forebear, a builder, built a small wooden chapel the following week on a local Christian farmer's land and then carried it on horse and cart, cutting down trees as they went, on the five-mile journey to Four Oaks ready for the following Sunday so they could avoid getting wet again! Such was the pioneering evangelistic spirit of these passionate Christ followers. That building then became the basis of much fruitful evangelism during the next century.

So, are new plants necessary for effective evangelism, now that we have lots of church buildings scattered around the UK? To unpack this, it helps to look at the life-cycle of the local church.

The life-cycle of a church

Stage 1

When a new church is planted, it is by a small dynamic team led by a faith-inspired entrepreneur who is comfortable to lean into risk. With God-given faith and creative energy, they embark on an adventure to break new ground and plant a new church.

Stage 2

Once the new plant starts to gather traction and people start to get saved and the new embryo church starts to grow, others are needed to organise the church. Initially this is great. The burden of organisation is taken off the creative workers, and what can be a slightly chaotic body of believers takes a more consistent shape.

Stage 3

However, it is not long before a battle ensues between the creatives and the organisers. The administrative organisers don't stop at the initial organising work. They want proper organisation because, as the church grows, health and safety forms need to be completed, risk assessments, budgets, GDPR, safeguarding, organisational committees and lots of processes suddenly get added. The creatives find all this restrictive and stifling. If churches are to keep on growing, this tension between the administrative organisers and the creative entrepreneurs needs to be maintained in a healthy way. The truth is they need each other for a church to remain healthy and keep growing. A thriving church needs good organisation, but organisation must never suffocate the life out of the creative evangelistic endeavour and zeal.

Stage 4

However, sadly established churches have a propensity to drift over time into organisational structures run by committees and ruled by rotas that focus on risk-avoidance and playing it safe. Maintenance of the status quo for core members' comfort takes front and centre stage, and maintenance of the building becomes the secondary focus. The risks often associated with evangelistic enterprise are limited to some missional work abroad, children's work or the odd special event where the main flow of the church services are not changed and the regular comfortable routine for rank-and-file members is not disturbed. At this stage of the church life-cycle, those who are creatively wired and gifted in evangelism become discouraged and leave. Some will leave church altogether, while others will start the cycle off again by planting a new church "free from the burden" of organisers who appear to them risk-averse.

I think that we can all recognise that cycle, either in our own local church or ones we are aware of. Once a church moves from stage 3 to stage 4. It is on the slippery slope to irrelevance and closure. If nothing is done to change direction, it may take 20 or even 30 years before the doors are finally closed and the lights turned out for the last time, but the depressing course is set. Phrases like, "it is a day of small things" become the mantra and a nostalgic look backwards to the "good old days" becomes a regular pastime. Meaningful evangelism beyond general seed sowing events have ceased, vision is never mentioned, and the local church dies.

Former missionary in South America and Professor of Church Growth at the Fuller Theological seminary, Peter Wagner, observed: '*The single most effective evangelistic methodology under heaven is planting new churches.*'[1] Written in 1990, those words sent a shock wave through the established church and became the catalyst for many church denominations across North America and Europe to review their evangelistic strategies and take church planting seriously again as a way of evangelising their countries.

A decade later, pastor and author, Tim Keller, published a brief article entitled 'Why plant Churches?' It soon became a must-read for all interested in evangelism and church planting. He wrote, 'The vigorous, continual planting of new congregations is the single most crucial strategy for (1) the numerical growth of the body of Christ in a city and (2) the continual corporate renewal

1. C. Peter Wagner, *Church Planting for a Greater Harvest: A comprehensive guide* (Ventura CA: Regal Books, 1990), p. 11.

and revival of the existing churches in a city.'[2] In Keller's view, if we are serious about evangelism, we have to be serious about church planting because it produces more converts both in the new churches and through catalytic inspiration of established churches that are treading water in maintenance mode.

The evangelistic fruitfulness of church planting was further underlined by Jeff Christopherson (Executive Director of Church Planting Canada and co-founder of the Send Institute): '. . . in Canada, churches planted since 2010 account for 71% of their Canadian Convention's baptisms.' Kevin Ezell, president of the North American Mission Board , is unequivocal that 'church plants baptise more people per attendee than do established churches—a 67 percent better attendee-to-baptism ratio.' 'New churches account for a significant percentage of evangelistic achievement in numerous jurisdictions.' However, he did highlight that it was not automatic that church plants will have a significant evangelistic drive. The key to having an evangelistic engine in the church plant is to start by focussing on 'disciple-making as their primary assignment.'

'Numerous studies show that younger churches consistently demonstrate a higher level of evangelistic proficiency than older, established churches', reports Steven M. Pike, formerly National Director, Church Multiplication Network, Springfield, Missouri. 'For example, a study conducted among Southern Baptist churches indicated that S[outhern] B[aptist] C[onvention] churches 10 years or older average 2.5 baptisms for every 100 active members, while SBC churches 10 years or younger average 10.8 baptisms per 100 active members.'

These studies and others completed more recently make a compelling case for the effectiveness of church planting in the role of evangelism.

For those who think that this is only a North American phenomenon, similar analysis can be found in the UK. Tim Thorlby's report, 'Love Sweat and Tears: Church planting in east London',[3] explains, 'Typical Sunday attendance of adults and children across the five churches has grown from 72 before the planting process to nearly 750 currently.' What is most interesting about Thorlby's findings is that the most growth in the number of people coming

---

2. https://redeemercitytocity.com/articles-stories/why-plant-churches, 1 January 2002 (accessed on 14.2.2023).

3. See https://ccx.org.uk/content/love-sweat-and-tears/, published in January 2017 (accessed on 14.2.2023).

new to church or returning to church is in those churches that are doing the most community action. This reminds us of the truth of the old adage, 'people don't care how much you know until they know how much you care!' People living in twenty-first century Britain want to know how being a follower of Jesus makes a difference to their lives and their community. When they see it in action, they are drawn to Jesus and his bride, the church.

As far as I can see, it is undeniable that, by planting churches with a primary focus on evangelistic disciple-making, we are committing to one of, if not the most significant, strategic decisions to bring the gospel to our communities and nation. But it does raise the question of why this is so. As a way of addressing that question I offer the following suggestions:

1. **Do or die**: Small plants have no option but to be evangelistic. If they don't reach out to their community with the gospel, they will either stay small or die quickly. This means risk and faith are embraced more readily.

2. **Speed of change**: They can be nimble and move quickly to take up new opportunities, while more established churches need more time before deciding to move into new areas of evangelism.

3. **Entrepreneurial leadership**: Church plants are usually led by creative innovators who bring an energy to the team which embraces risk and adventure. Established churches are more inclined to resist change and minimize risk, thereby unintentionally restricting new evangelistic ministries.

4. **Attitude to failure**: New plants are more willing to explore new ways of doing church and evangelism that may not always work out as hoped for. But if they fail, they are less likely to suffer recrimination. The process is seen as learning, not failure. Older churches can be harder on those who are perceived to fail, especially if the leader has changed a formula that used to work in earlier years.

5. **Age of team**: Church plants tend to attract a team of younger, more energetic people. This in turn enables more work to get done, particularly with families who instantly bring a wider and more dramatic impact as a result.

6. **Motivation**: Church planting is often referred to as the 'extreme sport of ministry!' Therefore, those who lead new plants usually have a strong sense of calling, which gives a higher level of motivation and commitment. As Ed Stetzer remarked, 'Church planting requires a tremendous amount of faith and a slight bit of gospel insanity!'
7. **Adapt to culture**: New churches have the privilege of a blank piece of paper and a chance to set the structure and culture in a way that they perceive is most able to connect with the world around them. Most churches inherit their culture from previous generations and as a result reflect what the culture was like in their community 50 or 100 years ago. This presents an extra hurdle to unchurched people, as they must engage not only with the timeless gospel but also grapple with the alien culture that they discover inside the church. Even unspoken rules forbidding clapping in church as irreverent can be problematic because in our culture today, if people like something, they clap. New churches instinctively adapt to cultural change so as to engage with the next generation.

If church plants are good for evangelism, what about the possible impact on sending churches and others in the area in which a new church is being planted? After all, it is well known in church planting circles that one of the greatest obstacles to church planting is resistance from existing churches because they feel threatened. In my own experience before I started replanting Forest Community Church, in Cinderford, I sent a letter to the leaders of all nine existing churches in the area, to explain that we were starting a church for those who didn't come to church. We were not after their sheep. I think that it is fair to say that most leaders appreciated the letter, but didn't believe me! However, we can say sixteen years later that we have kept that promise. We have actually sent more people on to other churches than we have taken from them! These were people who first connected to our church whom we were able to bless, but whom we sent on to one of the other churches in the area because they wanted a more traditional church culture than we were offering. We are taking a space in the church community that no one else is filling. We are after the 90% who don't go to church, not the 5–10% who occasionally do.

A new church is in fact a blessing to existing churches and sending churches in many ways. Here are a few:

1. Sending churches are inspired by seeing what God is doing and motivation is increased.
2. Sending churches have spaces for new leaders to step into which have been left by church planting teams. This raises up a new generation of leaders.
3. Sending churches receive the blessing of being able to give financial support to a new work as "it's more blessed to give than receive."
3. Existing churches have the opportunity to see, first-hand, different ways in which to do evangelism and learn.
4. Some lapsed churchgoers who are traditional in thinking may return to a church plant but be redirected to established churches as they are a better fit, therefore adding to their number.

Faced with all this evidence, where does that leave us? Are you someone who has ever thought about church planting or supporting a church plant? Is your church at a stage where you could release some of your people to plant a new church in your next neighbourhood and in so doing bring the gospel to that community and enrich your church at the same time? Are you actively praying for those involved in church planting in the same way as you may pray for those in front-line evangelism? If you care about bringing the gospel to your nation, these are important questions which you should be seriously considering.

* * * * * * * * *

Counties would love to partner with you if you or your fellowship would like to explore a calling to church planting. In 2018, Counties established Counties Planting Network to follow up and expand on two decades of work by the Church Planting Initiative. This growing network of first-generation church plants and planters is strengthening and giving fellowship to plants from within an independent stream of churches. As noted, a commitment to planting new churches can bring growth and transformation across a region, or within a city or town.

We have seen old chapels that had closed which are now occupied by thriving new fellowships, with the gospel again bringing living hope through a new community of believers. Ethnically diverse and cross-cultural plants are happening in central London, and new life is coming to rural and market town communities in the west of England, and to large housing estates in places like Cardiff.

Church planting can be an incredibly lonely calling, so in Counties Planting Network we believe in raising and planting through teams. Lead planters are led through an assessment, and they and their teams join the M4 process, where teams join together in a two-year journey of teaching and coaching. M4 is a Europe-wide tool, brought to the UK by Counties in 2019, and now partnering with other evangelical groups, networks, and streams to offer church planters ways of laying healthy foundations and setting church plants on the right course in the early challenging years.

To learn more, please visit https://www.countiesuk.org/

For discussion

1. What compelling reasons could you put forward for you or your church doing a church plant now?
2. What reasons can you give as to why this church plant has not yet been attempted. Analyse your reasons, asking are they valid?

Chapter 9

Gospel preaching

Bob Telford

An 85-year-old man was sentenced to serve thirty years in prison. He was stunned by the severity of the sentence and said plaintively, "Your honour, I'm 85 years old! I can't serve that many years." The judge looked down at him and in a kindly tone said, "That's alright. Just go away and do as many as you can!"

That story resonates with me because this chapter is about a huge subject and I have only one chapter in which to address it! Inevitably, I will not be able to say many things that should be said. I will say as many as I can!

The wonder of the gospel

First, we had better be clear what the 'gospel' is.

'Gypsy' Rodney Smith was an evangelist for over seventy years. Asked in his late 80's how he had managed to remain so fresh and vigorous in his preaching, he replied, "I have never lost the sense of the wonder of the Gospel." The gospel is a wonderful message. Mankind did not dream it up or think it up. It was given to us by God. It is about his Son. It is the channel through which God reaches lost people. In it is revealed a way to be right with God which does not depend on our being good!

There is no other message like it. We are not at liberty to change it, amend it, add to it or subtract from it. Its content does not change with the times. We needn't apologise for it or be ashamed of it. It will not suffer from comparison with other messages, and we must never pretend that it is equivalent to, but *no better than,* the core messages of other faiths. It is, quite simply, the best!

It is not a message about the general benevolence of God, the brotherhood of man, or how good it would be if we were all nicer to each other! It does not command us to live by the Ten Commandments, the 'Golden Rule', or the Sermon on the Mount. It is a specific message from God about one wonderful person, and two wonderful things that God has accomplished through him.

What God has done and the 'heart' of the gospel is stated clearly in 1 Corinthians 15: 3 & 4:

> **God has done something about the problem of sin**.
> 'Christ died for our sins'
> **God has done something about the problem of death**.
> 'He was raised on the third day'

These two facts must be at the heart of every gospel message. They are at the heart of Christianity. The death of Christ and his rising again are not truths for the periphery of a gospel sermon. They must not be 'shoehorned' in or bolted on to a gospel sermon. They are the essence of the gospel.

That is not to say that every gospel sermon must be a lengthy exposition of a so-called 'gospel text'. Nor must it be a graphic re-telling of the crucifixion story. But people must be told that what they need from God can be theirs only on the basis of what Christ's death and resurrection have done for them.

No less than proclaiming the death of Christ, a gospel sermon is a message which affirms the truth of Christ's resurrection. People must know that Christ is no longer dead, and that he is able and available to hear and help them.

Preaching—what we say and how we say it

When we are new to preaching, we give, I hope, a great deal of thought to *what* we will say. It may be that we think rather less about *how* we will say it. The result can be a sermon which is worthy but dull. It is 'worthy' because the truth is spoken. It is 'dull' because no attempt has been made to engage the interest of the hearers in the truth.

God can and does use truth when it is spoken, even if it is spoken poorly. He will not, however, endorse or use error or nonsense, even if it is very well spoken. What we say *is* more important than how we say it, but there should be no competition between the substance and the style of our preaching. We do not have to choose between being 'sound' and being interesting and clear!

How we should preach

> To be listened to is the first thing—be interesting.
> To be understood is the second thing—be clear.
> To be useful is the third—be practical.

I don't know where I came across that snippet of wisdom, but those words hang on the wall over my desk even as I write this. They are succinct, challenging and important.

Be interesting—don't be dull!

There is 'an elephant in the room' when we discuss preaching and preachers! It needs to be acknowledged that some people are **boring**. They just are! Whether they are talking about their holidays, children, jobs, or their ailments, the way that they express themselves is sleep inducing. It is a handicap which can be overcome, but the first step is to accept the need for us all to become more interesting presenters of truth.

'Not everyone can be what people call a "good preacher", but no one need be a "bad preacher".' Whether by virtue of natural ability or spiritual gifting, personality or something else, some people seem to have a flair for public speaking. Others, as I've already observed, do not. **All of us, however, regardless of our personalities or limitations, can become better at what we do.** We can train ourselves, and be taught by others, how to engage with an audience and capture and sustain their interest.

Being interesting does matter! The importance of being interesting can hardly be overstated. If people are bored, they will stop listening. If people do not listen, they will not hear. If people do not hear, they cannot believe. If people do not believe, they will not be saved!

We must think hard about how we can both begin and continue our message in ways that will capture and hold attention. We should work particularly hard on the introduction to our message. People make up their minds very quickly as to whether or not listening to us will be worthwhile.

We must not assume that, because someone is present at an event at which we are speaking, their presence in itself signifies that they are going to automatically listen to what we say. As someone once said, "If we think people are dying to hear us, we're half right!"

In his advice to preachers, C. H. Spurgeon said, 'Some [in your congregation] are dead and you must rouse them. Some are troubled and you must comfort them. Others are burdened and you must point them to the great burden bearer. Still more are puzzled, and you must enlighten and guide them. Others are indifferent and careless and you must warn them and woo them.'

Be prepared

Describing how he prepared his sermons, an old preacher said, "I reads myself full, I thinks myself straight, I prays myself hot, and I lets myself go!" If, when we 'let ourselves go', we are going to 'go' somewhere useful, we must not neglect the reading, thinking and praying aspects of sermon preparation. Reading, thinking and praying, and I would add writing, are the keys to ordering our thoughts and setting out our material. If we are unclear ourselves about the passage which we will be expounding, we will only succeed in spreading our 'darkness' around.

An old military adage says, 'Time spent in reconnaissance is never wasted.' A similar motto for preachers would be, 'Time spent in preparation is never wasted.' My Bible college principal used to tell his students, 'There will be no inspiration in presentation without perspiration in preparation.'

Clarity of expression begins with preparation, as material is selected, sorted, set out on paper, prayed over, edited, refined and re-written. We must not shrink from spending time, a lot of time, alone in prayerful and thoughtful preparation.

Our 'tools'—words

Words are the tools which we use to give shape and substance to our thoughts and to bring understanding to our hearers. J. B. Phillips said

> The preacher and the writer may seem to have an easy task. At first sight it may seem they have only to proclaim and declare; but in fact, if their words are to enter men's hearts and bear

> fruit, they must be the right words, shaped cunningly to pass men's defences and explode silently and effectually within their minds.

Perhaps we have a natural facility for finding the right words? Maybe we do not have that happy knack, and must work harder to clothe our thoughts in a striking and illuminating way? Whether words come naturally to us or not, we must be mindful of the responsibility that rests on us when we preach. The Bible says, that, 'If anyone speaks, they should do it as one speaking the very words of God.' (1 Pet. 4: 11) Speaking from God, and for God, requires us be as clear and comprehensible as we can possibly be.

Be economical

The average native-born English speaker has an active vocabulary of approximately 20,000 words, and a passive vocabulary of twice that many. Knowing lots of words, and more importantly knowing how and when to use them is a good thing, but an opportunity to preach is not an opportunity to use all the words we know! G. Campbell Morgan was pastor of Westminster Chapel. He was a prolific writer and a fine preacher. A reviewer criticised the simplicity with which this erudite and articulate man wrote:'This man obviously has no use for language other to make people understand what he means.' Intended as a criticism, Morgan took it as a compliment and pasted the review onto the wall of his study. He wrote underneath it, 'Lord, keep me right there!'

'To preach for more than half an hour a man should be an angel himself or have angels for hearers!' I'm not sure whether the evangelist, George Whitfield, took his own advice, but his words do point us in the direction of not preaching long messages.There is no hard-and-fast rule for how many minutes long a sermon should be. The lockdowns of recent months have inclined me, and many preachers, to preach shorter sermons. Shorter messages, it should be noted, are not easier to prepare than long ones. They require a lot of thought and the pruning away of any material that is not truly relevant can be a demanding task. Having only 20 minutes available, rather than the more usual 35–40 minutes, has a way of focussing the mind, as well as making it easier for others to concentrate on what they are hearing, especially if they are receiving the message via a laptop screen or smartphone.

Be gracious

The Devil has 'blinded the minds of unbelievers (2 Cor. 4: 4). Those to whom we preach are victims, not villains. There is no reason for us to be angry with them or to 'look down our noses at them' because they don't understand spiritual truth. Before coming to Christ, we were all in the same condition. That we now have a grasp on some spiritual realities cannot be attributed to our cleverness, goodness, insight, or merit in any way at all.

We must preach the truth, but we must also reflect the grace and kindness of God in the way we preach it. It is true, as Cambell Morgan said, that 'There is a sense in which preaching is a conflict with our hearers.' But we can and should be assertive, without being abrasive; candid, without being unkind; and bold without being belligerent.

Be a story teller!

"You can't beat a well told story, and a well told Bible story is best of all." Jesus was so convinced about the worth of a well-told story that he 'never spoke without telling the people a parable' (Mt. 13: 34). His parables make up approximately one third of his teaching. His normal response when asked a question was to frame his answer in the form of a story.

Stories, statistics, song lyrics, topical references, and anecdotes from our own experience, can help us to make points clear and memorable, and catch people's attention or re-capture it if we have lost it. A good illustration is one that is appropriate in at least three ways:

> *Appropriate to the point we are making*. We have all heard preachers who were determined to work into their message the latest good story which they had found, regardless of whether it really fitted. If an illustration doesn't genuinely illustrate the point, don't use it. If an illustration requires a further illustration to clarify it, don't use it. Use a better one in the first place.

Appropriate for the people who are listening. The age, experience, degree of familiarity with the Bible, and many other things about our listeners, need to be borne in mind when we are selecting sermon illustrations. For example, using an illustration about the purchase of a new car, or an anecdote about dining in an expensive restaurant, would be inappropriate for people whose greatest concern is how they are going to afford to eat the next day! Illustrations from the world of interactive, online war-gaming, will probably not be helpful to the residents of the local care home. We must match our illustrations to our audience.

Appropriate to our calling. Ephesians 4: 29 tells us that we should allow, 'Nothing unwholesome' to come out of our mouths. If we want the *Holy* Spirit to confirm our words to people and work through what we say, we must be careful not to offend against his holiness as we speak.

Illustrations can be found everywhere and in everything. If we can't find one that fits, we can always invent one, as Jesus did. His hearers were familiar with teaching being given in parabolic form. They understood the fictional nature of the characters that he spoke about. If we do use a made-up story, we can alert our hearers to the fact by asking them to imagine that such and such a thing happened. An invitation to the audience to use their imaginations sends a clear signal that the story is fictional.

Before modern architecture took to cladding the exterior of buildings entirely in glass, sermon illustrations were often likened to windows in a building. The windows were strategically placed to allow light in. Illustrations ought not to dominate a sermon. They are used to complement Scripture, not replace it. Our gospel messages must be more scriptural and substantial than just an unbroken string of stories.

Be structured

The apostles in Jerusalem were careful to give 'their attention to prayer and the ministry of the word' (Acts 6: 4). To 'minister' is to serve. A chef and a waiter in a restaurant 'minister' to customers as they serve up a meal. The food, in several courses which the waiter brings to the table course-by-course, would be just as nutritious and filling if it were given to the diner all at once in a bucket, but it would almost certainly be regarded as an unappetising mess, and sent back to the kitchen! The same food, cleanly plated up and served in separate courses on good china, will be more readily appreciated and more happily received.

The gospel preacher, no less than the Bible teacher, is involved in the ministry of the word. The 'meals' we serve to people should be as well presented as would be a meal in a good restaurant. We should make the various points (the 'courses') in our messages clear and distinct.

There is no rule that a sermon should have a certain number of points. The number of points that we make in a message must be driven, not by tradition, or the expectations of others. They must not be the result of a slavish devotion to preaching in just one way! The passage of Scripture which we are expounding is what dictates how many points we will make.

Sermon notes

These should be in a font big enough for us to see easily even in poor light. Assign headings (titles) to the sections of the message. Underline or highlight those headings. I use highlighting pens to colour code my notes. That helps me to glance very briefly at my notes, and know immediately if the next thing I will say is a Bible quotation (green), or an illustration (red), a main point (yellow), or a call for people to respond to what they have been hearing (orange)

Read the Bible, not your sermon!

"Firstly, he read it, secondly, he read it badly, and thirdly, it wasn't worth reading in the first place!" That was the comment of a church member about the visiting preacher's sermon. We should try not to be totally dependent on our sermon notes. If we are reading from our notes, we are not looking at the congregation. Eye contact has been lost. Sometimes we need to lower our eyes to read a passage of Scripture or refer to our notes, but we should be well enough prepared that we can maintain a high degree of eye contact with our audience, glancing only briefly at our notes. If we appear to be reluctant to look our hearers in the eye, we risk seeming furtive or fearful. Neither of those is a good impression to give! And if we maintain eye contact, we know whether or not we are engaging our audience, or whether their attention is drifting. We shall also have a good clue whether we are convincing them.

Be nervous!

'Every public speaker gets butterflies in their stomach, but in the experienced preacher, they fly in formation!' Experience doesn't banish nervousness, but with experience comes the ability to control it. It is not a bad thing to be nervous. It is a great deal better than being overconfident. Being nervous should cause us to pray and to rely on God for the strength and ability that we need.

When we begin to preach, it will help us if we breathe slowly and deeply, and deliver our opening remarks slightly more slowly and precisely than we ordinarily would. Nervousness can have at least three unfortunate effects on us. It can cause us:

> To look down at our notes rather than look out at the people
> To speak too quickly
> To speak in too high a register

A preacher who appears frightened, incoherent and squeaky is off to a bad start! Sensible people will not be disturbed or alienated when they see some sign of nerves in the preacher. Most people dread the prospect of having to get up and speak in front of other people. You have had the courage to attempt to do so, reasonable people will feel that to be admirable, and they will sympathise with your nervousness—up to a point!

Be enthusiastic

I have just read an online post from a church member in the USA. He was being honest about how his pastor's sermons disappointed him. He wrote, 'Sometimes I want to shake the preacher! I want to say, for the love of God, man, why are you talking about the most important things in the world, in a way that reminds me of a person reading the instruction manual for a new computer!'

Not everyone has a passionate nature. Not everyone wears their heart on their sleeve. But when we preach, it should be evident that we ourselves are moved and excited by our message. If we aren't, then we can hardly expect anyone else to be.

'Talking' with our hands

A preacher once told his congregation that he never knew what to do with his hands when he preached. Someone called out the suggestion that he should put them over his mouth! Abraham Lincoln said that if he had to listen to a preacher, he preferred to listen to one who preached as if fighting a swarm of bees!

We ought to be animated as we preach. But it is not necessary to wave our arms around vigorously, or to thump the lectern aggressively with our fist, or engage in any other gestures that are excessive. Until and unless we develop a physical way of emphasising our points which feels and looks natural, we can simply hold lightly to the sides of the lectern and use one hand to gesture when it is appropriate. In the many informal evangelistic events at which I speak, I don't use a lectern, even if one is available. I find that I can comfortably hold my slim-line New Testament in one hand and use my other hand to punctuate and emphasise what I'm saying.

Preaching in Africa, I was introduced once as, Bob Telford, our 'not loud' evangelist! Despite the lack of histrionics and fevered strutting up and down the aisle—perfectly reasonable for my African friends, but unnatural for me—God still made the preaching effective. We must find our own style!

Whatever we do with our voices and bodies, **we must impress people with the certainty that what we are saying really matters to us, that *they* matter to us, and that the gospel is to be taken very, very seriously indeed.**

Be urgent

Paul encouraged Timothy to, 'preach the word' (2 Tim. 4: 2) and to do it with an awareness that the clock was ticking. A moment earlier, he had reminded Timothy (v. 1) that his preaching was done against the backdrop of Christ's imminent appearing.

When we preach the gospel, we preach it to people who do not have time on their side. Life is uncertain and can end suddenly and unexpectedly. Christ's coming will close the door of opportunity for people to be saved. If we preach the gospel in such a casual way as to imply that people have all the time in the world in which to make up their minds about Christ, then we misrepresent the seriousness of their situation.

In churches we have become quite good at saying to people that they should, "Go away and think about what they have heard." That is legitimate, but sometimes we need to be saying, "Stay here and do something about what you have heard." There comes a time when people need to understand the urgency that underlies the gospel invitation.

Be expectant

God gets his work done by speaking! At creation, he spoke repeatedly and each pronouncement resulted in something happening. In 2 Corinthians 4: 5 & 6, Paul urges believers to keep on preaching Jesus Christ as Lord and he assures the Corinthian Christians that, if they do, God will turn the lights on for some people, just as at creation he spoke light into being.

You and I believed the gospel when other people told it to us. They were probably no better at communicating the gospel than we are, yet we believed. It is not fanciful or overly optimistic for us to dare to hope that other people will believe the gospel when they hear it from us!

Some who hear us may be in the process of coming to Christ. We do not know what God has been saying to them previously or how he has been preparing them to hear our message. When we preach the gospel, we should make clear to people how they can respond to it.

Do you know what it feels like to preach the gospel and have someone get saved? I'll tell you. It feels like you want to do it again! May God give all who preach the gospel the privilege of calling people to come to Christ, *and having them actually come.*

* * * * * * * * * *

You have read this chapter on preaching the gospel. Is preaching for you? Do you think you could or should or would like to preach? Try it! There is no need to wait for an invitation to preach at a Sunday service. There are many organisations and individuals who would welcome your partnership with them as they take the gospel message out onto the streets, or to students, or to the homeless. Preaching in the open air to people who can and will vote with their feet if they are bored or uninterested is a great (and slightly bruising) training experience for the novice preacher!

Try preaching. If you discover that you can do it, that you enjoy doing it, and that, most importantly, people are reached and helped when you do it, then it may well be something that God wants you to persist in and get better at.

'Go and give the people the message of this new life!' (Acts 5: 20 (NLT))

For discussion

1. Is the gospel 'preached' in your church? Why or why not?
2. Think of the best gospel sermon you have heard and explain why you think it was good.

Chapter 10

Preaching Jesus in all the Scriptures

Phil Davies

There are many moments described in the Bible when I would have loved to have been there in person. Imagine being in the court of Nebuchadnezzar when those three Jewish administrators announce, "Our God is able to rescue us but even if he doesn't, we will not bow down." Or out in the wilderness of Judea with David when he begins to strum those first chords and play with the words of that new song "The Lord is my shepherd" or to walk with Hosea as he sets out to hand over those coins to buy back his wife from prostitution.

But perhaps first among all these would be to walk on the road from Jerusalem to Emmaus (Lk. 24: 13–24) with Cleopas and his companion, discussing all that had happened over the previous few days when Jesus, their friend and Master, had been taken and crucified. Their lives had been totally devastated and torn apart, and yet the news that had filtered through during that morning was that the tomb was empty and angels may have been seen proclaiming that Jesus was alive. What could it all mean? Then this stranger (they don't recognise that it's Jesus) joins them on the road. And he doesn't seem to know what has happened. They are aghast and ask him incredulously, "Where have you been these past few days?" And for us, of course, as we know the end of the story, the rest of the story as it unfolds doesn't seem as poignant. But for them, they don't know it's him. As Jesus begins to share with them, "'How foolish you are, and how slow to believe all that the prophets have spoken! Did not the Messiah have to suffer these things and then enter his glory?" *And beginning with Moses and all the Prophets, he explained to them what was said in all the Scriptures concerning himself.*' (Lk. 23: 25–28—emphasis mine)

Wouldn't you have wanted to have been there! As Jesus scrolls through prophecies and stories, pictures, patterns, types and shadows of God's awesome rescue plan.

That is the joy of a pastor-teacher, an evangelist, a preacher and any sharer of this good news. The entire written revelation the word of God overflows with the person of the One who is the Word of God, God's final word and revelation of himself—Jesus (Jn. 1: 14, 18; Heb. 1: 1, 2). That should be true for any one of us as a follower of Christ.

One of the men who really influenced me as a student in the early 1980s, and then for many years after that in Operation Mobilisation, was Nigel Lee. He was a man who as a Bible teacher and evangelist radiated Jesus through his winsome smile and his gift in sharing of God's word. Sadly, at the age of 58, he contracted cancer and within a year passed away. Just before he died, his close friend, Professor John Lennox, went to see him and asked him, "What do you want me to tell them at your funeral?". Nigel replied, "Tell them what we have always told them: so soak your minds and hearts in the Word of God until you see and hear the Living Word of God"—until you see Jesus.

Preaching Christ in the Old Testament

The task of a teacher of Scripture is to bring out of the storehouse new and old treasures that point to Jesus (Mt. 13: 52). We have Jesus's words on it again in John's Gospel. Jesus is speaking about authority and testimony to the scribes and Pharisees: 'You study the Scriptures diligently because you think that in them you have eternal life. These are the very Scriptures *that testify about me,* yet you refuse to come to me to have life.' (Jn. 5: 39–40—emphasis mine).

Jesus is referring to the Old Testament Scriptures here. It was the Scripture that he read, as it was also for Paul, Peter, James, and John as they wrote what we hold now as the New Testament. It is this same Scripture that Paul uses in the synagogues of Galatia and Asia Minor as he opens the scrolls of the Law and Prophets and the Writings and speaks of Jesus from them. It is to the Old Testament that the writers of the Gospels refer as they tell the story of Jesus, drawing from the prophecies, pictures, stories, songs from the Old(er) Testament. Jesus himself is the one who said, 'Do not think that I have come to abolish the Law or the Prophets; I have not come to abolish them but to *fulfil them.*' (Mt. 5: 17—my emphasi) Or, as some have put it, to *fill full* these Scriptures.

Overall redemptive history

The writer to the Hebrews in the New Testament reminds us, 'In the past God spoke to our ancestors through the prophets at many times and in various ways, but in these last days he has spoken to us by his Son, . . .' (Heb. 1: 1 & 2) It is always of great value to keep firmly in mind the overall flow of the Old Testament narrative and purpose—God's Big Story or, in more theological terms, the *missio Dei* (the mission of God). This Big Story can be summarised as

Creation→Fall→Redemption in History→New Creation.

Immediately the preacher (and hearer) can see that Christ is central to this plan of God.

The God in community (Father, Son and Spirit), who says, 'Let us make humankind in our image' (Gen. 1: 26) **[Creation]**, reaches out throughout the Scriptures, and on into today, seeking to draw us into community in and with himself. And at the darkest moment of human history, when humankind through Adam and Eve turn their backs on God **[Fall]**, the offer of hope, a light that shines in the darkness, is held out through the cursing of the serpent: 'And I will put enmity between you and the woman, and between your offspring [seed] and hers; he will crush your head, and you will strike his heel. (Gen. 3: 15) As God sends Adam and Eve, and humankind through them, away from the Garden of Eden where he had walked with them; away from his presence, yet, as someone has put it so achingly beautifully, "He sent himself out after them." So, throughout the rest of the Old Testament, God reaches out in mercy and grace again and again to them **[Redemption in History]**: '"Come now, let us settle the matter," says the Lord. "Though your sins are like scarlet, they shall be as white as snow; though they are red as crimson, they shall be like wool."' (Is. 1: 18)

In the New Testament, it is the writer of the book of Hebrews who takes the most space to explain the Old Testament for us, as he traces God's plan as the promised Messiah, Redeemer, Sacrifice, Great High Priest and Covenant of God, resulting in the **[New Creation]** in Christ. which will find its "full filling" in the return of the King. Edmund Clowney writes, 'Preachers who ignore the history of redemption in their preaching are ignoring the witness of the Holy Spirit to Jesus in all the Scriptures.'[1]

Clear prophetic passages

Apart from the overall theme of the whole of Scripture pointing to redemption and rescue in Christ, there are the specific prophecies that point towards Christ in the Old Testament. Although the total can be calculated in various ways, it is safe to say that the Old Testament has over 350 specific prophecies of the birth, life, character, mission, death, resurrection, and return of Christ.

Chronologically, these start in God's prophesying in his curse on Satan in Genesis 3 (commented on by Paul in Galatians 4: 4–5) and end in Malachi 4 with the prophecy about John the Baptist as the forerunner of the Christ. Psalms alone include around 100 prophecies of this coming King, while Isaiah has over 120 predictions. In Isaiah itself, there is ample material to preach the birth, upbringing, life, ministry, death, resurrection, and future glory of Jesus, e.g., born of a virgin (7: 14), Immanuel—God with us (7: 14), Nazarene (11: 1), Root of Jesse (11: 1), Rock of offence (8: 14), Mighty God, Prince of Peace (9: 6), Judge (11: 4), the Lord, Saviour, First and Last, the Branch, the Banner, Servant, and Salvation to the ends of the earth. All these are before we get to such passages as the Suffering Servant, including Isaiah 53, which refer to his condemnation, suffering, death, and resurrection.

Seeing Jesus in the types and shadows

We move next into a more difficult, but no less thrilling, matter: that of the many types, pictures, symbols, shadows and visions. If you would like further assistance, refer to the studies by Clowney already cited and that by Fee and Stuart noted below.

The traditional interpretation of a type involves seeing an historical person, place, event, or institution as having a future historical fulfilment. The Old Testament character, story, or event can be seen as the type, whereas the fulfilment is the antitype. In the New Testament, the Greek word *týpos*, meaning 'example', describes a model or pattern in the Old Testament that is fulfilled

1. E. P. Clowney, *Preaching Christ in all of Scripture* (Wheaton IL: Crossway, 2003).

in the life and mission of Jesus Christ. The word *týpos* is variously translated in, for example, the King James Version as pattern, form, print, ensample, fashion, figure and manner. The truth is that one cannot fully understand Leviticus without Hebrews, or Daniel without Revelation, or the Passover, or Isaiah 53, without the Gospel accounts of the Crucifixion. The typology of the Old Testament is the picture language in which truths of the New Testament, such as the Atonement, are prefigured. For example, the brazen serpent is the type (Num. 21: 8 & 9) and the cross is the antitype (Jn. 3: 14–15). Therefore, in order to preach the truths of the New Testament fully, we need to be aware of the shadows in Old Testament.

In the New Testamnent, Paul writes of the journey of the Israelites to the promised land as 'examples [*týpoi*] . . . written down as warnings [instruction or admonition] for us, on whom the culmination of the ages has come.' (1 Cor. 10: 11). Hebrews sees the law as a 'shadow of good things to come' (Heb. 10: 1(KJV)), suggesting that the Old Testament type is a shadow of something more real, an imperfect revelation as such.

So, characters such as Adam, Melchizedek, Abraham, Isaac, Joseph, Moses, Joshua, David, and Jonah are often seen as types, shadows, or pictures of Christ. Events like the Flood, the Passover, the bronze serpent, crossing the Jordan, ceremonies like the offerings, the year of Jubilee, the day of Atonement also have New Testament fulfilment in Christ. Many books have been written to clarify typological objects and structures such as the Ark, the Tabernacle, and the Temple. Even the temple furniture, e.g., the seven-branched candlestick, and the Ark of the Covenant with its Mercy Seat, points us to Christ.

Types explained in their original context and story

There are stories or illustrations in the Old Testament that are explained in their immediate context and so point to their final fulfilment in redemptive history and in particular in Christ

An example is the story of Hosea and Gomer. Hosea is told to go and marry the promiscuous Gomer and have children by her (Hos. 1: 2). The immediate context is the unfaithfulness of God's people Israel and Judah. Sometime later, Hosea is told to 'Go, show your love to your wife again, though she is loved by another man and is an adulteress. Love her as the Lord loves the Israelites, though they turn to other gods . . . So, I bought her for fifteen shekels of silver . . .' (Hosea 3: 1 & 2) At some stage, she had left Hosea for another man and had been unfaithful, yet Hosea was called to love her again. The prophecy of Hosea is quoted eight times in the New Testament, and the overall picture of the grace of God is ultimately seen in full colour in the purchase of God's people, the church, by Christ on the cross.

Seeing Christ book-by-book through the Old Testament

There are many attempts to show how each Old Testament book foreshadows Christ. Here is one:

> Genesis—Our Creator and promised Redeemer (the seed of the woman)
> Exodus—Our Passover Lamb,
> Leviticus—Our Great High Priest
> Numbers—Our pillar of cloud by day and pillar of fire by night
> Deuteronomy—Prophet like Moses who became a curse for us
> Joshua—Captain of our salvation or Commander of the army of the Lord
> Judges—The Judge, Law Giver and Deliverer from injustice
> Ruth—Our Kinsman-Redeemer
> 1 Samuel—Trusted prophet
> 2 Samuel—King of grace and love
> 1 Kings—Ruler greater than Solomon
> 2 Kings—The powerful prophet
> 1 Chronicles—Son of David who is coming to rule
> 2 Chronicles—The King who reigns eternally
> Ezra—Priest proclaiming freedom
> Nehemiah—The One who restores what is broken down
> Esther—Protector of his people

Job—Ever-living redeemer and mediator between God and man
Psalms—Our song in the morning and in the night
Proverbs—Our wisdom
Ecclesiastes—Our meaning for life
Song of Solomon—Our loving Bridegroom and the Author of faithful love
Isaiah—Our suffering Servant
Jeremiah—The weeping Messiah
Lamentations—He assumes God's wrath for us
Ezekiel—Son of Man
Daniel—The stranger in the fire with us
Hosea—Faithful husband ever married to the backslider
Joel—Sending his Spirit to his people
Amos—Delivers justice to the oppressed
Obadiah—Judge of those who do evil
Jonah—Greatest missionary
Micah—He casts our sin into the sea of forgetfulness
Nahum—Proclaimer of future world peace
Habakkuk—Crusher of injustice
Zephaniah—Warrior who saves
Haggai—Restorer of our worship
Zechariah—Messiah pierced for us
Malachi—Sun of righteousness who brings healing

Types clearly understood only in light of the New Testament

Many incidents and stories in the Old Testament can only be seen to be types of Christ because the New Testament confirms that they are such. Examples are:

> Moses striking the Rock of Horeb (Ex. 17: 6), when compared with Paul speaking of Christ as the Rock in 1 Corinthians 10: 4.
>
> Isaiah's vision of the Lord in Isaiah 6, finding its fulfilment in Christ as confirmed in John 12: 41.

> Manna in the wilderness wanderings, foreshadowing Christ as the Bread of Life (Jn. 6: 30–35 & 1 Cor. 10: 3).

Sometimes a case can be identified when the writer, inspired by the Spirit, uses the two words ***as*** and ***so***: 'Just **as** Moses lifted up the snake in the wilderness, **so** the Son of Man must be lifted up, . . .' (Jn. 3: 14) and 'For **as** Jonah was three days and three nights in the belly of a huge fish, **so** the Son of Man will be three days and three nights in the heart of the earth.' (Mt. 12: 40).

The latter example was taken further by Tim Keller when he compared Mark's account in Mark 4 of Jesus's stilling the storm with the story of Jonah:

> [Mark's account is] almost identical to the language of the famous Old Testament account of Jonah. Both Jesus and Jonah were in a boat, and both boats were overtaken by a storm—the descriptions of the storms are almost identical. Both Jesus and Jonah were asleep. In both stories the sailors woke up the sleeper and said, "We're going to die" And in both cases, there was a miraculous divine intervention, and the sea was calmed. Further in both stories the sailors then became more terrified than they were before the storm was calmed.[2]

Keller made the point that there is one difference. Jonah says, 'If I die you will live' and they throw him into the sea. In Matthew's Gospel, Jesus says, '"One greater than Jonah is here"' (or I'm the true Jonah). By this, Keller suggests that Jesus meant:

> "Someday I'm going to calm all storms and still all waves. I'm going to destroy destruction, break brokenness, kill death." How can he do that? He can do it only because when he was on the cross he was thrown—willingly like Jonah—into the ultimate storm, under ultimate waves, the waves of sin and death. Jesus was thrown into the only storm that can

2. Tim Keller, *King's Cross: The Story of the World in the Life of Jesus*, (London: Dutton Redeemer, 2011), p. 57.

> sink us—the storm of eternal justice . . . That storm wasn't calmed—not until it swept him away"[3]

Christ appearing in the Old Testament

There are times in the Old Testament when God (sometimes in the person of Christ) seems to be physically present. Theologians through the years have referred to such events as *theophanies* (Greek: *theos* = God and *phaino* = I appear) or *Christophanies*. So these words mean 'appearances of God' and 'appearances of Christ' respectively. On a number of these occasions 'the Angel of the Lord' is described as appearing. These are events when the story and the experience of those present indicate that there was something more than an ordinary angelic appearance. For example,

> Jacob wrestles with a 'man' (Gen. 32: 24–25, 28–30) and yet declares 'I saw God face to face'.
>
> The appearance of the Angel of the Lord to the parents of Samson in Judges 13 and their response when they realise who it was: 'We are doomed to die . . . We have seen God' (Judges 13: 22).
>
> The fourth 'man' in the fiery furnace with Shadrach, Meshach and Abednego in Daniel 3 where King Nebuchadnezzar declares, 'the fourth looks like a son of the gods.' (Dan. 3: 25)

It is interesting to note also that the word that Paul choses to write and speak evangelically of Christ is the Greek word *Kurios*. From the Greek translation of the Old Testament (Septuagint) and Paul's use of the word, it is clear that the New Testament Church recognized Christ not only in type in the Old Testament, but also as appearing and being seen on occasion. For example, the Greek translation of Exodus, in describing the people of Israel fleeing from Egypt, uses the word *Kurios* for Lord separately from the name for God: 'And Israel saw the mighty hand, the things that **kurios** did to the Egyptians; and the people feared **kurios**, and they believed **God** and Moses

3. Ibid.

his servant (Ex. 14: 31). For a more detailed and helpful explanation of this, see Edward Clowney, *Preaching Christ in all of Scripture.*

B. Preaching Christ in New Testament

Preaching Christ from Gospel narratives

Most of our preaching of Jesus will probably come from the narrative parts of the Gospels. A number of points may help us as we do so.

First, it is helpful to preach through a Gospel, taking the story of Jesus as it happens. Examples are the emphasis on journeys to Jerusalem and feasts in John's Gospel and the stories that Mark or Luke choose in order to illustrate the message that they want us to hear of Christ.

Secondly, we may have to use our imaginations and watch for movement. With respect to John 8: 1–11, it helps to stop and visualise the scene when the woman taken in adultery is dragged to Jesus as he sits, teaching the crowd. Where is she left to stand? Why does Jesus stoop to write? What does this passage illustrate about the nature of God that Jesus seeks to declare (cf. Jn. 1: 18)?

Thirdly, always ask the questions that Rudyard Kipling referred to as his 'five friends':

> I KEEP six honest serving-men
> (They taught me all I knew);
> Their names are What and Why and When
> And How and Where and Who.

For example:

> Why does Jesus sigh as he heals the man who can't hear or speak in Mark 7: 31–35?
> What is significant about the appearances of Moses and Elijah on the Mount of Transfiguration with Jesus?
> And why a mountain?
> (Mt. 17: 1–13; Mk. 9: 2–13; & Lk. 9: 28–36)

Preaching Christ from parables

Throughout church history, there have been a number of ways that theologians, writers and preachers have addressed themselves to the parables. Some, like Augustine, used them in an allegorical way, so that, for example, Augustine even identified Paul as the innkeeper in the parable of the Good Samaritan—everything meant something. It is on safer ground, if possibly simplistic, to say that the essence of a parable is one clear message or point. *How to read the Bible for all its worth* should be read for its chapter on parables alone.[4]

A few things can be kept in mind as we prepare to preach from parables. Sometimes Jesus himself offers a clear interpretation, e.g., in the case of the parable of the sower and the seed (Lk. 8). Sometimes, light may be shed by the fact that the parable is in answer to a specific question. For example, the parable of the Good Samaritan is answering the question, 'Who is my neighbour?' (Lk. 10: 29) On other occasions, there are similar parables which shed light on each other. For example, why do we have in succession the parable of hidden treasure and the parable of the pearl of greatest price? (Mt. 13: 44–46).

There is also the question of where the parable sits in the wider Gospel narrative. Why does Jesus tell that particular parable at the particular point in the narrative? For example, in Luke 15, there are three parables which Jesus told to meet the criticism of the Pharisees and the teachers of the law that 'This man welcomes sinners and eats with them' (v. 2). All three parables have similarities—something or someone is lost, there is someone who seeks, there is rejoicing at the end. But what in gospel terms makes the third parable of the lost son or sons more remarkable?

Preaching Christ from the Letters and Revelation

The letters are written to inform, instruct and encourage the fledgling churches on what needed to be held and believed as they sought to live their transformed lives as new creations in Christ. Much is also written to correct, and also help the churches to take a stand as they witnessed for Christ in their contexts.

A number of the letters like Ephesians and Colossians have a pattern that gets the mind focussed on truth about Christ and faith in the first part of the

4. Gordon D. Fee & Douglas Stuart, *How to Read the Bible for All its Worth* (London: Scripture Union, ^{2}1994), pp. 135–148.

letter, followed by truth that was to be lived out in practice. Ephesians chapters 1–3 can be entitled Transformed Life (what is means to be 'in Christ', and the blessings and riches that come from him) and chapters 4–6 can be entitled, Transformed Living (being 'in Christ', how should we then live?)

One of the questions that we need to be asking constantly is, what does the writer want to teach this church about Jesus? As someone has commented, "the Gospel is Jesus; Jesus is the Gift."

Steps to preaching and sharing Jesus in all the Scriptures

If we are to take seriously the challenge to share Christ from all the Scriptures, there are three practical things we should be doing.

Read the Big Story

If we are to take seriously Jesus's words to the two on the road to Emmaus, then it is vital we should ourselves read continually and regularly the whole of Scripture. Set it as a goal to read through the whole Bible either every year or certainly within every three years. Get the Big Picture, the heart of God in his Big Story.

Some useful tools are (1) a Bible that takes you through the whole of Scripture in a year day-by-day. CWR produces an excellent one under their series *Every Day with Jesus*. They also have one in this series that orders of Scripture chronologically. And (2) a reading plan, such as that by Robert Murray McCheyne, which enables you read through the Old Testament in a year and the New Testament twice in the year (that is, roughly four chapters of Scripture a day). Another version of this takes you through the Old Testament in two years and the New Testament twice in the two years. The You Version Bible app will help you find these and similar plans.

Study and read around the Big Story

Continue to challenge and enlarge your thinking on the Big Story. Some books that you may find helpful are

Drama of Scripture: Finding our Place in the Biblical Story by Craig Bartholomew & Michael Goheen (London: SPCK, ^{2}2014)

God's big picture: Tracing the storyline of the Bible by Vaughan Roberts (Nottingham: IVP, 2002)

The Bible—a story that makes sense of life by Andrew Ollerton (London: Hodder & Stoughton, 2022)

How to read the Bible for all its worth by Gordan Fee & Douglas Stuart (Grand Rapids MI: Zondervan, 1993 & Scripture Union, 1994)

Preaching Christ in all of Scripture by Edmund Clowney (Wheaton IL: Crossway, 2003)

Preach, chat through and share the storyline regularly

As you seek God for your preaching, stretch yourself and look to go beyond where you would usually go by default. For example, see God's heart in Hosea's story, or see Christ in David's love for Mephibosheth (2 Samuel 9). Share what you learn. Bounce ideas, thoughts, insights off mentors and peers alike. Drill down together to what God's Spirit is seeking to reveal to you. Allow what you have read to infiltrate your conversations, enlarge your discussions, and be brought into your internet chats. Finally, constantly seek Christ in the passage you are reading, studying, meditating on. In the words of Nigel Lee, *soak your minds and hearts in the Word of God until you see and hear the Living Word of God.*

For discussion

1. Take one Old Testament passage and one New Testament and discuss how you would preach the gospel from each of them.
2. What turns a sermon into a compelling sermon?

Chapter 11

Preaching the gospel for a response

Bob Telford

> It's easy to be abstract, but it takes effort to be specific. Nothing becomes dynamic until it becomes specific. A well prepared sermon should be more like a bullet than buckshot! Know your purpose and aim right for it.—Rick Warren

All preaching, not least evangelistic preaching, should have a goal. The preacher should, as John Wesley put it, "Take aim". I am so convinced about this that I still, after five decades of preaching, write my aim for each message at the top of the page as I prepare it. The words stand out to me as I start to preach and remind me that I am there, under God, to get something done.

Regardless of when, how, where or what we are preaching, our preaching must be purposeful. The alternative to being purposeful is to be purposeless. Preaching without intentionality can too easily leave both preacher and hearers wondering just what the point really was.

Preaching for a decision

Answering people's questions, addressing their hostility or confusion, or simply sowing some good seed in people's minds are all good aims and it is necessary that we do those things. On occasion, however, we will both want to do more and feel that we must do more.

Appeals

A Scotsman was once asked, "What is it like to know Christ?" He replied that it was "better felt than telt!" That is, it was difficult for him to put it into words, but he knew inwardly the reality of Christ in his life. Knowing when it is the right time not only to call on people to respond inwardly to the gospel, but also to invite them to make a public response, is very similar. It is not something that can be reduced to a simple, one-size-fits-all explanation. Some preachers, the writer included, find that a sense of urgency and expectation comes to them as they prepare to preach. The passage we are studying, and what we know of the opportunity which is coming, combine together and stir us not only to cast out the net, but also to draw it in.

"You're not going to make appeals when you preach, are you? Please tell me that you won't." The enquiry came from the vicar of a church in Eastern Canada. I was there to lead a mission on a Canadian Air Force base. We were discussing the upcoming mission programme over a meal with other church leaders and Air Force chaplains. "Well", I assured him, "I can promise that I won't make an appeal *every* time I speak, but I'm not ruling it out altogether." "Oh! Please don't."he said, "It won't work; it's very un-Canadian!" Subsequent events proved that, while the Holy Spirit was aware of Canadian scruples and sensitivities, he was not bound by them!

Calling on people at the conclusion of a gospel message to respond both inwardly and outwardly may be un-Canadian and un-British, but, while custom and culture should be taken into account in our ministry, they must not be permitted to totally dominate it.

Not every time

As gospel communicators, we may find ourselves speaking in a range of situations in which to call for a public response would not be appropriate. We may be speaking to people whose exposure to the Christian faith is still at a very early stage, and we should probably not press people for a decision, but make ourselves and literature available to anyone who wants to investigate further. Presenting the gospel in those situations can reasonably be seen more as sowing than reaping. Even so, however, we should not rule out the possibility that the Holy Spirit may press us to press them a little harder to make their minds up about Jesus.

Response—inward and outward

There will be occasions when it *will* be appropriate for us to call on people to make an inward and spiritual response to the message, and to underscore that inward response by doing something outward and physical. Romans 10: 8–13 tells us that there is an inward, spiritual and invisible aspect to our response to the gospel. We must believe in our hearts. There is also, however, an outward, physical and visible aspect as we confess with our mouths. This Scripture is certainly about more than merely an initial confession of faith, but it *is* about that initial confession too. To call on people to believe, without calling on them to say or to show that they have done so, risks leaving them unsure about what they have done, and, because they have not identified themselves as having responded inwardly, they may well go away without getting the attention and the help which they need.

The positives

Making what is often known as an 'appeal' brings a number of benefits for all concerned.

An appeal brings clarity concerning the responder's spiritual interest. In many congregations, there are people whose exact spiritual condition no one is really sure about. When someone responds to an appeal, they reveal themselves to be seriously interested in spiritual things, to say the least. On the basis of that revealed interest, they can be approached and advised without impertinence.

An appeal underlines the truth that people need to 'Do something about what they hear and not just listen to it!' (Jas. 1: 22)

An appeal reminds everyone that deliberation should eventually lead to decision. Of course, we must be careful not to call people to a premature decision for Christ, but neither, by our unwillingness to challenge them, should we leave them in a state of permanent indecision.

An appeal teaches people that doing what Christ asks them to do must trump personal embarrassment or fear of what others will think.

When people respond to an appeal, that encourages and thrills God's people. They are reminded that the gospel 'is [still] the power of God at work saving everyone who believes' (Rom. 1: 16 (NLT))

An appeal sends a signal to everyone that there is more in coming to a service than sitting silently and passively acquiescing in what is being preached. It cuts across the cosiness and familiarity that may have become a hallmark of church services. When we listen to God's Word being preached, we are being called to do business with God. An appeal reinforces that truth.

The big problem: the fear of what people may think

Working more powerfully against making of an appeal than other people's scruples, cultural norms, theological reservations, or anything else, is anxiety about what people will think of us.

Just after I had made an appeal at his church, a young man asked me, "Bob, if you made an appeal and no one came forward, wouldn't you feel a bit embarrassed? I know I would!" "Yes", I answered, "I would: in fact it has happened more than once and I have felt a bit embarrassed. However, I can live with that. What I do not want to live with is knowing that God had asked me to do something and that I had failed to do it because of the risk of embarrassment." Driving home from preaching, I need to know that, even if I had been wrong on that occasion to make an appeal, I had done it because I believed that it was what God wanted me to do. I can handle the fact that I sometimes get things wrong, but the suspicion that, because of concern for my reputation or a failure to hold my faith and nerve, I had let the Lord down is far harder for me come to terms with.

Only the fear of God can drive out the fear of man

There may be several excellent reasons for not calling on people to respond publicly at a particular time, but fear of what others will think of us is not one of them. Someone has said, "Only the fear of God can drive out the fear of man." Gospel preachers must resolve that they are the Lord's servants, and that their commission is, as God said to Jeremiah, 'Get yourself ready. Stand up and say to them whatever I command you.' (Jer. 1: 17) (NIV). John Piper has pointed out that 'The person to whom we ascribe the most authority is the person we fear the most.' If we think of ourselves as being under Christ's authority and ultimately answerable to him, we will be more anxious to please him than we are to be popular or to be invited back to preach another time!

Above all else, we must pray about whether or not we should make an appeal, neither assuming that we should not, nor ignoring the possibility that we ought to.

Practicalities of making an appeal

Prepare believers for the appeal

Practically, this means we shall:

> Liaise with the service or event leader. Arrange that our message and appeal will be the concluding item on the programme.
>
> If a final congregational song is going to be intrinsic to the appeal, then musicians, a keyboard player at least, should be asked to remain in place during the preaching. Several musicians making their way from their chairs to the front, noisily stepping over cables, re-assembling and possibly re-tuning, will be an unhelpful distraction.
>
> Ensure that some believers are ready and able to come to the front and to stand alongside or just behind those who have responded. Make it very clear that they are **not** to come forward before any enquirers have begun to move forward: having Christians come forward in an attempt to encourage people to respond may be well-intentioned, but it is wrong-headed and, in my opinion, unethical.
>
> The role of the helpers is to show from the Bible how those who have made a response can be saved, and how they may be sure that they are saved. The helpers should also seek the information necessary to enable further contact (making it clear that the details will be held in confidence). The helpers play a critical role and should be chosen with care. Many

churches have a team of people who form a Prayer Ministry Team or something similar. They will doubtless be good and godly men and women, but we should not assume that the people in such a team are necessarily the right people to speak with those who have responded to an appeal, although it is to be hoped that they will be.

Arrange for space and seats at the front of the venue to be kept free so that conversations between enquirers and those alongside them can be uninterrupted.

Ensure that those who speak with enquirers have appropriate literature to give to them..

Prepare the appeal

Again there is a number of steps to be taken care of.

We should do this as carefully as we prepare our sermon. Unless we are very experienced, we will do well not to try to to make it up on the spot. Making an appeal requires a considerable degree of care and precision. Any lack of clarity will cause uncertainty as to what is being asked and work against what we are trying to do.

We must keep the appeal focused, and not send mixed or multiple messages. Our aim is that individuals will respond to the gospel. It is unhelpful, and in large measure negates the point of an appeal, if people are invited forward simultaneously for a variety of reasons. The most important thing that anyone can ever do is to respond to Christ in repentance and faith. That must be the focus of a gospel preacher's appeal.

Avoid giving the wrong impression. We must not give people the idea that walking to the front of an auditorium is what is going to save them.

Each preacher must operate within the bounds of their own theological understanding and conscience. I am careful personally not to call people to 'come and find Christ' or to 'Come to Christ' by walking forward. Jesus is no more present and available in front of the pulpit than he is in the row where the person was sitting a few moments before. He is *not* waiting at the front to receive them. He is present by his Spirit just where they are. I suggest that, while people are still in their seats, we encourage them to pray a prayer inviting Christ to be their Saviour. Then we can explain to them about the outward response of Romans 10, and invite them to show publicly that they have personally and prayerfully reached out to Christ. Walking forward then becomes not a way to be saved, but a way to signal that they have been or want to be saved, and that they are resolved to follow Christ and not ashamed of their decision.

Make the appeal

Here, too, there is a number of distinct points:

> Explain the two-fold nature of response to Christ (inward and outward).
>
> Lead in a brief prayer of repentance and faith. This should be prayed slowly and clearly, a sentence at a time, allowing time for people to repeat the prayer for themselves.
>
> Ask those who have prayed the prayer to leave where they are sitting and make their way to the front and stand in front of you as a demonstration that they have turned or are turning to Christ in their hearts and that they are not going to be ashamed, but are prepared to show that they have turned to Christ.
>
> Explain that, when they respond, someone will come and stand with them, to be on hand to give them some helpful literature.
>
> When people have responded, explain that they have taken a hugely important step, but that it is the first step in a life of following Christ. Tell them that you or someone else has something to give to them and will speak with them briefly before they leave.
>
> Ask those who have responded to sit down at the front and announce that service or event is over.

Tell people that those who have come forward will rejoin the families or friends in just a few minutes' time. At that point, the helpers should introduce themselves to those who've come forward and start to share briefly with them

What are you trying to do, preacher?

A teacher of homiletics once said, 'As I have listened to preachers I have generally had two questions in mind: "What is the preacher trying to do?" and "How well is he or she doing it?" I have often been unable to answer the second question because I could not discover the answer to the first!'

When we preach we must ask ourselves, what is it that we are trying to do? What changes do we want to effect, what impact do we want the preaching of the gospel to have? Without such determination, there is a danger that our messages could, as Donald Coggan[1], once said, 'meander like harmless, bubbling brooks; lacking drive, force and power, effecting nothing great in matters of eternal moment.'

God save us from that!

For discussion

1. Do you think there is a place for 'gospel appeals' in church today? Why or why not?
2. What do you think characterises a good appeal?

1. Archbishop of Canterbury, 1974–80.

Chapter 12

How ordinary friendships can result in extraordinary blessings

Beverley Bedford

It has been suggested that the average person requires five significant encounters with the gospel before accepting Jesus Christ as Saviour. One of the top influences leading individuals to come to know Jesus is having a friendship with a Christian believer.[1]

When I reflect on my own life, I remember significant encounters through friendships that encouraged me to consider the claims of Christ. I am thankful for those ordinary people who challenged me in an extraordinary way to follow Jesus.

A foundational influencer

First, there was my Sunday school teacher who intentionally prayed that God would bring all of her Sunday School class of ten children to a living faith in Jesus, and particularly that they would all be able to share their faith with others. Prayer was at the heart of her interactions with us. Dietrich Bonhoeffer wrote 'The activity of prayer and perseverance that often seems weak and inconsequential is the power to bring change and transformation in God's timing'.[2]

---

1. Paul Benjamin, *The equipping ministry* (Cincinnati, OH: Standard Publishing, 1977).

2. Dietrich Bonhoeffer, *The Cost of Discipleship*, (London: SCM Press, 1959) (trans. R. H. Fuller).

It was this Sunday school teacher who taught me to memorise Scripture that remains written on my heart to this day. I remember how, with deep conviction and a unique, animated style, she systematically shared the stories of the Old and New Testaments with me. I shall never forget how imaginatively she made the Bible come alive, and how engaged and excited we were as children when it was story time. We all thought our Sunday School teacher was awesome. She knew the Bible without looking at notes, always had answers for our questions, and prayed in a way that drew our hearts to heaven's gate.

This Sunday School teacher did not shy away from the dutiful work of weekly commitment and constant prayer. She always showed up with enthusiasm and passion to talk about Jesus. 'Transforming children into spiritual champions'[3] was the mission and assignment that she pursued faithfully every Sunday morning. It may not surprise you to know that most of the children in her class are now serving the Lord and sharing their faith.

It is hard to deny that our culture is increasingly opposed to Christian values, and the worldly influences bombarding and shaping our children's moral and spiritual development are difficult to contend with. So, I am ever thankful for praying, passionate **foundational influencers** who continue to impact our children's formative years by sharing God's word. Archbishop John Sentamu captures it: 'There is nothing more transformative, nothing more redemptive, nothing more able to turn a life around than the gospel of Jesus Christ.'

So, let me ask the question, where is your harvest field? Could it be in a Sunday school class, nurturing the next missional leaders? Is there an opportunity for you to be the 'footprint in the wet cement' of a young person's life that will lay a foundation for the Holy Spirit to draw that heart and life to Jesus? Is there potential to pray for a group of children that God could bring to living faith in Jesus, and particularly that they would be able to share their faith with others. The task of transforming children into spiritual champions is a calling of great importance.

---

3. To use George Barna's book title of 2003.

A motivational maker and shaker

A second friendship that set my course early in life was with my religious education teacher. She was a teacher who modelled friendship evangelism in everything she put her hand to. She was always looking for opportunities to engage us as children in local school projects that would demonstrate kindness to the community and connect us to church life.

It was this relationship above any other that taught me the importance of, and responsibility to undertake, social action in my community. I am thankful for the **motivational makers and shakers** who turn our eyes to the needs of others, who create a sense of conviction in us to speak out and stand up for those who have no voice and who are marginalised and ostracised in our society (Prov. 31: 8).

At school as a volunteer, I learned the value of community and being a visible presence for good. The joy of belonging, of knowing and being known, contributed immensely to the vibrancy of the village I grew up in. It provided effective opportunities to address the needs and aspirations of the local people. I discovered that the opportunity to serve my community affirmed me as a valuable member of school and church. I was grateful to be offered the chance as a young person to roll my sleeves up and be involved in a wide range of community activities and events, and witness first-hand the Christian community being salt and light in people's ordinary everyday lives. I felt the impact of engagement in the community on the lives of many, including my own.

Jesus didn't walk around with a programme under his arm. He got to know people, he got out among society, and most importantly he 'got real'. Jesus knew about the people he was talking to, he understood them, he had empathy with them. His stories captivated his audience because they were about what mattered to them. He spent time building relationships, he got his message across. He was in short, proactive. He built relationships and showed people that they needed him. In this, he demonstrated that he was the incarnate Son of God.

To understand this incarnational approach, our RE teacher each month took a themed real-life story of ordinary men and women who served God on mission. During her lunch-break, she established the 'adventure club', in which she retold the classic stories of missionary endeavour. They included Hudson Taylor, George Müller, David Livingstone, Amy Carmichael, Mary Slessor and Jim Elliot, to name but a few.They fuelled my imagination and inspired me to see what my life might look like if I gave it completely to Jesus.

The main focus and aim of 'adventure club' was always practical: that inspiration should be followed by application. Is there any point in just being inspired, if you are not prepared to do something? This passion for action, to make a difference in the world, was the outworking of the gospel that my RE teacher embodied. It was contagious and ignited a fire in my heart that was never to be extinguished.

As Dallas Willard claims, 'The world can no longer be left to mere diplomats, politicians and business leaders. They have done the best they could, no doubt. But this is an age for spiritual heroes—a time for men and women to be heroic in their faith and in spiritual character and power.' I pray that God will release in his Church a stronger prophetic voice to speak into society, to stand in the public square and declare the mind and will of God with a fearless heart. To speak out and stand up for the most marginalised, the most excluded, the most alone, so that people know the Church cares, and hope can be birthed in the hearts of those who need it most.

Pursuing Jesus, following Jesus, looks like something, and being intentionally engaged in the ordinary everyday lives of people will take us into every sphere of society, schools, education, hospitals and health care, business and commerce, government and politics, media, arts and science, our streets, our village halls the open squares of decision making and community life. There is nowhere we go that the Holy Spirit is not with us. So let's be carriers of his presence into every heart, every relationship, every conversation, so that we can bring life-giving, politics-changing, community-impacting, family-redeeming, individual-saving, body-healing CHANGE.

A constant companion

The third, and most memorable, friendship was with a Christian girl at my school. This friendship developed during the most difficult stage of my teenage years. I had lost my father who died when I was 4, and, when I was 11, my mum and brother had a serious road accident. This tragic event was to cause so much upheaval for us as a family: my mum suffered multi-injuries, including memory loss, and it took many years of rehabilitation to get her and my brother back to any kind of normality. It was following mum's return to the family home that I became her full-time helper, and it was inevitable that my school education was going to suffer as a result of all the exhausting hours that I spent with my four older brothers in a caring role. In God's perfect timing, in stepped a Christian who would become over the next few years a **constant companion** and my best friend.

Cathy and her beautiful godly family in effect adopted me and offered me respite from the mundane days, with occasional trips to the seaside and a commitment to drive me to school every day. I got to experience their happy healthy home, full of fun, laughter and Jesus, and for me their hospitality was an oasis in my desert. I look back with deep gratitude for their Christian support that was a lifeline to me when I was emotionally sinking and overwhelmed.

This devoted friendship was a gospel opportunity for God to open my eyes to his love and generous heart, and to have someone who was my peer demonstrating what living for Jesus really looked like. Cathy was the classic 'come-and-see-for-yourself' type of enthusiastic Christian. Like the woman at the well, she would invite, and I would willingly follow. I responded to her regular invitations to church without resistance because of our friendship and her enthusiastic way of getting me to try new things. Cathy never had an agenda, and one thing I was certain of in our relationship was that, should I never follow Jesus, I would always be her best friend. Cathy had a gift for just opening her Bible anywhere with anybody and talking boldly about Jesus, by saying things like "this is what I believe Jesus to be", and "this is why I believe he came", "but listen come to this youth event, service; come and see and hear for yourself." Cathy shone a gospel light straight into my heart, and taught me evangelism is not for just the full-timers or Bible college graduates or the extroverts of the world, but for everyone.

God has given each of his children the DNA to share the good news in natural ways that suit our style, personality and temperament. My friendship with Cathy drew me closer to God and lifted my head in the darkest of times, so that I felt loved and safe. It was a poignant period of my life when trauma and sadness caused me to explore more meaningfully the purpose of life, and some kind of theology of suffering that made sense. Cathy's friendship really influenced my belief system in a positive way, and caused me to consider the big questions of life and examine what the Bible had to say in contrast to my own world-views. It was a beautiful friendship in which her evangelistic fervour **signposted** the way for me on my journey of faith to Jesus.

I wonder, is God asking you to be generous in your love and gift of hospitality, to embrace someone who needs to brought in from the cold to the peripherals of church life? I have always felt that the church should be first in line to love its community in word and action. I know what that love feels like when you are broken and hurting. It is like someone putting a warm blanket around you. In the aftermath of a global pandemic, there is no end of opportunity to invest in the lives of others and to offer a friendship that says, "Come and see the difference God makes in our heart and home, and be part of the family."

Compassionate helper

The fourth and final person that impacted me with the gospel was a Christian nurse. For me, she was like encountering an angel because of her compassionate care for my mum following her road-traffic accident. It was transformational to witness how she delivered spiritual care and modelled God's love in action. Her Christ-like beauty and grace was stunning, and she was like no other Christian I had ever encountered in her practical approach to serving others. I often prayed in a childlike way as a result of knowing her: "Lord I want to serve people like this, I want to grow up and love people like this."

The most remarkable part of this friendship was her attitude, behaviour and personal qualities. It wasn't what she did for my mum, but how she was with my mum. This nurse with her professional skills was able to manage with such patience and sensitivity my mum's anger and frustration in her recovery journey. This beautiful human poured into our lives in gentle ways that were so profoundly powerful. I watched in awe as she wisely dealt with our everyday struggles and cheerfully listened to every grumble and moan (and there were many). I was more than impressed when she courageously embraced every opportunity to share her faith and beliefs in God. This Christian nurse put herself in our family picture-frame; she walked with us on a traumatic journey; she was a **compassionate helper** and taught me the essence of servant evangelism. I have absolutely no doubt that God sent this Irish nurse to us, and my memory of her was that peace permeated our home when she was present. It was so miraculous that she was always there, for every crisis, ready to minister grace and hope though the gift of friendship.

Evangelising and serving with compassion

To serve people with compassion and care, we need a big heart; we need God's heart, his agape love. In 1 Corinthians 13, we read that without love all we say is ineffective, without love all we know is incomplete, without love all we believe is insufficient, without love all we give is insignificant, and without love all we accomplish is inadequate. To relate to people, we have to identify with them, walk alongside them, journey together with them. Jesus was found in the marketplace, having meals with his friends; he invested time in listening, asking questions, responding to need, and understanding the people he engaged with. What would our communities look like if the Spirit of God carried us and used us in every context we find ourselves in? What would they look like if we authentically pointed to the Saviour who breaks his heart at the pain and suffering of this broken world; if we could pray and minister with compassion and care to those who are wounded, sick and sad, and comfort them as we have been comforted by God; if we could shine a gospel light and reach into the darkness of this world's despair though friendship that brings revelation of the truth that God is good and that his love endures forever.

Jesus demonstrated compassion to those who suffered, he fed the hungry, he healed the sick, and he lifted the heads of the forgotten. Jesus met physical and emotional needs and used it to point to the ultimate spiritual need of eternal life. Jesus didn't separate the ministry of compassion and mercy from the ministry of proclamation. Ministry is how we live out our vocation, the life that Jesus calls us to. It is, therefore, also the way in which we all fulfil God's mission for the world. At its heart is the incarnational principle of being with people in their context. Let's be vehicles of transformation so that we can bring life-giving, politics-changing, community-impacting, family-redeeming, body-healing, individual-saving, CHANGE into every heart, every relationship and every conversation.

Most people come to know Jesus because of a friendship with a believer whose life example and personal witness testify to God's love. Nothing communicates the truth of the gospel better than a life transformed by the power of God. It is evidence that this gospel works. In sharing your story, you are making clear the benefits of following Jesus Christ, the difference he has made, how your life now has meaning, purpose and significance. If you have friendships with non-believers, then you have so many opportunities to listen to their stories and share aspects of your own story, and build a bridge from your heart to their heart for Jesus to walk over.

Every church should be committed to proclaiming the gospel—this message of transformation and new birth. In 1 Peter 3: 15, the apostle writes that every Christian should be prepared to share his or her personal story in order to 'give an answer to everyone who asks you to give the reason for the hope that you have'.

Historically, on occasion, the church has been good at proclamation, but not at engagement within its community. It is also true that in more recent times the church has been great at engagement, but often pitches its message of the gospel too low. Proclamation with engagement really matters, and this was evidenced in the pandemic. The way we live out faith, the way we answer questions in response to the hope we have, have impact on our listeners and good relationships of friendship are a starting point for conversations about Jesus.[4]

One of the terms used most frequently in the New Testament which we translate as gospel is the Greek work 'evangelion', which means 'good news'. The English word 'evangelism' is derived from that word and it simply means 'sharing the good news' or gossiping the gospel. It is only as we are rooted in the gospel that mission can be outworked to those around us. Good news people have an instant responsiveness to whatever will help to proclaim and demonstrate the gospel of peace. The primary point of interface for the church with its community must always be the good news. Good news that brings hope when despair is eating into people's minds. Good news that is comforting when people embrace death, loss and sickness. Purposeful news that gives

4. See http://www.talkingjesus.org/ for a website which encourages and trains in evangelism through conversation.

meaning, significance, worth, and value to people's understanding of why they exist in the world. The world needs more than ever before that the church should live out the gospel in word and deed. Brothers and sisters, the gospel is the ground that we stand on; it is the soil we grow in; and it is where we pitch a kingdom flag as we advance; and it is where we co-labour in building the Church of Jesus Christ. This is our greatest pursuit as we follow Jesus in kingdom advancement. Is there any greater adventure? Is there anything more life giving, more demanding and more satisfying?

Archbishop Justin Welby said recently,'The responsibility of demonstrating in word and works the love of Jesus Christ, in a way that is deeply attractive is the responsibility of every single Christian. Always. Everywhere.' He went on: 'What draws people in, above all, is community. It's the fact that they belong. They are loved by others, they are accepted, they are welcomed.'

We are living in remarkable times that are full of opportunities to share our faith in compelling, compassionate and confident ways. Our nation needs God. It does not need a social gospel, a new method or programme, or a set of good ideas. It needs God in our communities. It needs churches in love with God and their neighbours, and engaged with society's brokenness. This is our moment! I dream of what thousands of ordinary Christians could do, who carry the Spirit of God unhindered into their communities: an army of foundational influencers, of motivational makers and shakers, of sign-posters, of compassionate helpers, in every stream of society.

I pray that, post-COVID, we have not simply gone back to buildings where we just gather, but that the church will break beyond what we have been in the immediate past. I pray that we are visibly moving into our neighbourhoods with a holistic, biblically-faithful, culturally-relevant, Spirit-dependant, and relationally-authentic approach to sharing our faith. When the history of the Church is written for our generation and the next, what will it say? I would suggest that it depends on our response to the gospel. We are in days of opportunity and advancement. So let us not retreat. Let's go beyond our comfort zones. There can be no social, political, economic change, there can be nothing of eternal worth, if we don't as a nation invite God to build our hearts, homes and communities. It is impossible to serve our chaotic, messy world, where the enemy has written his scandalous graffiti of sin over lives, without the help of God the Holy Spirit and without praying that the Lord of the harvest will send out his labourers into his harvest (Mt. 9: 38).

Counties seeks to equip churches to make Jesus known throughout the UK. The challenge to us as churches is, how missional and visible are we in reaching and engaging with the community? Counties invites you to be part of the growing number of local churches discovering the Neighbourhood Chaplains scheme. This scheme has the potential to become one of the most significant resources to help churches in our times.[5]

* * * * * * * * * * *

My objective in this chapter has been to inspire and challenge you. God used significant relationships in order to write my redemption story. God is seeking men and women who will be influencers, motivators, sign-posters, and compassionate helpers, to write someone else's story. I am confident that, as we proclaim the gospel and portray the biblical model of Jesus' compassionate servant heart, God will work and bless in exciting ways. Remember the gospel is not something we only hear; it's something that we live to tell. So, let us all live the good news and talk about those things that really matter, and intentionally seek friendships that can allow us to impact people's lives for eternity.

For discussion

1. What makes a good friend and what can I do now to be one?
2. What are the benefits and hazards of friendship evangelism?
3. What do you find most difficult in friendship evangelism? Why, and what can you do about it?

5. To find out more contact beverley.bedford@countiesuk.org

Chapter 13

Work as a gospel opportunity

Neil Summerton

Work is a necessary human activity. In the Christian perspective, it predates the fall of humankind, as Genesis 1 asserts that God himself works in creation; the human supervisory role that God gave to humankind entailed work; we were put into the Garden in order to tend and care for it (Gen. 2: 15); and the commandment specified 'Six days you shall labour' (Ex. 20: 9). It is only the *toil* of work which results from the fall and the consequent curse on the ground (Gen. 3: 17–19). Work can and does remain, however, a fulfilling activity because in it we do as God did and does.

Patterns of human labour have changed throughout history. The recent industrial period has perhaps been exceptional in the concentration of labour in factories and offices, though we should not underestimate the extent to which men, at least, went 'out' to work in former times: Jesus's parable shows that there were street-corner or village-centre daily labour markets in the Judea and Galilee in his day (Mt. 20: 1–16), as there still are in many parts of the world—I recall being struck by them in the suburbs of Beirut twenty-five years ago. And nearly 2,000 years earlier than the time of the Messiah, the obligation of young females to fetch water and water flocks certainly created the opportunity for social encounter through work (see Gen. 24: 13: 'the daughters of the townspeople are coming out to draw water' (NRSV); and also Ex. 2: 16–19, a few centuries later). The pandemic has influenced work patterns in the developed world, but it continues to be focussed on the workplace in manufacturing and production, distribution centres, retail, healthcare, and primary and secondary education; and even when working from home is physically and technically practicable, there has already been since the pandemic some swing back to a focal workplace for reasons of effectiveness and ensuring productivity.

The result is that the workplace competes with the home as a locale where waking hours are spent for those who are in employment; indeed, for many, more time is spent away at work than is spent in the home. It is also the case that those Christians who are economically active (as government economists and statisticians say) constitute a large proportion of many Christian congregations—larger still if students in tertiary and secondary education are counted as spending large amounts of time in workplaces.

All Christians are intended to be effective and successful witnesses for Christ: indeed, the infant Church spread as much through such witness as it did through the preaching of leaders, and their signs and wonders. In the Jerusalem church at the beginning, it appears that it was witness in social life which brought about daily addition of 'those who were being saved' (Acts 2: 47 (NRSV)); it was the proclamation of the nameless Christians who were scattered from Jerusalem by persecution that led to the expansion of the church throughout the eastern Mediterranean (Acts 8: 4 & 11: 19); and it was nameless Christians (strictly, then, 'disciples' rather than 'Christians') from Cyprus and Cyrene who established the first Gentile church in Antioch (Acts 11: 20 & 21).

It follows that those Christians who currently spend many hours of their lives in a workplace have an obligation to be witnesses there for Christ (and also, if they are regular commuters on public transport, to witness to any circles of travelling friends that they may build up over time). If we consider ourselves to be New Testament Christians, then our workplaces will be important arenas for outreach.

Being workplace witnesses in practice

How is this to be done to good effect in practice?

The first point to be noted is that workplace evangelism is essentially a branch of friendship evangelism. As mentioned elsewhere in this volume, the statistics over the past two generations at least (and it will probably be true over much longer than that) suggest that, among first-generation Christians (those not from Christian families), some 80% or more become Christians because they knew a Christian, that is, they had a friend who had a hand in the process by which they were converted to Christ. In this respect, workplace evangelism is no different from evangelism at school or university, or in our social lives at the bowls club or wherever, or in the social lives of retired people.

Making relationships

The first step is to have, to make, a relationship with those whom we seek to influence for Christ. We need to become friends with them in a way which establishes the right to speak intimately with them about emotional, psychological and spiritual matters. Indeed, it is not so much that we seek to make friends with people for the instrumental (some might say, cold-blooded) purpose of eventually having a gospel conversation with them. It is that, as we make genuine friendships with people in the course of work (as human beings inevitably do), we are then able naturally to engage with them in conversation about spiritual and related matters and, when the opportunity arises, to grasp it and share the essence of the gospel with them.

This does require us to make and create time to enable friendship to blossom. Here, the workplace may be becoming a more difficult place in which to make friendships: the tempo of work and business, the constant demand for greater productivity and efficiency (though the British have been peculiarly poor at increasing productivity in the last two generations compared with other advanced economies) may have squeezed out opportunity to develop friendship in the workplace. We rightly prize family-time, and children-time, in a way which may exceed that of earlier generations. As Christians, there are also the necessary pressures of church life on our time—though, in this respect, we are not different from non-Christians with their personal hobbies and social interests. Working from home may reduce the opportunities for social contact with colleagues in the workplace. But if we want to see our work colleagues become Christians, then we must make time to get to know them.

Quite apart from the pressures of the changing workplace, it is easy to compartmentalize our lives, so that work and the rest of life have no meaningful contact. This is particularly the case for commuters: in London, for example, work and the rest of life rarely meet for many, and employers and employees can be happy with an office culture which is in danger of treating staff as automata who are switched on when they arrive so as to do what their employers hope for, and switched off when they depart. This can be an obstacle to the relationship-building which is essential to workplace witness. We have to find ways and means of building real relationships with colleagues if we are to share fundamental aspects of our lives with them.

But, if it is true, as it often is for Christians, that the workplace is virtually the only place where we encounter non-Christians, then the question arises whether we need to prioritize our time so as to involve ourselves in the social life of our workplaces, whenever we can do that without moral compromise. It may also mean making time to lunch with colleagues, as well as taking an after-work coffee with them, notwithstanding the demands of the work that we are there to do. (Such contact may in fact be desirable for the better functioning of our work-team as well as for the gospel!) Here, discipline is needed, as well as properly agreed compromise with our spouses and families.

If work entails travel with colleagues (as it does for some), these are often fruitful opportunities for developing friendship and conversation, for example, in what the airlines euphemistically call airport 'lounges' or over meals—I well recall a life-sensitive conversation in a *bier-garten* in the hills above Vienna on a diplomatic visit on a warm summer's evening when a colleague and I agreed that our wives might be somewhat rueful to learn that this was among the rigours that diplomacy demanded!

Walking the talk is an indispensable gospel platform

An essential pre-condition of effective workplace evangelism is that we as Christians walk the talk. Curiously, but unsurprisingly if the Christian thinks about it for a moment in the light of Scripture, it remains the case that the most secular and pagan colleagues have a very clear idea of how Christians ought to behave and will seek to hold them to it, and will delight in expressing very public criticism if the Christian falls short by their lights. They may even expect cultural practices that used to be associated with evangelical Christianity in former times, but do not have particular scriptural foundation!

Walking the talk is certainly about matters of personal morality. As Christians, we shall be expected to be upright, particularly in matters of

Christian sexual morality, even if the non-Christian critic sees no reason why they should observe the code that they are applying. They will expect us not to be foul-mouthed, however much they may be themselves. They will watch us carefully as to our conduct with the opposite sex. They will be quick to call out the slightest hint of inappropriate conduct or inappropriate speech. In these days, even the hint of sexual harassment will be the death-knell of our Christian testimony. Some of our colleagues will be looking to call us out as hypocrites—remember that that is one of the limited number of arguments that non-Christians make against the truth and demands of Christianity, that Christians are simply hypocrites. Beyond that they will be looking to see kindness and graciousness in our lives, in our dealings with them as colleagues as well as acquaintances.

But it includes perfectly legitimate expectations in a number of ways which may not be so obvious to us, ways which may have particular benefit for them.

Walking the talk as a manager

First, there are points which relate to how we act as managers of colleagues, whether at a senior level or more junior levels. Because of their general demeanour, application, and seriousness, Christians often are made responsible for colleagues, even if it is only for a small section on the shop-floor. Here, our colleagues' expectations will be that we should be open and transparent, honest in our dealings with them, above all that we shall be fair, avoiding favouritism, and not being over-demanding in terms of our expectations of output.

None of this is entirely straightforward for the manager, of course. Colleagues do differ in ability and application. Some have personalities which do not serve as well as others in the team context. Our organizations do not exist simply for the benefit of workers, but for those whom the organization aims to benefit. Sometimes, it is necessary to challenge a colleague about their performance.

One of the more difficult circumstances with which I was faced as a manager was a colleague who had an alcohol problem, to the extent that his performance was very poor indeed. Some colleagues gave me the impression that they thought that I was less sympathetic than a Christian ought to have been towards him. Probably unknown to them, I did seek to get him help through the HR resources of the organization. But we owed to our masters (in my case Ministers and the public who had elected them) that the work should be done to a reasonable standard. And he did need to pull his weight, or the burden was thrown onto his colleagues or the work simply was not done.

Also the colleagues for whom we are responsible will expect that we shall not acquire airs and graces, and an inflated view of our own importance, that we do not 'think of ourselves more highly than we ought to think', chiming with Romans 12: 3. As Christians, let alone as good managers, we shall need to look to our style of management. For some managers, their only consideration is success in the task that they have been given, sometimes because they equate that success with their own chances of advancement; they will not mind exploiting their colleagues in order to achieve that success. Some managers are open or clandestine bullies, who enjoy dominating others, apparently for the buzz that they get out of it. As Christian managers we must, of course, do all we can to ensure that we achieve the goals that our own managers have set, that our section contributes to the success of the organization (if that success is something which is in itself unworthy, or questionable from the Christian perspective, we must ask ourselves whether we are in the right place as Christians). But how we achieve success also matters, and is a measure of ethical conduct. If as Christians, we succeed by climbing, or appearing to climb, over the backs and bodies of our colleagues, that will be noticed, and will certainly impair our Christian testimony. And if we are tempted to think that we can succeed only by adopting a dubious management style, then we need to be in constant prayer to our Lord and Master that we shall be enabled and allowed to perform well without adopting a style and practices which will call our testimony into question. Here, we should meditate on the experience of Joseph and Daniel in the Old Testament.

Further, secular workplaces (like churches and Christian workplaces, I regret to say) are very often the arenas of political and manipulative behaviour, where an individual's word is certainly not his or her bond, where others are kept in the dark in order to achieve sectional ends, and where majorities can be organized to achieve purposes. This leads to lack of transparency, openness, and straightforward dishonesty. If Christians behave in this way, testimony to Christ will certainly be impaired.

As managers, we need also to be seen to be exercising scrupulous fairness in reporting on the performance of those for whom we are responsible, whether or not there are formal reporting procedures. Some people get on in the workplace by gathering round them a coterie of friends and favourites whom they seek to advance alongside themselves. They can be unfair to others because they differ from them as personalities, because they do not appeal to them as people, and because they disapprove of aspects of their character or even the way that they do their work, even because they are too serious and committed! (I recall a colleague forty years ago who seemed to despise an industrious and conscientious member of his staff, I suspected because the staff member's Quaker background and approach showed only too clearly.) The Christian's reputation must be as a fair and open manager, one who is content with what is now known as 360-degree reporting. If we acquire reputations as unfair managers who consider themselves a cut above others, that too will affect our Christian testimony.

(In annual reviews, I was in the habit of asking the colleague concerned in each case whether he or she had any criticisms of me as a manager and if there were ways in which I could act differently so as to make their working lives easier, to help them to perform better. Typically, they would refer to my tendency to micro-manage and to want to understand the detail as well as the big picture, and my failure to delegate as much as they wanted. This was fair enough, but sometimes did not recognize the need for quality control across the board. But I did think that a colleague's comment that I was 'above all, a very decent fellow' was a rather English compliment to my Christian walk.)

Walking the talk as a colleague

Not all Christians will advance to positions of responsibility, even in a minor way, in their organizations. For some, perhaps many, the impression which they make as Christians will be as fellow-workers, working alongside others, nine to five, or as a shift-worker.

Our non-Christian colleagues will, just the same, be seeing and judging us as Christians if we are open about our profession of faith, as we should be. Some of what I have written above about the Christian as a manager will apply equally to us as co-workers. Our co-workers will expect us to behave as they think that Christians ought to behave, and they may go to some lengths to trip us up, to cause us to 'lose our rag', to catch us in bad language, and then publicly call us out for lack of Christian consistency. As Christians, we have no choice but to conduct ourselves uprightly and honestly, and to pray for patience and self-control, and to have the ability to turn the other cheek, to endure bullying which is in effect a form of persecution of the Christian.

At more senior levels, relations between Christians and non-Christians may be covered by a cloak of respectable behaviour and language. But on the shop-floor, conduct may well be more raw. There may be unwholesome banter and conversation, bullying, dishonesty, workshyness, work evasion, petty pilfering, and other practices which the Christian cannot be party to. This may in itself attract persecution, particularly when conduct is such that the Christian ought not to conceal it from those who are being short-changed or wrongfully deprived.

Especially in such circumstances, the Christian should be seeking a positive reputation with colleagues, not as a matter of show, but as evidencing Christian integrity. The Christian must be known to co-workers as someone who is reliable, who can be depended on, who works for the team as a whole, who does work to a good standard, and who sets an example.

They need to be known, too, as sympathetic and empathetic, as someone who takes an interest in the lives and circumstances of co-workers, who is interested in them as people, who shares in their trials as they become aware of them, who is unshocked even when privy to circumstances which they are unfamiliar with. In short, the Christian should be seeking to be an informal pastoral prop to their co-workers, to be known as someone who does not focus simply on his or her own concerns, but who is 'there for others', as people often put it when interviewed about someone who has just been unexpectedly killed. And all this will need to be done modestly, discreetly, and without show. We should be known and acknowledged by fair-minded co-workers as real Christians.

Talking the talk

It would be pleasant and encouraging if our Christian walk was sufficient in itself to bring many to Christ. In this life, we shall never know what contribution we have made to conversion in cases in which it is the privilege of some other believer to bring to Christ a person on whom our Christian life has had a real influence. But the fact is that the silent testimony of the Christian life, whether of one or many, is not enough in itself to bring an individual to Christ. Especially in days of relative truth, of your truth being different from my truth, the capacity of our co-workers to ignore, explain away, or simply not understand the significance of a well-lived Christian life is apparently limitless. Human beings have to be challenged by word of mouth if they are to become Christians, to be brought to conversion to Christ.

This is fundamental to God's relationship with us, and his efforts to restore relationship with fallen, sinful human beings. No sooner had humankind sinned, than God was 'calling' to them (and Adam was afraid of that voice by reason of guilt) (Gen. 3: 9, 10). Through Genesis and the Old Testament, we see God sending messengers (sometimes angels, more often prophets) to speak with those whom he wants to recall to himself or to be directed by him once they have responded. Occasionally, God speaks directly, as through the Ten Words on Sinai. Jesus himself comes as a teacher (a rabbi) 'proclaiming the good news of God' (Mk. 1: 14) and the eleven are in turn themselves to 'Go into all the world and proclaim the good news to the whole of creation' (Mk. 16: 15). Jesus's instruction in the upper room after his resurrection was that they were to his 'witnesses' (Acts 1: 8), that is, people who give oral testimony to Jesus 'to the ends of the earth'. Therefore, unsurprisingly, proclamation, heralding the gospel, is a keyword in the Acts of the Apostles, not always by the act of preaching, but certainly by 'speaking the word'. In the New Testament, 'speaking the word' to individuals is key to their becoming Christians, just as the Ethiopian eunuch needed Philip to explain to him the meaning of what he had been reading (Acts 8: 34, 35).

The apostle Paul formalized all this in his statement in Romans 10: 'how are they to call on one in whom they have not believed? And how are they to believe in one of whom they have never heard? And how are they to hear without someone to proclaim him? . . . So faith comes from what is heard, and what is heard comes through the word of Christ.' (vv. 14 & 17)

It is comparatively rare for people to come to Christ without the direct intervention of another human being and their explanation of the gospel. The explanation or proclamation can be by preaching on a formal occasion. But it is just as likely to be in quiet one-to-one conversation. (Occasionally, people do have a direct encounter with God, though usually drawing on what they already know of the truth. As it happens, I was converted in a wholly secular gathering at the age of almost 15 when God himself palpably shined the light of the gospel into my mind, but it was only because in a discussion someone, as it happened, David Pawson, doing his National Service as an Air Force chaplain[1], was asked to state what a Christian was, and did so in two sentences.)

If people are to be converted, in some way or another the gospel will need to be spoken to them, for action by them on the spot or subsequently. That is why this book emphasizes the importance of having gospel conversations with people (see especially chapter 15).

In order to have such conversations in the workplace, we need to pray daily that we shall have the opportunity for them, and pray that we shall have the courage to take the opportunity—how often do we have the opportunity for such conversations and fail to take them? For taking the opportunity entails the offence of the cross, 'the foolishness of our proclamation', which Paul explains at length in 1 Corinthians 1: 18–31 (and it may damage our reputation in our workplace and our career prospects!). We certainly have an enemy who is desperately anxious to keep us quiet rather than that 'the foolishness of our proclamation, [shall] save those who believe' (1 Cor. 1: 21). But the responsibility does squarely lie with us to take the opportunity to speak of Christ. How many will there be who are not eventually in the Kingdom because we have not taken the opportunity when it was there? As God said to Ezekiel, 'Mortal, I have made you a sentinel . . . whenever you hear the word from my mouth, you shall give them warning from me . . . if you give them no warning . . . their blood I will require at your hand.' (See Ezek. 3: 17–21, for the full statement.)

Of course, our gospel conversations will not always be successful, and they may indeed damage our reputations and prospects, if those with whom we

---

1. Of course, at the time, I had not the slightest idea who David Pawson was, and more particularly was going to be. However, that he did not shrink from speaking the word of the gospel in the circumstances has been to my eternal benefit (and perhaps too that of others who were present).

speak relate the matter to others in the workplace. But, by the grace of God, they will not be as unsuccessful as our silence.

It is not necessary for me to say more about the 'how to' of gospel conversations, because that is extensively covered by Jacquie Bodman in chapter 15 below. But there are some aspects of gospel conversations in the workplace that require comment in our times.

For some 200 hundred years or more in this country, it would not have been considered exceptional, or exceptionable, for two individuals to speak about spiritual matters in the course of their work or arising from it. No one would have thought it necessary that anyone should have to be protected from such spiritual conversations, or concerned that a doctor, nurse, teacher, lawyer or social worker was abusing their position in engaging in such conversation in the course of their duties, let alone in a conversation simply arising from a contact made in the course of professional duties. It is too easy for evangelical Christians to assume that the law and professional practice requirements now preclude practitioners from pursuing spiritual matters with clients and others, particularly when the conversation is initiated by the client; and some militant secularists are only too willing to give the impression that practitioners are so precluded by law—and, if not, to argue vehemently that they should be so precluded.

While I was drafting this chapter, I read a newsfeed report of efforts by the National Secular Society to argue once again that the charitable object of advancing religion is a loophole for promoting misogyny and homophobia.[2] In particular cases that have been raised with the Scottish charity regulator, it appears that the regulator has been arguing that religious belief is a protected characteristic under the Equalities Act 2010 and the particular views complained of were likely to be held by virtue of a manifestation of a religious belief. This is consistent with the reticence of the courts and regulators to allow encroachment on freedom of speech, including of religious speech, unless

2. See https://www.civilsociety.co.uk/news/regulator-urged-to-reform-loophole-for-scottish-religious-charities.html, accessed on 15.3.2023.

the law is manifestly clear that the particular expression infringes statutory requirements.[3]

So as Christians, we should not too readily assume that we cannot openly explain the gospel to individuals (including work colleagues) in private conversation and publicly on the grounds that the law and professional practice preclude us from doing so. Though it will take courage and fortitude, and perhaps risk to our careers, we should not over-cautiously accept what some might like law and professional practice to be, as distinct from adhering to what either actually requires. Our approach as followers of Christ should be to assume freedom until it is definitively demonstrated that law or professional practice preclude it.[4] And we should be prepared to stand our ground (while ensuring that we are well advised and make good, rational arguments within the context that we are required to argue).

In doing so, however, we should exercise due prudence, on the principle of being as wise as serpents and as harmless as doves (Mt. 10: 16). We should be careful about the context in which our gospel conversations take place, i.e., those in which we are seeking to explain the gospel with the clear intent that our hearer should heed and personally respond to it. There is no reason why in the workplace we cannot make our own Christian profession clear at any time—indeed, if we are faithful believers, we positively ought to do so.

But there are contexts in which it would not be appropriate for us to initiate a gospel conversation. An obvious example might be in the course of a formal annual appraisal of performance, or perhaps in a medical examination (though there are surely frequent circumstances in which there is an inevitable pastoral aspect to the consultation, or there ought to be, when spiritual comfort, tactfully given, would be far from irrelevant). In the normal case, it would be wrong, too, if gospel conversation encroached on time which was contracted to the employer or got in the way of work. But a clear distinction between

---

3. On this trend, and the tendency of the courts to resist it, see Neil Dickson, 'Un/free speech' in *Partnership Perspectives: The Christian, The Church, and The Public Sphere*, no. 71 (Spring 2021), pp. 48–58.

4. In this context, we should note that the requirements of professional practice probably vary between professions, depending on the extent to which professional thought has been penetrated by relativist philosophy and social theory. I shall not name the professions in mind.

working time, and the employees' own time, is surely relevant: conversation between friends securely based in established relationship—during breaks, in the canteen, or in a coffee shop after work—can hardly be regarded as precluded on the grounds of professional ethics, though it will always need to be handled diplomatically if a gospel purpose is to be achieved.

There are few professions which would preclude all social contact between advisers and clients—the criminal law might be one perhaps, but not other aspects of the law, and perhaps teaching because it entails relationship between adults and minors (though most educationalists presumably do not deny the beneficial effects which the example, not to say inspiration, of teachers has on children—and in this context what is the distinction between conveying the merits of a religion and the merits of a philosophy or political theory or ethic?).

There is a danger that here we are discussing hard cases, rather than the generality of the position with respect to the workplace. There can be nothing wrong with friendships, more or less close, that derive from first contact in the workplace, and no risk that legal or professional constraints preclude Christian witness and gospel conversation. But if we want those conversations to be successful in gospel terms, we need to be sure that we have earned the right to initiate them and that there is a winsomeness and tact about us that ensures that we shall be listened to. The greater risk is that the offence of the cross will keep us silent and therefore accountable for failing to speak the gospel into our colleagues' lives.

For discussion

1. What have been the biggest challenges you have faced in witnessing in the workplace and what have you learned from them?
2. If you could change one thing about your evangelistic style what would it be and why?

Chapter 14

Home as a gospel opportunity

Jacqui Mackinnon

The power of prayerful hospitality

I was sitting on the couch of my dear friend, Margaret. We were chatting about how it was being back at church in person after lockdown.

I first met Margaret and her daughter through the work of Christians Against Poverty. At that time, Margaret never left the house, spent day after day in her pyjamas, and was quite depressed and anxious as to what would happen when she died. The first meeting outside her home that I persuaded Margaret to have with me was for a coffee in a local café. As I left the café that day, I wondered how I would ever be able to share Christ with her. He was the only answer for her imprisoned life, and I prayed fervently in the days that followed. We drank tea and ate cake, and slowly Margaret opened up in a miraculous way. After a relatively short time, I began to see a glimmer of light and hope dawning in this woman's dark life as I spent time with her at a café table.

Later, Margaret accepted an invitation to church followed by Sunday lunch at my home. Soon this established for her a simple routine in which, after church each Sunday, she joined the weekly Sunday lunches at our home. As Margaret heard the gospel each week at church, and as we chatted about spiritual things over food, it wasn't long before Margaret came to know Christ for herself. As people got to know her at church, others started to show hospitality to her—inviting her to their home for meals also.

A knitting class in church became a favourite evening pastime. A little bit of knitting, a lot of chat, with tea and cakes provided. Then, our midweek House Group—studying God's word together with others—became a regular feature of Margaret's life, a time always ending up round the table for fellowship over supper.

Margaret was seldom at home now: a new social life, new friends, and a new freedom found in Christ.

As we sat and chatted after lockdown, Margaret commented on how church just wasn't the same now. No opportunities to talk to people at church, no longed-for hugs, no visiting other people's homes. "It's just not the same," she said. The Christian life had become hard for Margaret. The 'fellowship' was missing. Hospitality had been taken out of church through Covid-19 restrictions and something important had been taken out of Margaret's experience of the Christian life. There was not the same connection or interaction with the love, joy and support of God's people that had first drawn her to Christ, and which had proved to be a vital part of sustaining her in her Christian walk. Surely, this wasn't how God intended it to be—we are not to walk the Christian pathway alone.

Hospitality in and of itself does not save people. We know that: it is only a work of the Holy Spirit that can transform a life. But to show hospitality to one another is an instruction given by God to his people. It is clearly a window allowing unbelievers to see Christ in our lives and homes, and an encouragement to believers so that they can be sustained and discipled as we walk the Christian road together.

The meaning of biblical hospitality

Hospitality is a word used widely in our world today. We have a 'hospitality industry' where food and drink, tourism, conference and events, leisure and entertainment are provided. The Oxford English Dictionary defines hospitality as: 'the friendly and generous reception and entertainment of guests, visitors or strangers.' This is a good description, but biblical hospitality goes further—its definition stems from and operates at a deeper level.

John Raven from East Cooper Baptist church helpfully describes biblical hospitality as 'The welcoming and fellowshipping with believers and non-believers out of truth and love for Jesus Christ so that they may see more clearly and/or so they will join us as exiles themselves or join us as believers.' John lets us see that biblical hospitality is rooted in truth and love for Jesus Christ. He highlights that its scope is for all people, believers and non-believers. And he focuses our attention on the deepest motivation for biblical hospitality—that others may join us as believers. John the apostle would agree: 'so that you may have fellowship with us. And our fellowship is with the Father, and with his Son, Jesus Christ.' (1 Jn. 1: 3–4).[1] We should not be ashamed to say that, as we show hospitality as John describes it, we have an alternative motive—a supreme motive. Yes, we want to be friendly and generous to all, but we want to make Christ the centre and allow the love of Christ to overflow through us to others (2 Cor. 5: 14 & 18).

The Bible's focus on hospitality

Scripture makes much more of hospitality than western culture (particularly English culture with its ethic of 'my home is my castle') has been inclined to do for a number of generations now. We can discern at least three underlying principles.

Be generous with what you have

There are examples of hospitality right from the very beginning of the Bible. We might start in Eden where the LORD God "hosts" Adam and Eve and provides for their every need. There is another clear example in Genesis 18: 2–8. This is a beautiful description of the hospitality shown by Abraham to God himself (as became clear)! Abraham, the father of faith, promised the 'visitors' a little water, and a morsel of bread. But he did much more than that: he went out of his way to provide not only bread and water, but to kill one of the best calves in the herd, bake cakes from the best flour, and serve curds and milk. Then personally he waited upon them. We have been given much by the Lord and have been shown an abundance of provision for us. As we invite visitors into our homes to meet the Lord, it is good that we show them generosity similar to the amazing generosity that God has shown to us.

1. 'Fellowship' translates the Greek word *koinonia*, which means 'partnership; sharing in; a reality shared in common.'

Biblical hospitality is not practised so that others can reciprocate—it is an expression of the unconditional love and mercy of God towards us. There are many places in Scripture where God's heart for the stranger, the needy, the foreigner and the poor is clearly seen, and the exhortation extends to his people to be like him in this. Isaiah 58: 7 sums this up nicely with a clear instruction to share bread with the hungry and bring the homeless poor into your house.

Be joyful in sharing with others

In the New Testament, in Luke 19: 5–6, we read that the Lord Jesus went to Zacchaeus's house for a meal, and of the hospitality that he was shown. Zacchaeus didn't grumble at the thought that Jesus had invited himself to his house. His mind wasn't occupied by what he had in his cupboards or what was he going to manage to cook. Was he busy that evening, and did it fit in with his plans? Rather, he hurriedly came down from where he was hiding and received his guest with 'great excitement and joy' (v. 6). If having guests in our home, whether invited or not, becomes a chore, we are not truly practising hospitality as Scripture sees it.

Be devoted in winning others for Christ

There are many more examples showing the meaning and the practice of hospitality in the Bible. One of the most powerful is in Acts 2: 42–47. This great passage outlines for us another example of how we should behave in showing hospitality. Hospitality is seen alongside the apostles' teaching and prayer. Even the idea of the breaking of bread draws people through a meal (perhaps a specially designated meal) to the Saviour that we gather around—our Lord Jesus. When we are devoted to him, to his teaching, to relationship with him through prayer, and relationship with his people, then hospitality will be something that is part of our daily lives. Like those in the New Testament, we too will be in awe at the miracles that God can perform.

We can notice also from this passage that prayer goes hand in hand with hospitality. As we express friendship and generosity, kindness and grace to others, we pray for the miracle of seeing lost souls transformed and redeemed in Christ. A local church giving expression to these traits regularly is a healthy church, and such health results in growth: 'the Lord added daily to those who were being saved' (Acts 2: 27). We pray for one another so that the saving presence of the living Christ might be made manifest among us in our everyday lives.

I hope that we can also see from Scripture that there is a biblical pattern of intimacy, fellowship, support, and love which is intended to be integral to the concept of sharing a meal with one another. In eating together, we are intended in fact to be sharing life with one another.

Towards a practical theology of hospitality

Let me share one more practical experience of the power and influence of Christian hospitality before we try to reach some theological conclusions on the power of this ministry of hospitality.

It was our night for house group and we were expecting a new visitor. He burst through the door loudly, yet in a strangely anxious way. David's own unease was to be the predominant feature of his interactions for the next hour or so. He explained right from the beginning that he had only come to please his wife who had brought him. 'I'm an atheist.' David said, 'I just want to ask a few questions.' The 'few' questions turned into an hour of interrogation, and David held nothing back—straight talking, almost impertinent at times. Nevertheless, we answered clearly, quietly and consistently, offering our best responses to all his questions, in as gracious a manner as we could muster. Despite the bombardment of questions and the careful defence of the faith, we were apparently not any further forward in our attempt to try to convince David of the fact that Christ loved him, could forgive him, and that he could start a new life in a true and meaningful relationship with Jesus.

The small company which had gathered in our home that evening finally moved to sit round the dining table, as was our habit each week, to enjoy supper and less intense conversation together. We spoke of many things, the week that lay ahead, encouragements of the past, and challenges that faced us. We listened to one another and shared life. But as we did so, David grew less aggressive and quietly joined in the conversation. As time had gone, and the evening drew to a close, David rather quictly said, "I can't believe I've sat here with all of you round this table for the last hour while eating and drinking tea, and I've actually really enjoyed your chat and company. You are really quite a nice bunch. I've never experienced anything like this before." I believe that that evening we brought a faithful presence to bear upon David's life, as a testimony to the Lord Jesus being with us as the Spirit who dwells within us was manifest for David to see and experience.

David Fitch tells us in his excellent book, *Faithful Presence*, that a faithful presence begins with people who, restored to God's presence in Jesus Christ, are then able to be faithfully present for him in the world. This faithful presence is at the heart of what it means to be the people of God. This is especially seen when the close circle of Jesus-followers commune as a church with their Lord. Yet his presence with us is equally evident in our homes, where we can invite others to share in the presence of the Lord—he is there also. And Fitch reminds us that as the church is the extension of Christ's presence in the world, wherever we go, we too ought to tend to the presence of the living God in us, as he is making his rule and reign in the world visible and tangible through us.

So often these days, our Christianity is apparently only for Sunday. We attend church gatherings, do and say the right things, even feel the correct emotions, but we often fail to be the faithful presence of the Lord Jesus as we enter the business of our week. Christianity is not merely a Sunday thing or going to a church building for worship. It is meant to infiltrate and pervade all of life. This is what the gospel should look like as we invite others into the living and saving presence of Jesus. Peterson's paraphrase in *The Message* of Romans 12: 1 & 2 suggests this idea of a holistic approach to Christian living—one that constantly invites others to experience the faithful presence of the Lord through his people:

> So here's what I want you to do, God helping you: Take your everyday, ordinary life—your sleeping, eating, going-to-work, and walking-around life—and place it before God as an offering. Embracing what God does for you is the best thing you can do for him. Don't become so well-adjusted to your culture that you fit into it without even thinking. Instead, fix your attention on God. You'll be changed from the inside out. Readily recognize what he wants from you, and quickly respond to it.

This is how God changes the world, and it starts with ordinary people like you and me, and the sharing of ordinary lives with others, in full consciousness that his presence to save and restore is always among us. Fitch in his book describes this concept as Christians being present to his presence wherever they may be. Whether in our church settings, in our own homes, or in the local McDonalds, there is opportunity for us to demonstrate 'hospitality' as we invite others into the presence of Jesus. Fitch convincingly asserts that this is the starting point for changing the world. But he didn't think of this first: Jesus did. The great commission requires it of us: '*Go out and teach everyone you meet*, far and near, *in this way of life*, marking them by baptism in the threefold name: Father, Son, and Holy Spirit. Then instruct them in the practice of all I have commanded you. *I'll be with you as you do this, day after day after day, right up to the end of the age.*' (Mt. 28: 19–20 (MSG); my emphasis).

For discussion

1. What prevents Christians from using their home for evangelism?
2. What are the dangers and benefits of using the home for evangelism?
3. What practical things could you do to become better at home-based evangelism?

Chapter 15

Creating gospel conversations

Jacquie Bodman

Everyone, even evangelists, can baulk at the thought of creating a gospel conversation, as it can convey the thought of artificially manufacturing a conversation which is purely about the gospel. But creating a gospel conversation is not quite as it sounds! In our everyday conversations, we have opportunities to bring in what is important to us and what we are passionate about. As Christians, we are passionate about Jesus and all that he has done for us! In this chapter, we will look at how we can intentionally grasp gospel opportunities within our normal interactions and conversations.

What is a gospel conversation

There are four elements to creating a gospel conversation.

1. Remember that this is a divine appointment, so seek the Holy Spirit's help in your mind throughout the conversation.
2. Be really interested in having a genuine conversation with the individual. Do this by showing your interest in them as an individual, asking questions about them and their life in a conversational way.
3. Look for the common ground that you have together, to facilitate an easy and genuine conversation.
4. Look for the opening that gives you the opportunity to share naturally your personal witness and the gospel message.

I want to help you to see how natural this can and should be, by asking a simple question: what are you passionate about? It's not a trick question, but, before you read any more, please stop and think: what or who are you really passionate about? Once you've answered that, think about how you would bring your passion into a conversation? Would you have to try really hard? Would you have to engineer or manipulate the conversation in order to make it happen? Or would it come in naturally because you love that thing so much? In most cases, it would be a very natural process, purely because that person or item is your passion and you are really interested in them.

Creating a gospel conversation is just like that. If you are in the joy of your salvation, your identity will be in Christ. Your passion for Jesus, and all that he has done for you, is your DNA and the joy of it is bubbling away inside you, bursting to get out. I understand that from day to day we may ebb and flow in our enjoyment of this; but, if we are talking about creating gospel conversations, we need to have the joy of the Lord in our hearts. Without that, we will struggle to share his love and salvation in a genuine and living way.

We need to remember the art of conversation. When we are beginning a conversation with someone, we are making a connection with them at some level, whether it's with a stranger in the street, at the bus stop or the doctor's surgery, or with a friend, acquaintance or family member. In all of these cases, we are talking to them in order to make a connection. Exactly how we begin the process depends on how well we already know them, and what the subject matter and ultimate purpose of the conversation is.

Creating a gospel conversation is no different. You are talking to them because you are interested in them and you care about them. But even more than this, you want to share the good news about Jesus with them, as you want them to be saved and have the joy, peace and assurance that you have in the Lord.

Remember that this is the Lord's work and it doesn't all depend on you! Take some of the pressure off your shoulders and know that the Holy Spirit is there with you. He is over this chat and he will help you.

I find that I pray quietly in my head throughout a gospel conversation, asking the Lord to help me and guide me, as I know that he loves the person in front of me so much that he died on the cross for them! He knows them intimately and he has arranged this conversation. So I lean on him totally, but I recognise that I need to do my bit as well!

Active listening

We must genuinely care. We can't just have a gospel conversation as a tick-box exercise or we won't show that genuine interest in the individual.

Because of our care for them and interest in them, we actively listen. We demonstrate this by keeping ***natural eye contact***, by being aware of our ***facial expressions***: we smile when they smile, and frown when they do. This is called mirroring and is something we do naturally when we are comfortable in a conversation, but we may need to give this a bit more effort, as it won't feel entirely natural at first.

Our ***body language*** will speak volumes about how much we are listening. During a conversation, leaning in slightly to hear them better, nodding or shaking your head when appropriate, and having a relaxed stance, are all ways of showing the individual that we are actively listening to them.

It is also important to ***avoid distractions***. As useful as our mobile phones are, we need to be aware that they can easily distract from the conversation you are having, as well as other things happening around you.

Here are a few tips that I have learned along the way:

> repeat, comment on or emphasise something they say every so often. This helps to reaffirm that I am listening and taking in what they are saying.
>
> ask the Holy Spirit to help you to remember key points of what they are saying. He will help you as he is even more interested in this conversation than you are!
>
> try to not to interrupt. It can be really tempting, but remember what the goal of this conversation is that you are building a connection and therefore you want them to feel safe and listened to. This way you will build their trust in you, which is essential so that they can trust the message that you are going to share with them.

Remember, the Lord has set up this conversation and you will find a connection through something that you will have in common, be it work, family, hobbies, interests, and so on. It will be in there somewhere and once you've found it, chat around it. You will know where the opening is to bring in the gospel message, as you will feel the prompting from the Holy Spirit. That now is the opportunity.

For some, the flow of conversation will come more naturally than for others. If you are not naturally good at making conversation, remember God is: so just relax, trust the Lord to speak through you, and don't be too pushy or intense. Remember God can speak through anyone. As we see in Numbers 22, he even used a donkey! So let him speak through you, and don't try and make a gospel conversation happen in your own strength. If you do that, it won't go anywhere, and it will be strained and weird for both of you.

An example of creating a gospel conversation

Imagine sitting down next to someone on public transport.

> *CHRISTIAN:* Ah, what a relief to sit down!
> *NON-CHRISTIAN:* It certainly is!
> *CHRISTIAN:* Did you find it busy in town today?
> *NON-CHRISTIAN:* Definitely! Especially in New Look.
> *CHRISTIAN:* Yes, it was! I just popped in to look for something for my daughter, but walked out as it was way too busy. Was it a big sale or something?
> *NON-CHRISTIAN:* Yeah, everything was at least half price, so I decided to get all my daughters' birthday presents in one trip. So I was in there for hours.
> *CHRISTIAN:* Oh, bless you! Well done, I bet that was exhausting!
> *NON-CHRISTIAN:* Yeah, it's a case of having to, as it's the only way I can afford all their birthdays.

In this short exchange, you will have found out potential common ground in the complexities of being a mum of children who needs to be careful with money. There is now the opportunity to chat about the ages of the children, schooling, parenting, family life and even work. Somewhere in all of that, there will be an opening for the gospel. I have found that often, without realising it, they have asked the question that enabled me to share my faith and share the gospel message with them.

Don't overstay your welcome

In all these conversations, it is important to remember that they are two-way interactions. The other person must never feel talked at or trapped, and they must feel free to finish the conversation if they want to; to be able to leave it at any time.

Again, continuing on the public transport theme, if during the conversation they start to look at their phone, start texting or get their head phones ready to put on, these are clear signals that, for them, the conversation is finished. It may be that they don't know how to say it, or have the confidence to say it; so read their body language and respond to it accordingly. The way to do this is maybe to answer it in your body language or say something to reassure them that you've noticed, like "oh well, I'd best ring my other half to let him know I'm on my way".

On the other hand, they may get a text message or phone call during your conversation and apologise, saying they need to quickly take the call. While they do, pray and when they have finished, wait for them to continue the conversation with you. They may do this by initiating the conversation with you again, or in their body language, for example, putting their phone down and turning to you with a smile.

Recognising an opening

Having found your common ground, continue to chat with them and, as they get more comfortable with you, they will start asking you questions too. As human beings, God has created us with the need to socially interact with others in some form or another (obviously the extraverts more so than introverts!). If they are chatting comfortably with you, they will want to connect with you too.

Any question that they then ask you could be an opening. For example, a question about your life could allow you to share about your faith, as that is such an important part of your life. To illustrate, here are some examples of how questions about our everyday lives may open up a gospel conversation.

QUESTION: I can hear by your accent you're not originally from these parts: what brought you here?
ANSWER: My husband and I are Christians and God moved us here by a set of amazing miracles twenty-two years ago.

QUESTION: How on earth did you manage four kids—it's killing me with just these two?
ANSWER: Sometimes we barely managed! But I'm a Christian and it's only with God looking after us that we did manage. At different points in our lives when we were really struggling, he provided us with food and money by amazing miracles and that helped us get through.

QUESTION: What do you do for work?
ANSWER: My husband and I lead a church in town and we are as surprised as anyone else to find ourselves in this position!

Or it may be a comment, which then gives an opening for you to share a bit more:

COMMENT: It's so impossible to own property in Cornwall. You're one of the lucky ones: most of us will never have our own home.
REPLY: Yes, it is so tough, but we're Christians and we would never have our home without God's help. He worked some amazing miracles to make it happen.

These are just a few examples, but there are many more possibilities and you will have your own examples personal to you and your life. Be assured, most people will want to know more when you make a statement about a miracle-working God who you believe has had an effect on your life, as most will not have thought about his relevance in today's society.

Throughout the conversation, you will have built up a rapport. You have shown that you are interested in them and are listening to them, but they are interested in you too and want to listen to you. Be prepared, as they will invariably ask you to explain more, which opens the way up for you to share with them your personal testimony and the good news.

The opening may come with something that they share with you about themselves and you will recognise this. I tend to find that people pour out their problems to me, so to go back to our public transport scenario, they may mention something around concerns for their children or their marriage. This would open up an opportunity to inquire whether they know of or access any church support groups in their area.

Many people in wider society have never considered that church-based support groups are available for all in the community and are surprised that they can access support, even though they don't attend the church. When you explain that they don't have to attend to access all that the church has to offer (the love, support and community work), most people would question how or why we would do this.

This is your opening. You can answer their question by sharing the message of Jesus' love for them, explaining the gospel message and that this is at the heart of all that we do.

How to start talking to people about Jesus

Unless your conversation is with family, friends, acquaintances or people attending the groups at your church, many conversations will have a time limit. Don't put yourself under pressure to "try and get them saved" in this one conversation. Remember what the Apostle Paul said, 'I planted the seed in your hearts, and Apollos watered it, but it was God who made it grow. It's not important who does the planting, or who does the watering. What's important is that God makes the seed grow." (1 Cor. 3: 6–7 (NLT)). This is the Lord's work and you could be anywhere in this person's spiritual journey. All you are asked to do is to share the gospel message. It's the Holy Spirit's work to convict them.

With some conversations you will be aware from the beginning that there will be a time limit, for example, as in our scenario on encountering someone on public transport. So, in the first few minutes you will be listening and remembering what you are being told, finding what you have in common, and chatting together. When you have seen the opening and stepped into it, it is important to bear in mind that you may be talking to someone who has no idea of who Jesus is or what it means to be a Christian.

Most people don't understand Christian jargon words, so we need to be careful what terms we use. Also, some will have had bad experiences of what they perceive as religion and possibly of other evangelical Christians, and will bundle all this up together with Christianity and resist what you have to say. Don't feel that you have to defend Jesus (he's big enough to do that himself). Rather, listen to their hurts and misunderstandings, showing that you care and understand, while praying silently for the Holy Spirit to give you the words you need. If you jump to the defensive, you will potentially create a wall between the two of you, and you may lose the gospel opportunity.

Although it is easy to make the simple statement, "I am a Christian", it is much better to bring this in as part of the conversation. In other words, give the reason why being a follower of Jesus affects your life. For example, in our scenario on public transport and the mum's concern for her children, I may say, "As a Christian, I find myself constantly asking God to look after them and keep them safe."

Further on in the conversation, you may develop this a bit more. If we were talking about worry and concern for their children, I would share about the time when my 19-year-old daughter was on mission in Cambodia and phoned me from an internet café. Her phone ran out of battery during the conversation and I knew that she had to walk back to her home alone in the dark, in an area where there was a big problem with sex trafficking. I would then explain the comfort that Jesus was to me at that time, that I knew how much he loves me and my daughter, and that in the Bible, he has promised never to leave us. So even though I didn't hear from my daughter for nearly two weeks, I had to really trust Jesus to look after her and keep her safe, when I didn't know if she was safe or not.

In sharing this experience, I now have her attention as she understands how desperate I would have been, as we have already established that our common ground is in being mums of daughters. I would use this as a springboard to relate it to her and her situation, and explain that God loves her so much and understands her circumstances. I would then bring in a personal message of the gospel explaining how God understands how she feels, and that he died for her sorrows as well as all the things she has done wrong. And I would share why she needs to be saved from the things that she has done wrong and how Jesus died on the cross to save her personally.

I would explain that he knows that her shoulders can't carry all the worry of being a parent alone. So he organised for us to sit together on this transport so that I could share with her how much he understands and loves her. I would encourage her that, if she could trust Jesus and give her life to him, he will help her through all the difficulties and trials she has experienced. It is important here to name some of those things she has mentioned, to personalise the gospel message to her. I would then ask what she felt about what I had shared and go on from there.

Many people struggle with the concept of giving their lives to Jesus and don't understand what it means to have faith in someone that they can't see or that they can't be sure is real. At this point, I would go through some of the normal things in our daily lives and point out how many times she had acted in faith that day:

> how do you know any of the food that you are eating isn't contaminated? You don't; you think in faith that is wholesome.
>
> unless you check a chair all over and get someone else to test it before you sit on it, how do you know it will hold you up? You don't, but you sit on it in faith
>
> when you stepped onto this bus you had faith in the driver, in the mechanics that serviced it, and in the other drivers on the road.

Every day, many times a day, we have faith in what we cannot see and have not verified for ourselves, but maybe we haven't seen it before as "faith".

Once we have covered all of her questions and doubts, I would ask again what she thinks about what I have shared and, if she no longer has questions and concerns, I would invite her to ask Jesus into her life. If she was ready for this, I would go through a prayer of repentance with her, but it is never good to pressure someone into this if they are unsure. Remember that this is God's work, to be done according to God's timetable.

Before leaving the conversation, it is important to leave them with a contact, whether for you or your church, and offer to meet them again, if possible.

A few points to help you in a gospel conversation

There are a few points on which you can prepare in advance for gospel conversations:

> It is good to have a two- to three-minute testimony prepared and practised, focusing on what your life was like before you became a Christian, how you came to Christ, what he has done in your life and what he is doing now.
>
> Have Christian literature with you, e.g., gospel booklets and cards with church contact information.
>
> Make sure you know how to help your contact to download to their phone a free Bible app and/or a good devotional app. You never know when you may need it and you won't have the time to trawl through and find the best one for them on the spot.
>
> A good prompt to have with you in a gospel conversation is the Counties tract, "Loved".

Examples of gospel conversations

What I have suggested is not simply theory: it results from experience with a variety of gospel conversations over the years. Here are three examples which I hope you will find encouraging:

1. During the second COVID lockdown, I was speaking to someone who was dabbling in drugs and the occult and who had become very paranoid as a result. I established some common ground in our love for animals, and he mentioned that he had only got through his situation because he had his dog with him. This was my opening to

use the "Loved" tract, and I talked him through the gospel. When I finished, I asked him what he thought, to which he replied, "Well, it's obvious: I need salvation. God is clearly telling me I need salvation." We prayed and he gave his life to the Lord Jesus. My husband and I had to do some deliverance ministry with him because of what he had been involved in. However, he has now moved back to live with his parents. We heard recently through a friend of the family that he is now a changed man. The Holy Spirit used the "Loved" tract to convict him.

2. A man came to the church one day and asked if we could give him a home where he could have his daughter to stay. He was living with his mum and she refused to have his daughter in her home. I could see that he was desperate and we were his last chance as he had exhausted every other avenue. I knew there was no way we could help with the house, but we could help him find Jesus which would be his answer to everything. I therefore said to him that I couldn't offer him a home, but I could offer him Jesus. He was a bit taken aback and asked what I meant. I shared the gospel message with him and then asked him what he thought about it. He told me that he could see that he needed Jesus in his life, so I asked if he wanted to pray and accept Jesus as his Saviour. He did and we prayed. I gave him a Bible, and he came to the church every day for about a week, where he read his Bible and we talked and shared with him, and discipled him. When I last heard of him, he was living further away from us in his own flat and his daughter was able to visit him. In this case, I didn't find our common ground; I responded to his urgent, desperate need, and the Holy Spirit did the rest!

3. One of our regular ladies in the Toddler Group came to the church one day, a week before her wedding, to tell us that her fiancé had left her. As a church, we all prayed for her and I had many conversations about how much the Lord loved her and cared for her. She always got stuck on needing to have faith to give her life to Jesus. She could see he was good because of his love for her which was demonstrated

by the church, but she couldn't make the leap herself. Her salvation was worked out over the following two years, as she became more involved with church activities and services. It wasn't until her two younger children were saved, that she gave her life to the Lord. She still struggles to completely commit to the Lord at times and her walk with him can be a bit up and down. But she knows the Lord and prays to him regularly throughout the day and is always open to discussions about him and his goodness, as well as accepting prayer for her and her family.

These are three very different examples, but they are all gospel conversations through which the Holy Spirit has worked mightily and I've just followed his lead.

Make sure you don't force a conversation, but as you follow the leading of the Holy Spirit, he will use you. And when he does, remember that it is all for the glory of Jesus—Hallelujah!

For discussion

1. What has helped you to begin gospel conversations and what have you struggled with?
2. What have you learned from this chapter that could help you and how could you apply it?

Chapter 16

Evangelism in today's youth culture

Dave Symons & Neil Summerton

Evangelism among young people today, and the manner in which it is attempted, needs to take close account of the vast changes which have taken place in the past two generations in both youth culture and young people's basic knowledge of Christianity.

In the closing stages of the First World War, an inquiry into the religious attitudes of British servicemen (by definition largely younger males) expressed deep concern over their lack of knowledge about and interest in Christianity as a group. From our perspective over 100 years later, we can only wish that young people had anything like the knowledge of and interest in Christianity that the men of the Army were likely to have had in 1918. It is true that our Victorian forbears were shocked to discover from the church attendance census of 1851 that less than half of the population attended church on Sunday, but that compares with 5% or less today.[1] Church membership (not the same thing as church attendance) has declined from a little over 30% of the UK population in 1920 to about 7% now.

The dramatic decline of personal involvement in church life in the twentieth century, and particularly since the Second World War, has been paralleled by changing attitudes in the UK to religion and specifically to Christianity. A century ago most of the UK population would have identified themselves as Christian, even if only a minority would practically have been such in the terms of Scripture. The legal requirement was that schools should include

1. Estimates for church attendance in 2020 are 4.9% of the population in England, 6.7% in Scotland, 4.4% in Wales, and 21.2% in Northern Ireland.

religious education in the curriculum, and the expectation was that that would be education in the Christian religion, though there was usually a contrast in the energy with which it was propagated between church and county schools because the legal framework called for factual knowledge rather than experience. At the level of the family, there was frequently a belief that children and young people needed education in Christianity, and this was reflected in the high levels of Sunday school attendance, and involvement in church youth clubs and camps, in the first two-thirds of the twentieth century: the strength of Brethren churches at the time owed much to their effectiveness in reaching children and young people, including outside their own ranks. This was evident even in London in 1960s and in places elsewhere well into the 1970s.

How different now: Sunday schools rarely reach outside the children of the church, while youth clubs and even some camps struggle to maintain numbers. For many in the population, Sunday is now a day reserved for family activities with a focus on children, who are no longer sent elsewhere so that parents can have time to themselves. Family services often fall between stools and leave some, whether parents, singles, young people, or children, feeling that no real effort was made to engage with them. Weeknight clubs for children can be popular and meet a need for working parents, but in educational value they can fall far short of the Sunday schools of earlier years.

At the same time, the character of religious education in schools has changed markedly. Now the teaching focusses not on Christianity but on comparative religion and secularized ethics. How far school students are now familarized with the central doctrines of Christianity is in question. Also at the same time, young people are now exposed to ideological, if not blatantly religious, thought through the media, entertainment, and the arts in ways and in an intensity which were unknown 150 years ago. Time was in Europe when the Christian religion in its various forms had virtually no contest from such types of competition—which was one reason why rulers sought to control the Christian religion in their own interests. This crucial change has been long in the making, in fact since soon after the introduction of print with movable type: so-called 'chapbooks' (rudimentary fiction) were very popular in the seventeeth century. But this competition with religion really got underway in earnest in the late nineteenth century, initiated first in the reaction of high culture against the evangelicalism of their parents' generation. This reaction, in the name of absolute individual freedom and moral autonomy, did not gain real traction at the popular level until the availability of film, recordings, radio, TV, and now the internet, all energized by profit-seeking capital which saw the advantage of appealing to human instincts, one might say base human instincts. Since the Second World War, these vectors been increasingly aware of the potential of youth markets. These platforms have also advantaged celebrities, including youth idols, who have not been slow to promote their own ideologies and quasi-religious ideas: to understand this it is necessary only to think of the 1960s and the Beatles' hostility to the Catholicism which they knew in Liverpool, promotion of half-baked understanding of eastern religion, and life-style experimentation. The approach has been replicated by countless stars since then, sometimes in significant political interventions.

The success of these messages may be judged by religious and non-religious trends among the young, some of which can be seen in UK Census data, thanks to the optional question which has been included in recent censuses. The following table[2] gives figures from the last three censuses for the overall population, and from the 2021 census the figures for the younger age group which are the focus of this chapter.

Year	**No religion** (% of population)	**Christian** (% of population)
2001†	15	71
2011¶	25	59
2021¶	37	46
10–14 age group	41	38
15–19 age group	44	34
20–24 age group	50	30

† Figures are for Britain (i.e., England, Wales, and Scotland).

¶ Figures are for England and Wales (92% of the population of Britain in 2021).

Anthropologists and sociologists would probably regard social change as normally a gradual process. What is striking about these figures is the speed

2. We acknowledge the assistance of Peter Brierley, of Brierley Research, in compiling these figures.

of change through which we have been living in recent years with respect to religious attitudes (bearing in mind that 'Christian' in the table is the result of identification by the person completing the census form for the household: the column is certainly not referring to the percentage of Bible-believing Christians). Those of whom 'No religion' has been declared doubled in the first twenty years of this century and 'Christian' declined by more than a third. The proportions of 'No religion' declared with respect to the 10–24 age groups all exceed the average, and it is said of half those in the 20–24 age group that they have no religion (though the biggest proportions of those so declared were in fact men between the ages of 55 and 75, of whom 55%-60% were declared to have no religion). This scepticism among males can be seen in younger age-groups: significantly more than half of males in the 10–19 age groups were said to have no religion in the 2021 census.

This analysis demonstrates the challenge to evangelism among the 10–25 age groups. At least half of people in those age groups are sceptical, particularly about Christianity in view of the bad press that Christianity receives in Britain. Doubts probably afflict many of those whom the censuses identify as Christian. The minds and attitudes of the age groups as whole are shaped by the non-Christian forces that have been outlined. They are likely to be suspicious of Christianity, particularly on the grounds that they are 'just a bunch of hypocrites' as exemplified by the reports of historical child abuse in the major denominations.

In this assessment, it is also desirable to call a spade a spade: much of the revolution brought about in personal morality in the West over the past 100 years has been about individual sexual freedom; about throwing off the shackles which confine sexual activity to lifelong marriage between two persons of opposite sex; about accepting, even trumpeting, that celibacy is impossible for healthy human beings after puberty and is psychologically dangerous. The result has been to normalize and make respectable and acceptable all consenting sexual activity post-puberty (or at least, in the UK, post 16 years of age), bearing in mind that the vast majority of human beings are heterosexual in their desires, whatever the enthusiastic narrative of the chatterati might be. Here peer pressure among young people is very important, but also parents these days often effectively accquiesce in and facilitate conduct which they would in fact prefer that their children were not engaging in at tender ages. The challenge to orthodox biblical evangelism in this particular respect is that to many young people the cost of discipleship seems very high indeed, and deeply counter-cultural (though one suspects that some, perhaps many given the idealism of youth and pressures to behave in ways that at heart they instinctively dislike, might secretly be attracted by it).

How then are young people to be introduced to the gospel in this very different and unpromising cultural situation? That will probably not be by persisting with and hankering after methods which worked a century or more ago in conditions which are quite different from today. Nor is much likely to be achieved among teenagers by occasional church youth events or by weeknight clubs which are largely social in character with a superficial, five-minute God-slot. Such clubs may be effective in making a contact between the local church and unchurched families. But they are unlikely in themselves to contribute much to conversion and discipleship.

What we offer in the remainder of this chapter are some guidelines and principles which may lead to effective gospel work among young people.

Youth evangelism is cross-cultural evangelism

Against this background, we need as a first step to recognize that reaching out to youth today can often be as much cross-cultural as if we were seeking to reach a people or tribe with little or no knowledge of Christianity. We should not make assumptions about the knowledge that they have, or that they will be familiar with Scripture, or that they will have heard many or any Bible stories. They may well be approaching Christianity from a quite different perspective.

This means that we need to take time to explore and understand what they believe, a process which may open up conversation which scratches them where they itch. We need to probe what they understand about spiritual and religious matters, and identify what work in apologetics we must do with them, before they can begin to understand their own spiritual needs and how the Christian gospel meets those needs.

Whether they are aware of it or not, this will be a process of introducing them to the basic biblical worldview and the key features of the gospel. Above all, this is about making meaningful connection with our interlocutors, and we can only do that if we have put in the hard yards to have some understanding of youth culture, of where young people are at. It is important that we should not be taken by surprise, or be visibly shocked by or censorious about what they believe and how they conduct themselves. We should be careful not to be perceived as putting them right about matters of behaviour before they are actually Christians (unless they are putting themselves at serious risk, when we need to handle the matter with diplomacy and fluency). On such matters, as many will be under 18, we need to remember our safeguarding responsibilities, including when we are acting on behalf of the church and its trustees.

Build relationships—unchurched young people need to feel that they belong in the group

Here we return to a point made in a number of places in this book: that evangelism depends on building real relationships with individuals. If young people are to 'hear' us, and not simply dismiss us as fuddy-duddies who are by definition unsympathetic to them, we must demonstrate that we are interested in them and genuinely care about them. This is not just about outreach by older generations: it must be true of their peers within fellowships as well. If the impression is given that there are insiders and outsiders, and they are outsiders, then there will be no reason for them to be impressed by what we believe nor what we are trying to teach them. Like others whom we are seeking to reach, they will need to feel that they belong to the group, have confidence that they have a trusted place in the group, before they will start listening to us. They must feel that we as individuals care for them, even love them, for who they are.

The role of apologetics in the evangelistic process

In order to turn to Christ, young people, like anyone else, will need to grasp the core of the gospel and what it means for them, and accept that it is for them in a profound way. That individuals could do that in former generations at virtually first contact with a particular group of believers was a product of their environment, with their familiarity with the basic tenets and requirements of biblical Christianity. They would already have accepted that God was the Christian God, with knowledge of the Christian story. Many young people (and indeed others) in European society are not in that happy position. This means that there is apologetic groundwork to be done with them before they are in a position to trust Christ for salvation, though we might be wise never use the word 'apologetics' in their hearing!

This runs counter to some thinking in evangelicalism, which is inclined to argue that the problem in human beings is not intellectual but spiritual and moral. That is true from one perspective, and all must come eventually to see that that is so if they are to become Christians in biblical terms. But if young people have real intellectual problems with, for example, the existence of God, or that science has disproved biblical Christianity, or because they are ignorant about the basic framework of Christianity, they are likely never to get to the point of realising that their fundamental problem is sin and that they need to repent, or that a personal God actually loves them personally.

Evangelism cannot be confined simply to the key tenets of the gospel itself, depending on the starting point of the hearer. If we require biblical proof of this, it is necessary only to compare the way in which Paul presented the gospel in the Jewish synagogues on his missionary journeys (e.g., Acts 13: 15–41) with the way in which he presented it to the simple pagans of Lystra (Acts 14: 14–17) on the one hand and the sophisticated pagans of Athens on the other (Acts 17: 22–31). We can assume that Paul's and the other disciples' daily disputations for two years in the hall of Tyrannus (Acts 19: 9, 10) went much further than the essentials of atonement. There will be circumstances in which our evangelism also will need to go much further if young people are to see that the atoning work of Christ is for them. It follows that we may need to brush up on how to do apologetics with young people today without their really noticing!

Recognize that young people think independently and need to be convinced—don't dumb down the truth or the gospel

This leads conveniently to a signficant point about our general approach to young people in evangelism. We should not underestimate them and their ability to grasp and understand arguments. We should not underestimate their ability to come to grips with Scripture, and therefore we should be unafraid to present Scripture to them, in the light of the Spirit's ability to make the Word living and powerful in their understandings (though we may need to convince them as to why Scripture can be taken seriously). There is no need to treat young people as children, to be simplistic in our presentations or arguments, to dumb down the nature of the discussion. We need, too, to meet their arguments head on, and not to sidestep or be dismissive of, still less sarcastic or mocking about, the points that they make. If we bring them to grips with Scripture, we shall open the way to the work of the Spirit in their lives and consciences. But, of course, individuals vary and how we discuss matters with each of them needs to be adjusted to their knowledge and experience. We shall need to pitch the discussion to our specific interlocutors. We should note the importance of discussion and dialogue with young people, rather than dogmatic, one-sided presentation, partly because of what they experience in education these days.

Form small groups which allow consistent engagement with young people over time

It follows that the process of evangelism with young people in these essentially cross-cultural circumstances may be more drawn-out than in earlier years. The need to establish relationships, to improve basic knowledge of Christianity and the gospel, and to allow for dialogue, point in the direction of evangelism through small groups which allow consistent engagement with young people over a period of time. This will take time on our part, and will entail consistent commitment. It will require patience and prayer. These groups can be church-based, but they can also be free-standing. There is still the opportunity for Christian Unions in schools, especially if there are young people available (usually Christians) who are prepared to request the school authorities to allow them to form a group.

It is important that such small groups should be Bible-focussed, engaging in serious and systematic study of Scripture, preferably with programmes which are designed to introduce the group to a basic understanding of the biblical worldview, to see Scripture as God's revelation of himself to humankind, and leading to an understanding of the way of salvation in Christ. The content should aim to give the chance for Scripture to speak to individuals by the Holy Spirit.

Such groups are likely to have a dual purpose in practice—on the one hand, to introduce unchurched young people to biblical truth and the biblical worldview, and on the other hand to disciple those who become Christians, to deepen their faith, and lay firm foundations for life-long commitment to Christ. Managing these dual objectives in a single group may not always be easy, but it is likely to be inevitable because of the difficulty of managing things so that groups for non-Christians are kept separate from those for Christians.

Make use of Christian young people (if they are available) in these groups

Such small groups are likely to be all the more successful if they can incorporate young people who are already committed Christians who are growing in their Christian lives. Those who are not Christians are likely to be more impressed by peers who challenge and teach them than by older generations whose ideas can easily be dismissed as being out of touch with what young people regard as real life. What is important is that young Christians should be able to draw others into their orbit, rather than vice versa. Local churches often have excellent work among toddlers and primary-age children which gives the church connection with unchurched families. The challenge which they face, however, is how can children of the fellowship be brought to real Christian commitment so as to ensure that in their teenage years they do not drop out of church and spiritual life in favour of immersing themselves in the culture of their peers? And how can the church's contacts of childhood years be brought to real commitment which will have the same effect? For the fact is that increasingly it is teenagers and the 20—30 age group who are missing from Christian congregations (as well as males of maturer years). Among other things, this augurs badly for the future of local churches.

A small group of teenagers which intentionally seeks to illuminate from Scripture the Christian worldview as well as the way of salvation can address these challenges, the more so if children of or closely connected with the fellowship can form an attractional core for other unchurched young people. If those teenagers who are already committed Christians can have a strong role in teaching and discussion in the group, this is likely to benefit their own spiritual growth and challenge their peers who are not yet committed believers.

The role of intensive events, weekends, camps in clinching decision and encouraging commitment

None of this is to say that there is no role today for more traditional aspects of Christian youth work, such as gospel events, weekends away, and Christian camps. The latter, at least, can continue the serious intentionalism which it has been argued should lie at the core of the small group as a vehicle for bringing young people to Christ and discipling them as young Christians. It is factually so, that weekend houseparties and week-long camps which are the one hand good and enjoyable fun for young people and on the other include serious teaching and group discussion lead to life-changing and life-shaping decisions by young people (as well as providing the context for early steps in Christian leadership). They are likely to be all the more effective where year-long small group teaching and discussion has prepared the ground for such choices.

Conversion and baptism need to be followed up with systematic discipling

A word needs to be said about conversion and baptism and how they relate to systematic discipling (and 'disciple-making'). It is true that evangelism which focuses only on 'decisions for Christ' and 'saying the prayer' can result in shallow, transient 'conversions' which do not result in lifelong commitment to Christ. But we should be careful not to denigrate what God did in the past through revivalism and the crusade evangelism of the twentieth century (and is still doing in the Majority World through Pentecostal campaigns of healing evangelism). The undeniable fact is that these campaigns very often resulted in life-long, life-transforming commitments to Christ through conversion. Where the church of Christ would be today worldwide without the nineteenth-century revivals and revivalism, and Billy Graham's campaigns in particular in the twentieth century, scarcely bears contemplation—the Church of England ministry, and the resurgence of evangelicalism in the Church of England in the second half of the twentieth century, owed much to those converted in Billy Graham's campaigns in the 1950s.

This is not to argue that this specific method of evangelism any longer has traction in the kind of societies described in the early part of this chapter. It is also the case that George Müller, for one, saw a very clear need for deeper discipleship of young people converted in the 1859–63 revival and the subsequent campaigns of D. L. Moody and others, and set about doing something about it in his worldwide preaching tours in old age—as did the Open Brethren movement as a whole, whose system of church life was calculated to produce first-class Christians. And we have the parable of the sower to remind us that not all genuine conversions will result in lifelong, fruitful discipleship.

But there remains questions about the relationship between 'making disciples', the importance of discipling, and conversion to Christ.

First, in some modern systems, the command to 'go and make disciples' in Matthew 28: 19 is made to do a great deal of work, when it can be argued that, in the context, it means 'make them followers of, or believers in, Christ', baptising them immediately they have made this decision (not after they have learned a great deal—as became the practice of the Patristic church), and then 'teach them to obey everything that I have commanded you', i.e., disciple them (bearing in mind that a disciple is a 'learner' or 'pupil'). Incidentally, we should remind ourselves that we are to make them disciples of Christ, not of us as teachers—in contrast with the rabbinical system; disciple-making should not become a cloak for heavy shepherding.

Second, the emphasis on 'disciple-making', good as it may be, should not result in a de facto denigration of, or glossing over of the need for, conversion. The New Testament doctrine of salvation by faith in the substitutionary atoning work of Christ implies that salvation is an instantaneous event in human life. It is true that trust in Christ can have long antecedents in the individual's life, probably in every case in fact. It is also true that that many true believing Christians cannot say when exactly they trusted Christ for salvation, when exactly they were converted. But this does not alter the fact that at the moment of repentance and true faith in Christ that person receives forgiveness and passes from death to life. And, of course, from that moment the believer becomes a disciple, a follower of Christ, who needs to grow in grace and understanding (with the assistance of careful and effective discipling). Without true conversion to Christ through faith, disciple-making will not be more than the Christianization of the individual concerned.

The emphasis in this chapter on evangelism and discipling in small groups, focussing on teaching the Word (as the whole counsel, or purpose, of God—Acts 20: 27), has in mind both bringing young people to the point that they see the need to be saved and can experience genuine conversion; and discipling them in the faith once they have believed.

An epilogue about the importance of music

Music plays an important role in almost all human religion. The combination of melody and lyrics have played an important role from the beginning in Christianity, both in worship and in reinforcing the teaching of the faith. Music has an important role in youth culture, both as a background to life and study, and through music festivals. Its significance may be judged by the nostalgic place which popular music has in people of maturer years: Glastonbury has, it can be argued, become a religious rite for a large segment of society, not just young people. We shall be missing an important trick if we do not see that music is a key vector for connecting with young people, in evangelism as well as discipling. The challenge is to ensure that both music and words are faithful to the gospel, and connect with those whom we are seeking to reach.

Online resources to help with apologetic discussion with young people:

Bible Questions Answered (GotQuestions.org)
Christian Apologetics & Research Ministry (carm.org)
Be Thinking – making sense of the big questions about life (bethinking.org)
ABR Apologetics – compelling evidence for God and the Bible (alwaysbeready.com)
Chatnow – help topics (chatnow.org/help-topics)

For discussion

1. Of all the changes mentioned in this chapter, which do you think makes youth evangelism the most difficult and why?
2. Why do you think disciple-making is such an important component of youth evangelism today?
3. In what ways does your church need to adapt in order to make it a youth-welcoming place?

Chapter 17

Sharing the gospel with children

Paul Willmott

May I first direct you back to the earlier chapters of this book. Given the wealth of experience of the writers, you will no doubt already have collected some very helpful nuggets of advice. But there may be more to be found by considering what you have read from a different viewpoint—that is, with a specific child, or group of children, in mind. Throughout Scripture, we are instructed to teach our children, as in the command, 'Teach them to your children and to their children after them.' (Dt. 4: 9) And this we are instructed to do, *so that they in turn can teach future generations.*

If thinking from this perspective highlights something new from earlier chapters, this might be a good time to think and pray about how you can implement this within your church or family.

Children are people too

Let me begin with this bold statement, *Children are people too*. It may seem a little obvious, but we can often think of children as junior humans or, worse, we can end up treating them as less than people. Maybe this is because they are young, with lots to learn and much growing to do. Children do have much to learn, but then so do all of us. Certainly, learning about God never stops. Remember Nicodemus. Jesus acknowledged him as 'Israel's teacher' (Jn. 3: 10), yet he did not understand about being born again. But for Nicodemus, Jesus was there to instruct him.

I recently experienced children's ministry in a country in the Majority World which had better be nameless. Here is how a typical Sunday school lesson is planned. The pastor of the church stands to begin the service, maybe opening with prayer and some songs. Then it is time for the sermon and the pastor says, "Michael, I would like you to teach the children today." and off Michael goes to teach the Sunday school. No warning, no planning, no way to teach children! The children were being treated as second-class people: they even had second-hand Bible teaching.

Jesus taught positively about the way that children can respond to God's love, but not always so positively about the way that some adults do. The Gospels of Matthew and Mark both note that Jesus called a child to stand with the disciples. Matthew tells us (18: 3) that Jesus said, "You need to change and become like little children." What would that have been like, to be looked at like this, by Jesus? We also read in Acts 1: 8 that Jesus said, 'But you will receive power when the Holy Spirit has come on you, and you will be my witnesses in Jerusalem, and in all Judea and Samaria, and to the ends of the earth.' We don't read, 'and then the power of the *Junior Holy Spirit* fell on those who attended Sunday school lessons'. The same Father, Son and Holy Spirit is available to all, whatever our age may be. Then in Acts 2: 39 we read: 'For the promise is for you and for your children and for all who are far off, everyone whom the Lord our God calls to himself.' This shows that God's forgiveness is available to all, regardless of age or location. Children are clearly highly rated by God.

Accountability and responsibility

So is there an age at which we become spiritually accountable? The Bible gives no specific information about a person's age of accountability. In practice, it probably varies a little from child to child. I would suggest that a child reaches the age of accountability when he or she is capable of making a faith decision for or against Christ. Charles Spurgeon's conclusion on this subject was that 'A child of five can as truly be saved and regenerated as an adult.'

One of the common myths in today's church is that children cannot be zealous, God-loving, faith-drenched, Bible-devoted, prayer-uttering disciples of Jesus Christ. The truth is that children can be just as ardent in their Christian faith as adults. **Children are people too.**

Of course, we do have to be responsible in the way we teach and share faith with children in our homes, churches and schools. There are also many different views about this both within church and outside of church. For example, Richard Dawkins has written,

> Indoctrinating your opinions into the vulnerable minds of your children is bad enough. Perhaps worse is the defeatist assumption, almost universally made by society at large, including secular society, that children as a matter of fact *do* automatically inherit the beliefs of their parents and our language should reflect this. Non-religious as well as religious people buy into the notion that children should be *labeled* with one religious name or another.

I would agree that 'indoctrinating' is wrong in many ways. However, introducing children (or adults for that matter) to faith, informing them so that they can make their own decisions, is essential as in other aspects of life. We cannot make intelligent choices without information. A dictionary definition of indoctrination is the 'process of teaching a person or group to accept a set of beliefs uncritically'. The Bible asks us on occasion to test, ask questions, and be critical. Let's be honest, indoctrination doesn't really work anyway, certainly not in a faith context. If someone is not completely committed 'in spirit and in truth' (Jn. 4: 24) and not utterly convinced, then ultimately they are living a false life.

When we are teaching children biblically and theologically, we do of course need to take great care that we are not indoctrinating, not because of Professor Dawkins, but because we would want each individual to be living a renewed life, demonstrating faith in the way that they live. And most of all, we would want them to be following Jesus out of choice and love, not because they are being told to do so.

Parents and responsibility

We also have a responsibility to the parents of the children whom we are teaching. In school, there would be regular contact and, of course, parents' evenings. As churches, we need to ask the question how well we are communicating with the parents of the children that we teach? This is important for parents who are members of our churches, but it is key for families who are not members of our churches. Do the parents know what faith principles we are teaching to their children? If not, how can they reinforce these principles at home?

Who is really responsible for teaching our kids about faith? RE lessons at school can teach facts and figures. In the playground for many children, as it was for me, it will be other children who teach wild and crazy ideas. In Sunday school, by the time you have taken out the welcome, songs, craft, and games, teaching maybe accounts for 10 minutes per session. But, even when we bear in mind that children also learn by watching us, they are still only with us in church for a short time each week, even in normal times.

So with whom do they spend a good portion of time? That would be with their family—parents, carers, all those in their households. But not all of these parents are known to us, still less members of our congregations.

When we are teaching children the Christian faith and how to follow the way of Jesus, it is a good principle to be completely open with their families, whether they are part of church or not, about what we are teaching and why. Let's be clear with parents about the faith journey that children may have begun. Even better, we could aim to be teaching the whole household at the same time. Why not run an 'Alpha' style event for the whole family? Or if you want to connect with those families outside of church, how about a lunch club. Through local schools, we have engaged with families who would benefit from free meals. We then invited a few of those families to join with key families from the church in a good cooked meal. There was no message or preaching, but there was plenty of time for targeted conversation. Following the meal, we had a few planned activities that the children could choose, while all the parents were left to talk with each other. Not only was the gospel shared through targeted conversation, but also friendships were made. Let's try to be connected with the whole family, not simply children.

How well do we even know the child's family? Are the family connected with the church? Maybe they are still to become a part for the church. At my church, as a direct result of school assemblies, followed by family events (a pancake party and light parties) and a summer lunch club, one family was drawn into church life. This family (mum, dad and four kids) became hooked by the friendship that they were shown, the passion that they experienced, and for them it led to growing faith. Let's be ready to invite new families to our events, so we can get to know them and welcome them into God's Family.

A finding from the Church of England's Church Growth Research Programme Report (2014) noted that

> half of the children of churchgoing parents do not attend as adults. It would seem that twenty-first century Christian families are facing their own unique challenges when it comes to successfully passing on God's redemptive story. Of course, nurturing Christian faith in the home is always with the intended goal that the child—accepting and embracing a living relationship with Jesus Christ for themselves—will choose to stand in the living tradition of the faith. However, generational dropout, declining church membership and falling church attendance in the UK point to signs of a failure in intergenerational transmission.

If we can encourage faith at home through real godly conversation, not only will individuals be strengthened but the household will be living church together. However, home life is constantly changing and we as parents can often leave our faith conversation at church on Sunday. There are so many different responsibilities that take up our time as parents. There are growing expectations from schools about how parents should be supporting the education of their children. There are many after-school activities and sport clubs to take part in. If parents are separated, visits from children to the separated parties must be arranged. And of course there is all that time we must spend on social media, and there is the growing need to binge-watch TV shows. So how does even a Christian family make time to talk faith at home, and nurture children in godly discipleship?

Maybe some of this responsibility does rest with the church, in equipping parents to share their own faith stories and helping them to be prepared to answer those unnerving questions from children. So how can that happen? We can look for resources and conversation starters in book or video form, and make this available to parents and prospective parents, and also to young people and children. In a typical Sunday service, the congregation will listen and watch, maybe have a brief conversation with friends, and then go home. Perhaps we could be encouraging conversation during the service. If we can encourage each member of the family to talk, then maybe we shall inspire the whole family to share faith at home.

During COVID restrictions, children spent more time at home with their families. This no doubt caused conflict and disagreement, but it also created the opportunity for family conversation. There was also much more time for people think and reflect about life. My prayer is that in all of this God met people where they were—at home!

Let me now consider a little more those conversations and ask, "What do children know about theology?"

Kids and theology

Can children talk theology? In his book, *Little Theologians*, Dave Csinos talks about the theology of children. Here's how the book begins:

> Children are not simply passive consumers of theology; they actively generate theological meaning for themselves. As they do, they take in information and experiences from their contexts as raw materials and tools for building theology . . . their congregations have a hand in providing them with sources and methods used in theological meaning-making.[1]

So, can children talk theology? I mean really?

Do you remember those conversations you had as a child in the playground when you talked about all sorts? How about those conversations you had about God? Can I suggest that this was theology? As a child in the school playground, I remember talking about how that world was made, how the rain was God's tears, how the earth was a speck of dust on God's arm. Plus many other even more ridiculous ideas. You can probably tell me about childhood conversations like this? Did we get all things right? Of course not. Does that matter? It is certain that as a child I had a lot to learn, but even as adults we still have lots to learn. But those discussions about which we can be nostalgic were theology.

---

1. David M. Csinos, *Little Theologians: Children, Culture, and the Making of Theological Meaning*, (Montreal: McGill-Queen's University Press, 2020).

Simply put, theology is the study of the nature of God. And that is what we were doing: we were studying and asking questions about the nature of God. Trying our best to fit God into the world that we knew. Of course, God was much bigger than our humble ideas, and we had no idea that we were trying to fit God into a human box. But that was the beginnings of theology.

Leading a child to Christ (is it a one-time conversation?)

When did you become a Christian? I have often seen the figures telling us that the majority of adult Christians today made a first decision under the age of 18. But what about you? Do you remember what it was that clinched the deal for you? For my daughter it was a "click" as she called it, when the final things of what she needed to hear fell into place. For me, there was a point when it all seemed to make sense. I had heard many of the Bible accounts at Sunday School; I had even heard a few adult preachers. But then, at the age of 11, I heard a clear presentation as a simple "A, B, C.": Admit, Believe and Commit. It was as I was sitting there that I realised that if all of this I heard was real, then I needed to make my own decision to follow Jesus and be committed to him.

And so that is where my faith journey began? Well actually, no. My faith journey began way back in Sunday School classes. With my brother and sister, I was sent along to Sunday school. Did our parents want a good spiritual upbringing for their precious children or did they want a quiet Sunday morning? I am not sure. But it was these Bible lessons, taught by faithful teachers, that became the foundation of my young faith. Let's not undervalue these lessons learnt at an early age.

So that is where my faith journey began? No, I would suggest not. It was more likely to have been when I was even younger. I was talking the other day with a friend about childhood. I found myself recounting that my mum repeated to me a bedtime prayer each evening. My parents were good people, but I didn't really see them engage with Christianity until I was in my late teens. But that didn't stop God working through them and ministering to me. They were after all the ones who sent me to Sunday school.

So where do we start in leading a child to Christ? How can we help a child take their own steps into an independent Christian life? The following seem to me to be key points.

1. **Let's allow and encourage conversations to happen?** (Remember those playground conversations.) Maybe these conversations can be guided in the home or through Sunday school lessons, or maybe by other members of church in targeted chatting at the end of a service. It is when we begin to explore the truth about God and begin asking questions that God will begin to reveal his presence to us. Children can talk theology.

2. **Let's *actually* present the gospel to our children.** As with those whom Paul had in mind as he dictated Romans 10: 14–17, if they don't hear, they can't know. If they don't know, they can't respond. This may need to happen with an illustration of a wall blocking the way, or a tube full of rubbish that blocks a perfect relationship with God. Or better still, why not tell your own personal story? We love telling friends what we have done since we last met.Why not share what God has done in us too? Most of us are a little nosey about others and intrigued as to why someone did or did not do something. The Bible is often described as God's story, and we are invited to allow our story to meet with his story. How wonderful that God allows his story to connect with our story. We all have a wonderful story to share.When did you last share your 'God story' with someone?

3. **Let's be living out God's story in our lives.** Children can often be visual learners, and can pick up what is going in around them. They learn from the world, especially what they see and experience. How are you living out your God story? Children have this knack of being able to tell when you are being genuine. What is your God story? Do you remember any of your actual Sunday school lessons? No? Me neither, but I am sure that you remember your Sunday school teachers or school teachers, and how they treated you and how you felt. How did they live? Are we ready to teach the gospel by the way that we live?

4. **Let's be ready.** The experience that I recounted earlier in a Majority World country was not a great way to teach children. We can look at it from another point of view. You are sitting before the pastor in that congregation. How do you feel? It could be you this week. You could

be asked to teach the children. Are you prepared? What will be your teaching for them? In 1 Peter 3: 15 we are instructed, 'But in your hearts set apart Christ as Lord. Always be prepared to give an answer to everyone who asks you to give the reason for the hope that you have. But do this with gentleness and respect. . . .' (NIV). Peter says be prepared to answer 'everyone who asks': remember, people don't always ask verbally. Children can be at church events because they are asking, without even having a specific set of questions. Perhaps my Majority World experience meant that everyone in the congregation had to be ready to teach in case the pastor called them. When God calls are you ready?

Where do you begin? If I was going to present the gospel, I would be sure to talk about these key points:

> God as creator, creating the world and people, to love and share it with him.
> Through bad choices, sin entered the world. People began to value other things before God. Therefore people are separated from God.
> Then Jesus, as God the Son, became human as part of our world, and lived a perfect life. He stood in our place at the cross, to restore our relationship with God.
> To complete this, the Holy Spirit (not the junior holy spirit) lives with us as our comforter and guide, to help us live rightly before God.

Of course, you would have to choose your own level of words depending on whom you were talking with or presenting to. I would also (and this may sound obvious) pray and ask the Holy Spirit to take the lead in your words, that we would speak in the most kind, yet engaging ways. Let's remember that it is the Holy Spirit who does the work in people's hearts.

But is this only a one-time conversation? What next?

I believe that if we only present the gospel as a lovely, neat presentation, and then walk away, we are leaving children, or anyone, short. We are also responsible to be discipling all people. As recorded in Matthew 28: 18–20, Jesus said, 'All authority in heaven and on earth has been given to me. Go therefore and **make disciples** of all nations, baptising them in the name of the Father and of the Son and of the Holy Spirit, teaching them to observe all that I have commanded you. And behold, I am with you always, to the end of the age.' Jesus instructs us to **make disciples**. To be a Christian is to become more like Jesus; it is a growing process, and we all need feeding and nurturing.

It is the role of parents to care for, nurture, and train their children, but then ultimately let them go into the world—it is to be hoped, wiser and able to make good life-choices. As God's family, we have the same responsibility to the children who are under our care. Communicating the gospel may well only be a one-time conversation, but it is a (key) part of our ongoing spiritual conversations, enabling children to learn more about God and be more like Jesus. If we nurture and train our children well, then they in turn will nurture and train the children under their care. Remember Deuteronomy 4: 9, as quoted at the beginning of this chapter, and also Proverbs 22: 6: 'Train up a child in the way he should go; even when he is old he will not depart from it.'

This said, we also need to be sure that we actually present the good news of Jesus to our children. During my Sunday school years, I don't actually recall hearing the gospel. Each week was full of good Bible teaching, and those years became the foundation for my early faith. Maybe my spiritual eyes were not open to see; maybe I simply wasn't listening. But I do see and hear of many churches and children's groups who have the most wonderful teaching programmes, from the Old and New Testament, looking at characters, mountains, geography or history. But the actual gospel message can sometimes be missing. So let's be sure that the gospel message definitely features in our teaching, while we are supporting parents or carers also to ensure that the gospel features in their teaching too.

Do you remember the time that you were brought into God's Kingdom? What was it that clinched the deal for you? Whatever it was, it was a key point for you, and a thought or idea that captured you. But let's remember that whatever worked for you, doesn't work for everyone. This is true. However, it might still be a good place for you to start when you are sharing the gospel with children.

We are all God's children, and children are people too.

For discussion

1. What are the most important lessons in this chapter that you could apply to your church?
2. If you were to 'upskill' your church to be better at reaching children, what would you do and why?

Chapter 18

Cross-cultural evangelism in the UK

Rupert Abbott

Daily in the late summer of 2021, chaotic scenes from Kabul airport were shown on our TV screens and newsfeeds, of people desperate to leave Afghanistan after the sudden takeover by the Taliban. At the time, the UK Government pledged to receive 20,000 Afghans. They would join 80,000 who were already settled in this country. Now, here's something to challenge us: Afghanistan is one of the toughest mission fields and yet there are 100,000 Afghans in our country, living in our neighbourhoods and working as part of our labour-force; and their children are attending our schools. This is a significant missional opportunity.

It is not only Afghans who have come to the UK. Others from war-torn, corruption-ravaged countries are seeking refuge and a future that holds some prospect of hope for them and their children. For example, in 2023 there are nearly 210,000 Ukrainian refugees in the UK.

Then there are those who migrate, for example, to join family already here, for work, or for study. According to the Annual Population Survey, in 2021 about 9.5 million of the UK population (about 14.5%) were foreign-born.[1] Of these, 70% were in the age-group 26–64, compared with 48% of the UK-born, that is they were skewed towards those most likely to be economically active. Almost half of the foreign born were concentrated in London and the South East. 37% of the population in London were foreign-born, compared with 10% in Yorkshire and Humberside, the North West and Scotland. Nearly

1. Only about two thirds of this number are of non-UK nationality, partly because of naturalisation as UK citizens among people in the overall total.

10% of the foreign-born were from India, followed by 7% from Poland, nearly 5% from Pakistan, and 4% from the Republic of Ireland. This means that, by way of religious background, many of the foreign born are Muslim, others Hindu, and a more significant number than we probably imagine are of Catholic background (particularly from the Republic of Ireland, Poland, Portugal and Italy) and are a significant potential strategic vector for eventual evangelism in their home countries.[2]

Another perspective is given by the response to the 2021 Census question on religious affiliation. Until very recently, figures have been available only for England and Wales, but they suggest that nearly 7% of the total population are Muslim, and nearly 2% are Hindu[3] (the proportions being considerably higher in certain areas of London and the South East, and in Leicester, Bradford, and Blackburn, for example[4]).

Those who migrate may be particularly ready to question views acquired in their upbringing. Also, 14% of the foreign-born from the European Union were in the UK to study, and 17% in the case of those from outside the EU. Students are a group who are particularly open to revising the ideas with which they were brought up. They are also a strategically important group because a substantial proportion may return to their home country sooner or later—and it is better that they return as advocates for Christ than simply as advocates for UK culture.

These data underline that there are more people on the move in our world today than ever before in history. There are major opportunities for cross-cultural mission here in the UK, especially in London and the South East and

---

2. The figures given in this paragraph are drawn from analysis of Annual Population Survey data by The Migration Observatory at the University of Oxford (see https://migrationobservatory.ox.ac.uk/resources/briefings/migrants-in-the-uk-an-overview/, accessed on 17 February 2023.)

3. See Peter Brierley, 'Making sense of the Census' in *Partnership Perspectives*, no. 75 (Autumn 2022/Winter 2023), pp. 52–55.

4. In the 2021 Census, 26% of the population of Harrow self-identified themselves as Hindu, and 18% of the population of Leicester (see https://www.ons.gov.uk/census/maps/choropleth/identity/religion/religion-tb/hindu, accessed on 17 February 2023), while 29% of the population of Slough identified themselves as Muslim, 30% of the populations of Birmingham and Bradford, and 35% of the population of Blackburn with Darwen (and about 20% in many of the old towns and cities of Lancashire and West Yorkshire) (see https://www.ons.gov.uk/census/maps/choropleth/identity/religion/religion-tb/muslim, accessed on 17 February 2023),

the old industrial centres of the North. International students continue to offer a fertile and priority field for evangelism. Significant numbers of such migrants, often from hard-to-reach or closed countries, are coming to faith in the Lord Jesus! Do we stop and ask the question: what is God doing in our day and generation? How is God asking us to respond to the opportunity to reach out to people living in our midst from many tribes and tongues, peoples and nations?

A few years ago, when I was asked by a church to take their mission weekend, rather than focussing on mission abroad, I felt that I should highlight the opportunity to reach the world on our doorstep. For, as people rightly observe, mission is no longer from here to there, but from everywhere to everywhere.

I found that my friends from this church were involved in a local charity which was assisting refugees and asylum seekers and had befriended a couple of Syrian families. One of these refugees had been a chef in a good hotel, so it was decided to ask him to cook the lunch that was usually provided by the church members and to invite the other family to share about their experiences as refugees after the shared meal. The chef produced a wonderful spread of middle eastern food, after which the other family shared their experiences of escaping the city of Aleppo—about what it is like to hear reports on the news about cities being bombed when you have family members living in those very places; and about starting school in England and adjusting to our culture. Whatever the political opinions of those listening with respect to migration to the UK, one could not help but be moved by the personal stories, the courage and the heartaches, that were shared by this Syrian Muslim family now making their home in this church's neighbourhood. I was encouraged by how this different approach to doing a mission weekend evidently helped to break down barriers, overcome prejudices, and alleviate the fear of the unknown that exists in society generally, as well as in our churches.

To the outsider looking at the way in which immigrant communities appear to have taken over some parts of our cities, a natural reaction can be one of resentment. (Such responses can be tempered by an awareness that the first migrants came at the invitation of the government to make up the depleted labour force following the Second World War.) However, the more recent history of 9/11, the subsequent war on terror, and atrocities like the

Manchester Arena bombing, can instil fear of all Muslims, fear that can be exacerbated by reports of Christians being persecuted in countries around the world. All this can create barriers rather than build bridges between our church members and migrants.

The best way to overcome the resulting negative stereotypes is to get to know migrants personally. My attitude towards Muslims is greatly coloured by the friendships that we established when we moved into an inner-city area of Birmingham with a 60–70% Pakistani population. Pakistani people are naturally hospitable, and we developed good relationships with our neighbours through exchanging food, our children playing together, and birthday parties that included sleepovers. Our terraced house had an unusually big back garden where we kept animals and grew vegetables. This reminded some of our neighbours of the villages they had left behind in Pakistan's rural Punjab or in Azad-Kashmir. It was only when, later, we visited some of our neighbours from Birmingham in their village homes in Pakistan that we appreciated the huge contrast that many of these immigrants experienced. They had exchanged an open-air life in a rural village, via Islamabad and Manchester airports, for being cooped up in the back room of an inner-city terraced house. No wonder many experienced mental health issues. Of course, things change for subsequent generations born in this country, for whom the question of identity becomes a very real issue.

To build bridges as individuals and as churches, and to be comfortable with welcoming people of other nationalities and faiths into our homes and to our community-based church-run activities, it helps to learn something about cultural differences. With reference to Pakistani Muslim culture, this would include things like separation between males and females—and what can happen if you are invited for a meal; halal (acceptable) and haram (forbidden) food; and attitudes towards dogs, cats and other pets. It may help to amplify these points.

First, Muslim homes commonly have different rooms for men and women, and men greet men with a handshake and embrace, and women greet women. In our experience it is not unusual, if making a visit as a couple, that we are split up on arrival and meet again as we leave. That came as a bit of a surprise when it happened for the first time! (On one occasion, when a Muslim contact came to church, he was greeted by one of the church ladies with an all-embracing hug. This was culturally inept and best avoided!)

Secondly, Muslims do not eat pork, and other categories of meat, all of which is "haram"; permitted meat will have been slaughtered following certain rituals, and this is "halal". If you are cooking a meal for a Muslim friend, make sure you use halal meat (it is readily available). If you have Muslims coming to church activities, such as Mother and Toddler groups and you are planning an occasion with food, it is a good idea to do a "bring and share", as this is a guaranteed way to ensure there will be food that they will be happy to eat.

Thirdly, Muslims who sincerely practice their faith pray five times a day and it is important to them to be clean for their prayer times. They consider dogs to be unclean and if they were to get dog hairs on their clothes, they would consider themselves unclean for prayer. So if you keep a dog, keep it out of the way when your Muslim friend visits and make sure you have put the hoover around beforehand.

Sometimes people are surprised to find that it is easier to have a conversation about what you believe with a Muslim than with someone who is white, secular and British; people of faith understand people of faith! But to be confident in talking about matters of faith, it helps to know about common misunderstandings and to learn ways for starting and developing conversations, and to learn approaches that avoid unnecessary offence or arguments that get nowhere.

Muslims revere the Prophet Mohammed as the last and greatest of the prophets, and they misunderstand the description of Jesus as "Son of God" (they understand this in a literal sense). I have found that a useful way to have a profitable discussion about your differences in belief is to say to your Muslim friend: "You follow the Prophet Mohammed and I follow the Lord Jesus. Why don't you tell me in ten minutes why you follow your prophet, and then I can tell you in ten minutes why I follow the Lord Jesus." In this way, you earn the right to be heard and you can talk about the uniqueness of Jesus' birth and his character, his words and his works, his death (including that he predicted it), and his resurrection.

Muslims find it impossible to believe that God would have allowed Jesus, whom they consider to be one of the greatest of the prophets, to be crucified.

I have often been told that God made Judas to take on the likeness of Jesus so that it was Judas who was crucified, while Jesus was taken up into heaven. So how do you explain to your Muslim friend why Jesus's mission was fulfilled through his death on the cross? Here is one way:

> Q: "Do you believe that God is Just?" *[A: "Yes, most certainly!"]*
> Q: "Do you believe that God is Merciful?" *[A: "Oh yes, indeed, God is Merciful!"]*
> Q: "How can God be Just and Merciful at the same time?" (Give that question a little time to be thought about.) "This is how I believe that Jesus Christ died on the cross: it was where the Justice of God met the Mercy of God." (There is a good story that can be told to illustrate this—and, for dialogue with Muslims, it is wise to learn to become a good storyteller).

Muslims will often tell you that the Bible has been changed. You can reply by asking when and where this was done, as there are verses in the Quran that affirm the Bible and so, if the changes were made after the time of the prophet Mohammed, the Bible was in many different countries by then, so how can all the copies of the Bible have been changed? It is good to familiarise yourself with the Quran, but it is best to be known as someone who knows their own book (the Quran refers to Christians as "The People of the Book"!). I have found the passage in Luke 24: 25–27 very useful, when the risen Lord Jesus explains to the two dispirited disciples on the road to Emmaus (who also couldn't get their heads around his death on the cross), that he had fulfilled all that was written about him in the books of Moses and the prophets. (THINK: What prophecies could you point to that Jesus fulfilled in his life and death?)

Although knowing the way in which a textbook would present Islam is helpful, it was a revelation to me to be told, and then to experience, the extent to which the Muslims whom I have met were influenced by folk Islam. This meant being fearful of the evil eye and of the powerful influence of evil spirits; the fear of being cursed and learning of the practice of using talismans (verses from the Quran placed above a doorway or worn round one's neck) for protection; and of the influence of Pirs (holy men) and their belief in the efficacy of prayers said at the tombs of Pirs. (On this, see *The Unseen Face of*

Islam by Bill Musk.[5]) In this context and through experiences in Birmingham and Pakistan, I learnt that a powerful way to share a testimony of what God has done for us in and through our Lord Jesus is by using Psalm 34: 4: 'This poor man called, and the Lord heard him, and delivered him from all his fears.'

This will be much more understood than an academic discussion about God and sin, especially when what is understood by both terms varies so much. When you find people, as I have, genuinely disturbed by evil spirits, then to share stories from the Gospels that demonstrate the authority of the Lord Jesus over forces of evil, and to pray for them in that authority, is a powerful way to communicate the truth of the gospel.

I found the same contrast between theory and religious practice in Buddhist Thailand. You could learn about pure Buddhism, but what you saw being practised every day on every street corner bore no relationship to the text-book religion, but rather was an expression of a fear-bound superstition that dominated the way people viewed the world. Of course, the same is true in societies dominated by nominal Christianity, but understanding this helps with how you present the freedom that can be found through faith in the good news of the Lord Jesus. Having lived in both Islamic and Buddhist countries, I have become much more aware of a spiritual dimension to life that could be experienced in time (an oppressive atmosphere at certain festivals) and space (the oppressive feeling in a certain place) in a way that brought a different understanding of the spiritual warfare that we are engaged in as we seek to shine for God in the darkness of this sin-soaked world.

In both Islamic and Buddhist contexts, I also learnt the power of witnessing to the gospel through means where words were not needed. For twenty years I was on the board of an eye hospital in North Pakistan. We started a Blind School for children who had been born blind. Typically, these children had no purpose in life—they were well cared for, but nothing was expected of them. At the blind school, they learned to read and write, to play musical instruments, to make bricks and to knit and crochet, and even to play cricket! All the patients coming to the hospital on seeing this could witness a living parable illustrating the impact of the gospel in the lives of these (worthless)

5. Bill A. Musk, *The Unseen Face of Islam* (Crowborough: Monarch, 1989).

blind children: people were being given purpose and hope where they had none; people who were at the bottom of the pile (Jas. 1: 27) to whom dignity had been restored.

In a similar way, in Thailand we demonstrated the compassion of the gospel by running a small Riding for Disabled project. In a Buddhist worldview, dominated by "Karma", if you are born disabled, it is because you deserved it; it is seen as the consequence of misdeeds in a previous life. So, to care for disabled children, which we did by giving them horse-riding experience and by training a pony to pull a cart so that we could give these children a fun ride around where we lived, was to treat 'the least of these' (Mt. 25: 45) with dignity in a way that demonstrated the love and grace of God. By the way in which we welcome all comers, cater for all comers, and live out what we believe by what we do, we can live the gospel in ways that speak to those among whom we live, whatever their origin, backgrounds, or beliefs.

This chapter has reflected the cross-cultural witness experiences that have been part of my ministry for over forty years in Birmingham, Pakistan and Thailand, first with the Birmingham City Mission and then in mission overseas with Echoes International (EI). In the last few years, EI has made cross-cultural witness in the UK a strategic focus, so it has UK-based mission partners reaching out to Iranians, Arabs, Syrians, Jews, Pakistanis, Turks and others. The ministry of a number of Counties evangelists has a special focus on cross-cultural witness. Both EI and Counties can help to equip churches, groups or individuals to reach out more effectively in cross-cultural contexts.

For discussion

1. On a scale of 1 to 10 (1 being 'poor' and 10 being 'brilliant'), how good is your church at reaching out to people of other nationalities and faiths?

2. What proportion of your town would be people of other nationalities and faiths?

3. What practical steps could you take to get better at reaching people of other nationalities and faiths?

Chapter 19

Sharing the good news online

Matt Rich

The pandemic brought many challenges and hardships, but one of the exciting developments that we saw was the way in which churches really grabbed hold of the importance of occupying the online world.

I have been working as an online evangelist since the year 2000, and over the twenty years up to 2020 I tried again and again to encourage churches and others to take more of their mission online—some churches dabbled, some ignored my encouragement, but God used the pandemic to force our hand, to make us go where the world already was! The pandemic caused an even more rapid growth in online adaptation by the whole population, as everyone shifted even further into doing things online as the norm.

If you are reading this chapter, and your eyes are already beginning to glaze over, and you are considering flicking to a different, more relevant, chapter of the book—can I implore and encourage you and your church with these simple words: "Don't go back!"? As God's people, we mustn't step back. Whether we have returned to the old normality or a new, different normality—please don't breathe a sigh of relief and think, "Great! No more need to be online!'

Many businesses today are spending more than half of their advertising budget online, even those whose main business is things that take place offline. Whether we like it or not, the online world is where most of those we are seeking to reach are spending an ever-increasing amount of their time. It's the go-to place to discover new things, to look for help, to explore ideas, to read about new concepts, and meet new people.

Now that so much of the church was forced to take itself and its message online, we mustn't step back, we mustn't retreat, we mustn't withdraw. Instead, we need to learn how to do even more online, and how to do what we do in the most effective way with the resources we have.

Johannes Gutenberg, the German publisher who used movable type for the first time to produce the Gutenberg Bible in the 1450s (one of the most important technical and intellectual developments in history) wrote:

> Religious truth is imprisoned in a small number of manuscript books, which confine instead of spread the public treasure. Let us break the seal which seals up holy things and give wings to Truth in order that she may win every soul that comes into the world by her word no longer written at great expense by hands easily palsied, but multiplied like the wind by an untiring machine. . . . from which shall soon flow in inexhaustible streams the most abundant and most marvellous liquor that has ever flowed to relieve the thirst of man! Through it God will spread His Word. A spring of pure truth shall flow from it! Like a new star, it shall scatter the darkness of ignorance, and cause a light heretofore unknown to shine among men.

The Gutenberg printing press created wonderful new opportunities to tell people in print about the Lord Jesus Christ. But printing has also resulted in a proliferation of evil content. The same can be said of the Internet. The opportunity to use the Internet for good is as large as the opportunity to use it for evil—those flooding the Internet with unhelpful and unhealthy things have just become better at it, as they are more convinced than most of the church that it's the medium to use for their purpose. We need to make sure we use it too, and don't waste a wonderful, God-given opportunity to spread the good news.

In a recent Online Nation report, Ofcom reported that adults are spending an average of four hours a day online.[1] In other research,it was discovered that

1. www.iabuk.com/news-article/ofcom-time-spent-online-hits-record-levels

two-thirds of our population use social media, with the user averaging 1 hour 50 minutes every day.[2]

In the words of Jesus to the Father in John 17: 18, 'As you sent me into the world, so I have sent them into the world.' Just as the early church gave time and effort to taking the gospel into the world where people spent their time, so we need to take the wonderful news about King Jesus to where people today are spending an ever-increasing proportion of their time.

Each of our churches, and every one of us as individuals, will have different levels of ability and experience, time and resources to draw on as we seek to use the Internet to make an impact for the Lord God in our local communities. All churches should prayerfully do something. But also they should only do what can be done well, avoiding doing things poorly because what we do represents God, as we are his ambassadors: 'We are ambassadors for Christ, God making his appeal through us.' (2 Cor. 5: 20)

Here are some suggestions about what your church could do online.

The basics: your website

The look and feel of your website is incredibly important. If you don't have a church website, please create one and have the church web-address prominently displayed outside your church. If your church website is more than five years old, think about creating a new one! If you don't have the necessary skills in the congregation, then maybe your church regulars could ask their family whether they know anyone who could help, or seek help from another church, or pay someone to make a simple, smart, easily-editable website for the church. Your website is the first impression that many people will have of you and could easily affect perceptions about the relevance of God's message to them today. Always remember to test your website on a smartphone: it needs to look good on small devices because most websites are more often viewed from a smartphone than by someone sitting at a computer.

Aim your website at the right people. Don't create a website for the people in your church: design it for those whom you are aiming to reach out to. Think about what information they will want easily to discover or learn about you.

---

2. www.tigermobiles.com/blog/how-much-time-do-people-spend-on-social-media

Avoid Christian jargon, and make everything that is important to them easy to find. Most people are very lazy online; each extra click feels like hard work and can be enough to lose people along the way! The more committed someone is to your church already, the more work they will be prepared to put in to find what they want. Your church regulars need to be the ones who have to do the extra clicks, not those you are seeking to reach out to in your local community.

Keep your website up-to-date. It's so important to keep a website current, making sure that you are not promoting an event that has already happened: people will happily allow you two or three days' grace before they consider an old event that you are still promoting as proof that the website is out-of-date. Information that is a week or two, or more, out of date will cause them to doubt other things written on the website. Put it in the church diary to review the whole website annually, and consider a major redesign or overhaul every three to five years.[3]

Intermediate suggestions

Video your in-person Sunday services

Record your Sunday service, and upload it to YouTube or Vimeo on the same day, and provide really clear links to it on your church's website and Facebook page. If in-person meetings were to become impossible again at some point in the future, then still put together a service with all the normal parts—using a variety of people from the church and making use of online resources for sections of the service that might be difficult (e.g., songs).

Facebook

Post regularly to your church Facebook page. Make sure you post at least once a week, but the more often the better. Encourage church regulars to actively look for church posts in order to 'Like', 'Comment' on, and 'Share' them—all such interactions on a Facebook post increase the number of other people locally who will be shown the church's post because Facebook assumes people

3. For additional practical advice on church websites, see 'Some tips for improving and maintaining your church website' in *Partnership Perspectives*, no. 67 (Autumn 2019), pp. 46–50 (viewable online at https://fliphtml5.com/bookcase/vbavv).

are interested in what you have written and so tries to show it to others in your locality to see if they might be interested too.

Social media advertising

Advertising a Sunday service, or a one-off or regular outreach event, on social media is really quite cheap and effective. The easiest place to begin is Facebook Boosting or Facebook Ads (Facebook Ads are also automatically shown on Instagram too). The most effective adverts often use brighter, more eye-catching coloured images with a person clearly in the image (or at least a face clearly visible). Please be careful with permissions from the person(s) in the image or copyright in the photo(s). Select a small geographical area for Facebook to show the image to, and link the advert to a specific page on your website where readers can easily find more information on whatever you are promoting.

Advanced suggestions

Live stream church services

Make your services available live on the Internet as they happen—live-stream on Youtube and/or Facebook, but still make sure you that you post the same service online for viewing later by those who were not able to be present or to view it live online.

Social media WhatsApp group

If you have a number of people in your congregation that are pretty active on social media, then set up a WhatsApp group for them, so that when the church posts something on social media the group can all be quickly and easily informed, enabling them to go immediately online to find the post and interact with it straightaway. People commenting on the post, and then others commenting on their comments, is an effective way of encouraging Facebook to show what the church has posted to people in the local community. A WhatsApp group, or similar, can also be used to enable and encourage online fellowship between church members and others, and for instant communication of news and prayer needs (with the permission of the subject when necessary, of course).

Video stories of hope

People enjoy watching short, real-life stories about local people. Record two- to three- minute video stories of hope, life, encouragement, testimony, and so on. Make sure the videos are short, snappy, and have a genuine feel about them. Video someone at church talking about an aspect of their life and, with an unbelieving audience in mind, ensure that they talk about how their faith in Jesus has made a difference to them in a specific situation, and how their faith has brought hope.

What about personal evangelism online?

The beauty and the ugliness of interaction between people online is that many people choose to say things that they would feel uneasy about saying to the same person if they were physically standing in front of them. The Internet removes many inhibitions, many reservations, and also a lot of the normal cultural protocols that most people follow in face-to-face contact. A high percentage of people feel free to respond very frankly, harshly, critically, and instantly to what others write online, which is why discussions by email and on social media can easily escalate into polarisation of positions rather than listening, weighing, and learning. When we seek to use the Internet for evangelism, it is important that we are very conscious of this tendency, so that we don't slip into the same pattern. We need to read, re-read, and re-read everything that we are about to send, because words and sentences can so often be taken in different ways, depending on the emotional intonation filter through which we choose to read them.

Eight tips for personal evangelism online

1. *Don't argue with people in online public places.* It is very rare that arguing in public achieves a good result; more often, it is detrimental and the opposite of the injunction in 1 Peter 3: 15, 'But in your hearts revere Christ as Lord. Always be prepared to give an answer to everyone who asks you to give the reason for the hope that you have. But do this with gentleness and respect, . . .' It is a very small number of people who are spectacularly good at debating in public online

spaces. But most of us should avoid it, as it too easily wastes a lot of time and mostly achieves very little.

2. *Show genuine interest in people.* Try to show a real interest in the people you interact with online—be interested in what they are interested in, be interested in their families, their personal lives, their opinions, in what they write and share online. When people can see that you care about them and the things they feel are important, then they are more likely to listen to you and to the things you feel are important.

3. *Imagine you are wearing a large hat with the words, "I'm a follower of Jesus"*, emblazoned on it in bright, bold letters. Realise that, because you are wearing this big imaginary hat, everyone already thinks you are a little bit odd for being a follower of Jesus, so now you don't need to hide your faith and nor do you any longer need to force it unnaturally into what you write to people.

4. *Be natural about things.* Aim to be genuine about your beliefs. If it's relevant to mention your faith in what you write, then write about it, bring it up naturally, don't hide it. The more at home and comfortable you feel about your faith, the more it will feel less awkward and odd to others to ask you questions about it. Write about spiritual things in passing, showing how much church, the Bible and your faith in Jesus are a natural part of your life. To start with, you may need to look actively for these natural opportunities, until you begin to get into the habit of being yourself and genuine about your beliefs and the effect that they have on your life.

5. *Know what you believe about Jesus and how to explain it in normal everyday words* that will be understood by someone who doesn't know anything about God, or who has never been to church, or never read the Bible. The more you are able to simplify things and still make sense, the more confident you will be about talking about God and the less worrying it will all seem to you.

6. *Trust that God is taking people on a spiritual journey* and so it is okay to be only one part of that journey. Understanding this will free you to

realise that you don't always have to share everything with everyone all of the time. Sometimes being part of the journey is more important than trying to explain everything we know in one go. However, be careful not to use this as an excuse! Always be ready to go further, and always be prepared to explain it all.

7. *Realise that sharing your faith online is very similar to sharing your faith offline.* Whether we are online or offline, God wants us to have genuine concern for people, to be confident in what we believe, and to walk in the Spirit as we write or talk about Jesus, in ways that show how important he is to us, and in as natural a way as possible.
8. *Actively look for places to share your faith online.* Why not set aside some time each week to be intentional about sharing your faith over the Internet. You could choose to do one or two hours a week split over a couple of days, for example. There are many ways you could spend this time, but be very gospel-minded in your intentions. E.g.,
   - Join a discussion forum on a website of particular interest to you, so as to meet people with similar interests to you, with whom you can share Jesus as well as your mutual interest.
   - Spend the time on social media specifically looking to foster relationships with people in your local community whom you have not physically met before.
   - Volunteer to help with a Christian organisation that already has a specific evangelistic online strategy (e.g., Chatnow).

   Whatever you choose, remember that these couple of hours a week are intentionally about gospel opportunity—whether immediate opportunity or as part of a longer strategy. We need to remember at all times why we are doing it.

Chatnow

If you enjoy talking to people about Jesus and you are happy to spend time online, then volunteering to take chats from websites like chatnow.org would be a great fit for you, because you don't need to go looking for people to talk to: rather, an organisation can bring them to you!

chatnow.org is a website that is primarily evangelistic in aim and offers anyone, anywhere in the world, the opportunity to chat live one-to-one with a Christian at any time of day or night. The aim is that people who don't believe in Jesus will take one step closer to becoming his disciple through the time they spend visiting the website and chatting with a Christian online.

Last year, 185,000 people visited chatnow.org, and this resulted in 40,000 one-to-one online chats taking place. That is the equivalent of your sitting on a bench in the middle of your nearest shopping centre and watching people queue to sit down and talk to you about deep, heartfelt, life issues, with someone new arriving every 13 minutes, giving you the opportunity to have 110 chats every day of the year (that is, if you worked 24 hours every day)! Those wanting to find hope come from all over the world, with chatters arriving from 140+ countries each month. Some of these chats will be with Christians who are struggling in their faith, and others will be with those that follow a different faith or no faith, but who are exploring Christianity or simply looking to hear if there is an alternative hope somewhere out there!

There is a number of other websites across the world that also bring in evangelistic conversations, and Chatnow is working together with many of them to form one team of volunteers. Having an international team of Christians across the world willing to take conversations enables better continual coverage, with volunteers available 24 hours a day, every day of the year.

There is a number of different ways a church or an individual Christian could be involved with the exciting work of Chatnow. Here are three suggestions:

1. The easiest way to be involved is by simply placing a link on your church or personal website, to offer website visitors an opportunity to chat with a Christian.

2. You could sponsor local social media adverts which will be shown to those living in your area. These online "posters", offering the opportunity to chat with a Christian, are very good value and can reach thousands of local people, as they scroll through their social media accounts. In 2020, every £25 spent on local social media

advertising resulted in the online advert being shown to 5,000 people, in Chatnow's case, 150 of them clicking on the advert.

3. The most time-consuming, but also the most fulfilling way to be involved, is to join the international volunteer team and make yourself available to talk to people about Jesus online. All of Chatnow's chats are typed conversations rather than spoken: Chatnow never uses video, audio or anything that makes its volunteers identifiable outside of the chat software system. Each volunteer varies in how much time they help out: the minimum Chatnow asks for is 2 hours a week, but some volunteers are willing to commit up to 20 hours!

All the information about how to be involved in the work of Chatnow, how to support the work financially, and how sign up to receive its newsletter, is available on the chatnow.org website, or you can email matt@chatnow.org to ask for more information.

Conclusion

As I began, can I implore and encourage you and your church, not to go back to where you were before the pandemic? We mustn't step back. Whether we have returned to the old normality or a new, different normality—please don't breathe a sigh of relief and think, "Great: no more need to be online!". Instead, we need to learn how to do more online, and how to do what we do in the most effective way with the resources that we have, and to do it as well as we possibly can.

Remember a church's online presence is worth spending time, money and effort on, as it will affect your local community's perception of your relevance to them, and therefore also their view of the relevance of the message of Jesus that you bring.

For discussion

1. What practical obstacles do you face in sharing the gospel online?
2. What practical steps could you take as a church to get better in this area?

Chapter 20

Blended church—a new awakening?

Aderyn Taylor-Roberts

During the pandemic and its lockdowns, many churches struggled and some even closed. But many other churches learnt new ways of doing things. My fellowship, Forest Community Church in the Forest of Dean, was one such church. Here, I am sharing lessons that we learned that may help others adjust to a new mindset and new opportunities.

For the analogue (non-digital) church, the Covid experience was like a mission trip. At first, we thought we were going on a short-term trip to a place that felt foreign. We got there and had immediately to learn some new languages and methods. It turned out that over a two-year period, it was more like a long-term mission assignment. But meanwhile, from this "digital Babylon" (as David Kinnaman, the President of the Barna Group, termed it), we reached people whom we never thought possible. Looking back, we can say that it actually led us to a stronger, more relevant and durable way of doing ministry with traditional tools, digital tools, and everything in between. As Nicky Gumbel summed it up, 'We have tasted something better.'

In true Twitter/X style (direct and provoking), let's get straight to the point: as Peter Phillips, Head of Digital Theology at *Premier Christianity*, tweeted in late March 2020 as the pandemic began: 'We really need to get over this idea that church has to be physical. God isn't. Faith isn't. Prayer isn't. Worship isn't. Church is a community of people worshipping God, seeking to follow Christ. We can do all of that online regardless of a virus.'

The lengthy lockdowns brought a more nuanced approach in which we largely proved that the church and other Christian activities could exist online.

We were forced to practise what we preached—that 'we are co-workers in God's service; you are God's field, God's building' (1 Cor. 3: 9) and that there is nowhere to 'flee from His presence' (Ps. 139: 7–12). But is existing, and merely being present online, enough?

Moving swiftly past the theological question of whether we need to meet physically in order to be church, let's look at where we are now with the blending of the physical and spiritual church, the offline and online, fixtures and fittings and swipes and zooms. The pandemic has taught us so many lessons and made us rethink our attitudes and perceptions regarding church, mission, and the place of online church. While the building closed during the early lockdowns, the church did not. We continued to worship, pray, teach, and minister both online and offline. Churches upskilled in diverse ways and moved quickly to continue to witness to the mission of God despite buildings being closed.

That said, it took the pandemic to get the bulk of the church to understand that there is a desperate need for the church to go digital. For certain, a few churches were rethinking their digital presence long before 2020, but most viewed the digital world at best as a tool and a last-minute add-on to their "normal" activities. There were only a few outward-thinking churches that saw it as a ripe and abundant mission field.

For our church in the Forest of Dean, rather like the masses, the pandemic abruptly awakened us to become culturally relevant in the digital age—we had to be released from the shackles of the physical, because the option of meeting in our building simply wasn't there. Before that, real, missional, online church was always on the backburner, an afterthought because mission was always considered to be only authentic in the flesh. What has changed now is our perspective: what started by merely trying to hold our church congregation together quickly evolved into a new attitude and recognition that the digital world is only secondarily a tool; it is primarily a mission field.

The pandemic brought us to the crossroads of whether we choose to sit back into the well-worn, comfortable but rigid pew of the church building or whether we harness the power of the internet and technology as a tool for renewed engagement in mission.

It's not as though the church is unfamiliar with renewal. In Acts 15, the early church found new ways to welcome Gentiles. With Constantine, renewal came again (with all its up and downs), as it did with William Tyndale when, through the printing press and new Bible translations, the church was propelled through yet another renewal. I think you get my point: there have been many variations of renewal in our history, but the constant is that the church could not stick in its previous state. The COVID era was a time for renewal, and we cannot go back.

In the summer of 2021, church buildings re-opened, in-person meetings were restored, and church community activities resumed. But we should not be simply turning our backs with relief on digital and online possibilities. Here are seven starting points for churches to engage with as they seek to involve themselves fully in the new mission field of blended church.

1. A broadcast Sunday service is just the start

Broadcasting our Sunday meetings by internet is an obvious evangelistic tool that enables people to check out their local church while remaining anonymous. However, live-streaming your physical meeting, while giving valuable insight into your church and providing a platform for the gospel to be heard more widely, is simply putting your physical church service online. It is a one-sided conversation in which the viewer becomes a consumer, not an engager; indeed, it is not a conversation at all.

Livestreaming is just the start for blended church. The deeper question is how do we convey online the in-person experience of church that offers warm hellos and greetings of "how's things?" that actually wait patiently for the real answer, drinking coffee and eating biscuits, and sharing communion? If we only offer a broadcast service, we deny those who are searching the rich, multi-sensory, and authentic experience of God's intention for his church. They will be in danger of peaking at the church's perimeter without knowing what church is really meant to be like. This point also raises a hidden question about our physical meetings as church: by holding in-person 'services', are we restricting ourselves to what a limited set of middle-class people want or expect, while in our generation many more ordinary people are looking for something more informal and authentic in the encounter?

We now have access to a plethora of platforms: YouTube, Zoom, Facebook, Google, Teams . . . The list is endless. They provide a variety of pathways for connection that is real and authentic. A key question has already been touched on: is the particular mechanism in mind a one-way mechanism, or does the mechanism permit interaction and participation, and so promote relationship? It takes longer and more perseverance, but true relationship can be found. At Forest Community Church, we have placed huge emphasis on the importance of staying and being connected online in various ways, through Zoom Coffee Meetings, Prayer Groups, WhatsApp conversation, Facebook Interest Groups, Small Group studies, interviews online, quiz evenings, worship evenings, open gardens (yes, we did this online!), collaborative worship videos, and more.

In seeking interaction and participation online, here are three more detailed guidelines:

> Utilise all that is available to you and make sure to invite the housebound, vulnerable, disabled, the anonymous to connect.
>
> Being truly blended does not stop with adding digital to in-person meeting. We can utilise the phone, paper letters, mobile. It is in the true blending of all these that we can form genuine connections.
>
> 'All these are the work of one and the same Spirit, and he distributes them to each one as he determines. The body is a unit, though it is composed of many parts. And although its parts are many, they all form one body.' (1 Cor. 12: 11 & 12)

2. Put your money where the mission field is

For the future, church leaders need to realise that people who are engaging from home or other places need to count just as much as those who attending in person. What we have to understand is that this trend of more people accessing the church online and choosing to participate from home, isn't about people dropping out. It's about people who are leaning in. And to continue to serve those and reach out missionally, our budgets need to reflect this. Pastor Carey

Nieuwhof recently stated that he now encourages churches to spend 50% of their staffing budget on online services. This may initially seem crazy, until you realise that during the lockdowns over 90% of all church staff were online pastors or producers. Since then, most have returned to their day-jobs, but the opportunities of online church remain. With all the "normal" ministries having started up again, is this need being met? Are we just dropping out of this mission field, going back behind the wall, or are we allocating sufficient resources to online church and evangelism?

Every budget line needs to be scrutinized. Questions that need to be asked are:

> What does this enable us to do?
> Does this help us accomplish our mission?
> How can we measure the success of this programme?
> What should this programme look like if we want to serve both our physical and digital communities?
> Is our church the best one to create or own this programme, or should we partner with the work of another organization?

Every pound that you free up from old, outdated programmes is a pound you can now invest in reaching people in ways that are culturally relevant, measurable, and effective.

3. In an age of excess, simplicity is key

As highlighted above, many in our churches assumed that the post-lockdown era would see a return to the "normal" hubbub of activities in church life. But can we be more effective if we focus on simplicity as we prayerfully seek to forge new paths in this developing mission field? Can we keep the church lean, while reaching the most that we can? I call this Back-to-Basics—a return to the true calling of churches: discipleship. It requires churches to focus on doing a few things well and trimming the excess. There is a correlation between what you do and what you get: if we return to trying to do a scattering of everything from our building and now also online, we return to being another social club, community centre or fan page. That in turn draws us away from discipleship,

discipleship not as a programme but as the entire aim of the church. Just as we can't be everywhere physically in our community, we can't be everywhere digitally, and we must often evaluate and return to the basics when needed.

At Forest Community Church, we have taken the post-pandemic years as an opportunity to reset—to look in-depth at our ministries and question all we have been doing. We have re-evaluated our mission and vision statements to be more in line with the era we are now in. And each ministry now has to be in line with this vision and moving together with the church to fulfil the mission. Far from being a top-heavy or stifling experience, it has brought a much more cohesive approach to our church body, and its ministries are feeling more supported and engaged.

4. There's no replacement for face-to-face experience together

But does that mean digital is impersonal? Quite the opposite. Here's what one pastor told me:

> I was a critic of digital ministry until we were forced to switch. I'm completely converted. The quality and depth of the conversations I'm having with people online is incredible. Never have I been able go so personal, so quickly as I am right now. People are willing to share very personal things with me that they would never talk about in our building.

Not only can personal interactions be surprisingly intimate online, but it's also now possible to know more than ever before about your community, and your engaged audiences (whether online or physically present). Churches are using macro-level information to learn things such as:

> What are the demographics of the communities that we serve?
> Are the marriages in our church healthier now, compared to a year ago?
> How many people are visiting our website for a first, second, or third week in a row?

What are the spiritual postures of people in different neighbourhoods nearby?

These questions and many more can be answered, and can lead to incredible ministry opportunities. Churches can attract, get, keep, and grow people more effectively now than ever before.

5. Blended is diverse, in every way

You don't need a big budget to make effective use of digital tools. In fact, congregations from all over are finding creative ways to reach more people than ever before. At Forest Community Church, we started with a simple mobile phone, and we still make use of it now, even though we have had significant upgrades. But what is the thing that's working? Is it our tech upgrade? It's not slick production, fancy lights or multi-camera setups. Those are nice-to-haves. What reaches people is authenticity.

When our pastor, Tim Cracknell, goes live for a three-minute honest comment on a smartphone, the engagement is significant. How do we know? Do we just look at insights from digital data? Well, yes, we do, but it's the private messages we get, in-person conversations and real-life connections that have taken place because of these honest and real, short snippets of his life, spiritual struggles and biblical wisdom have touched people in places where a 30-minute sermon cannot.

Further, digital pathways provide the means for any congregation to reach any individual—crossing the lines of ethnicity, community, and social station. Groups are not left behind. The digital platform is multi-ethnic and multi-generational, and it becomes our primary faucet for disseminating the gospel.

6. Blended is both gathered and scattered, and is neither

Is small group still small group when it's over video? Does virtual prayer count as a meeting for prayer? Can a person grow spiritually in a community that interacts through screens?

I'm not arguing that Matthew 18: 20 is irrelevant. But what if 'where two or three are gathered' could extend to new definitions of "gathered?" Could God still move through pixels? Some analysis may help:

- Things that can only be done in person:

  Face-to-face fellowship
  Corporate worship
  Community care and outreach
  Local ministry

- Things that can only be done online:

  Streaming
  Targeted communication
  Personalization
  Data-informed leadership
  Measuring growth over time

- Things that can be better with a blend of in-person and digital together:

  Worship
  Bible teaching
  Prayer
  Evangelism
  Giving
  Groups
  Leader Development

Followers of Jesus, shaped by biblical understanding, are in a good position to appreciate this blended approach. The Bible itself is divided into Old and New Testaments, because Jesus fulfilled the old covenant between God and his people and brought in a new one (Hebrews 8). The old was not simply rejected, but rather superseded by bringing its original intention to new expression. The old and new were not just bolted together—Jesus said that new wine needed new wineskins (Mt. 9: 17). But what was of value in the old was carried into the new in fresh ways—the new was in continuity with, and completion of, those values. Jesus said that every scribe who has been trained for the kingdom of heaven is like a master of a house, who brings out of his treasure what is new and what is old (Mt. 13: 52)

7. People may not be looking for church, but they are looking for answers

If we think about the five core areas of human flourishing, our world is disrupted in all of them: spiritual, relationships, finances, vocation, and health. If your church is preaching Scripture, then you have something to offer your community in all of these areas! The question is, will you be able to reach these people in the new ways that will be necessary if you are to reach them?

Reaching people through an aspect of their lives where they are conscious of acute need can lead to gospel conversations, spiritual formation, and deeper discipleship opportunities. This applies in person, and it applies online. The arrival of digital communication challenges us to think about how to be a more externally focused church.

As we face this new era of renewal and uncertainty, there is a danger that, as people return to their 'old' roles, all the hard work and investment in online services, discipleship and community will be lost—not entirely because of lack of desire, but because we aren't implementing it. Let us plan and work for forms of blended church that put the gospel at its very core, both online and offline, digital and analogue, blended in a variety of ways. Let's recognise the blended church for the gift it is: a rich and effective tool to draw individuals forward on their spiritual journey. Let's recognise that relationship is the catalyst for growth, where intimate, life-on-life discipleship often involves in-person connections (as it should), but we can make vital use of additional tools in the process. Not just as an alternative, but to enrich the personal connection!

Let us truly recognise that the pandemic may have been the salvation of the church in many ways. For us at Forest Community Church, it liberated us from a Sunday/weekend-centric approach. It forced us online and into social media. It also made us open to change, to being creative when previously we were neither creative nor open to innovation. It also got us back down to raw mission—what is our mission? Add all that up, and it is dangerously close to an awakening.

Ultimately, let us remember that the gospel message is not tied to any one delivery mechanism, and regardless of medium, it never returns void: 'It is the same with my word. I send it out, and it always produces fruit. It will accomplish all I want it to, and it will prosper everywhere I send it." (Is. 55: 11 (NLT)).

Many are hearing the groans of a broken world in need of a saviour. The gospel message is more needed now than ever.

Let us not fear the uncertain path for 'The Lord himself goes before you and will be with you; he will never leave you nor forsake you. Do not be afraid; do not be discouraged.' (Dt. 31: 8)

For discussion

1. How would blended church help your church and why?
2. What good things that your church did during the 'pandemic' should continue and why?

Chapter 21

Healing broken lives[1]

Allan S. McKinnon

Forever changed

Our afternoon routines were interrupted by an urgent 'hodi hodi!', the Tanzanian equivalent of 'knocking the door'. Bursting into our rural home, a local teacher quickly explained that a young girl aged 14 had a broken leg—would we rush her to Nkoaranga hospital, high on the mountain? Drawing on our first aid manual, 'Where there is no doctor', we sprang into action. The girl was in agony with a broken femur which we carefully splinted. Paracetamol, and sugary tea to dull the pain and deal with shock. Carefully, we manoeuvred her into our make-shift ambulance, an ancient Land Rover 109, where she lay out on the floor of the back compartment, while she cried out and hollered. The noise subsided for a time but, as we climbed the rugged road to the hospital, bumps and jolts drew from the young girl the most terrible screams. There was nothing I could do to make the journey smoother. I felt helpless. But then the Lord spoke to my heart: 'reach out behind you, lay your hand on her leg and pray for healing.'

My heart and my flesh were in turmoil. My stomach churned, my thoughts reeled, my mind debated, my head believed, my heart doubted. For 40 mins that seemed to last an eternity, I wrestled with God, but refused to act according to the Spirit's prompting. Finally, we arrived. The medics took over. She got her leg set in plaster and was forever grateful. I was forever changed. This

1. This chapter does not rehearse the debate around the continuation of the sign gifts to the church, but assumes God can still apportion these gifts as he wills.

incident changed my theology of healing forever. I swore to the Lord that I would never again refuse the promptings of his Spirit or the request of others who are suffering to pray for their healing. The rest is upon the Lord.

The mystery of healing

Someone has said, 'The subject of healing is one of the greatest mysteries of the universe. We are big enough to ask the questions, but we are not big enough to understand all the answers.' The story that changed my perspective on healing was not the story of a miracle, but of what might have been. It is in this place of tension that the mystery of healing lies. In personal experience, I have seen God answer prayer miraculously for complete physical healing and restoration to full health within my close family: a case which was 'verified' as such by the medical consultant who 'ran out of scientific explanations'. I could also recount how the pursuit of a miraculous intervention in the lives of others who have suffered badly from physical illness and disease has resulted in no such miraculous provision. We have many questions about healing. We often are short of answers. We have no answers to explain why or how healing comes. We have no answers to offer when it does not. Nevertheless, this mystery seems unable to stem the ever-rising hope that we have as human beings that what is wrong may be righted, what is painful might be relieved, what brings suffering and tears might be exchanged for joy and gladness.

Healing may be defined in different ways. Physical healing as cited above is the assumption that most people make when the subject of healing arises. Yet there is more to healing than mere physical wholeness. The gospel of the Lord Jesus Christ offers so much more than merely 'fixing' our temporal bodies. Neither does a human body necessarily define who we are, or how we feel. Dis-ease may be in the mind. Gladness and joy, peace and acceptance, may yet be found in a body that is considered by some to be 'broken'. Healing perhaps ought to be better defined as the restoration of health or well-being. With such a broad definition to hand, the mystery of 'healing' remains—it may yet be found in the midst of a fallen and broken world.

That mysterious pursuit of wholeness and well-being is an age-old trait of human beings. As those made in the image of our Maker, this should not surprise us. Fundamental to our understanding of who God is, the assertion that God is good, drives us away from everything less than good (even by our poor measure of it). We know that God wants us to be whole—fully and completely as he made us to be from the beginning. The biblical origins of suffering and disease, illness and the general brokenness of our world, are written into the account of the fall of mankind in Genesis 3. Yet God's good purposes to redeem and restore his fallen world speak loudly from the same pages. God is good. His purposes are good. His intentions towards all that he has made are good. Even physical healing is clearly part of God's good design, built into the DNA of our biological make up: wounds usually heal, illness is often only for a season until wellness is recovered. We enjoy the healing and restoring touch of the Almighty more often than we care to acknowledge. He heals us, he saves us, time and time again.

Our broken world

Not only are *we* in need of saving, but we brush shoulders with *people* every day who are in need of saving, of rescue from the dis-ease of suffering and pain. The pain of suffering and evil run much deeper than physical or psychological pain. Steven Anderson writes, 'There are too many people, both in the church and outside the church, living their lives subject to all manner of fears, inner pain and torment. Many of these people feel as if they are in the grip of an enemy too powerful for them to overcome.'

This sense of being oppressed or down-trodden, of suffering and pain, that arises in the hearts of many aligns well with the biblical perspective on our broken world. Suffering and disease are closely bound to questions about the nature and origin of evil. The universal experience of humanity's suffering may well vary in kind, or intensity and frequency for different groups and individuals, but the Bible makes it clear that suffering was not part of God's original design. Rather pain and toil and hardship are an outcome of human sin and rebellion against God's ways according to the biblical narrative (Gen. 3: 1–19). An Enemy has deceived and tricked us into pursuing our own selfish ends and the outcome of our foolishness is darkness, depression and despair. Nevertheless, this Enemy has been overcome by one stronger than he—the Lord Jesus himself (Ps. 18: 16–19; Mk. 3: 27; Jn. 10: 10–11). This is the good news that a broken world of broken people needs to hear.

Yet, we discover in the biblical story that, in the providence of God, even the broken world, and the consequences of our suffering arising in this world, can be used by God for good. Joseph's perspective on a life of suffering and injustice was '. . . you meant evil [misery, distress, injury] against me, but God meant it for good [welfare, benefit, happiness], to bring it about that many people should be kept alive [be restored to life or health], as they are today' (Gen. 50: 20 (RSV)). Clearly, God sometimes allows suffering in the world for reasons that may be beyond our immediate comprehension. God sometimes allows suffering so that his glory might be displayed in the life of the sufferer (Jn. 9: 1–3). On other occasions, suffering is interpreted as a learning experience (2 Cor. 12: 7–10) that leads towards maturity of character and Christlikeness (Rom. 5: 3–5) and even to assist us in ministering to others (2 Cor. 1: 3–7). But none of this is to exclude or erase the clear promises of God to heal and to deliver, to rescue and to save. Instead, the complexity of the biblical teaching on healing leaves room for mystery. And it gives us hope of the in-breaking Kingdom of God, promising us a taste of a world that is yet to come in all its fulness—ransomed, healed, restored and forgiven.

The LORD our Healer

There is no question about the revelation of God in the Bible asserting as it does so clearly, that 'the LORD God is Healer' (Jehovah Rapha) (Ex. 15: 26). The occasion of such a clear statement assures the people of God that, as they walk in obedience to him, then he will not bring upon them any of the diseases that he brought upon the Egyptians. The fact that it occurs in relation to a miraculous provision of palatable water points us to the Lord's commitment to bring (the water of) life and wholeness to his people now and forever (see also Ex. 23: 25–26; Jn. 4: 10–14; Ezek. 47: 1–12; Rev. 22: 1–2).

This agenda from God's story of redemption is spoken of in Psalms where 'salvation' extends not only to the forgiveness of sins but also the healing of 'all our diseases' (Ps. 103: 1 &2). That this blessing is to be extended to 'many nations' (Is. 52: 15; 53: 11–12) is secured by the Lord's servant who will suffer on their behalf so that they may not suffer (Is. 53: 3–5). In Matthew's Gospel, he interprets these verses concerning the Lord's servant as being descriptive of the ministry that Jesus himself conducted among the oppressed and the sick, "He took up our infirmities and bore our diseases." (Mt. 8: 16 & 17). Matthew's theology of a God who heals is set squarely in the midst of numerous incidents of miraculous interventions by Jesus and is a commission for his disciples to do likewise (Mt. 8: 1–10: 1). 'He gave them authority to drive out impure spirits and to heal every disease and sickness.' Other Gospel writers chime in with their accounts of Jesus' own perspective on his ministry. Luke recounts the reading of Isaiah's scroll in the synagogue at Capernaum, where Jesus sets forth his identity as the Lord's servant and his corresponding manifesto: 'The Spirit of the Lord is on me to proclaim the good new . . . recovery of sight to the blind, to set the oppressed free, [19] to proclaim the year of the Lord's favour.' (Lk. 4: 18 & 19; compare Is. 61: 1 & 2). Even Mark wants it to be clear that Jesus has this kind of authority over sickness and demonic forces. In his opening chapter, the news of Jesus' healing ministry results in many following him, but Mark is quick to remind us of deeper healing that is required at the hands of this Physician who said, 'It is not the healthy who need a doctor, but the sick. I have not come to call the righteous, but sinners [to repentance].' (Mk. 2: 17).

Jesus and his disciples ministered healing to the sick. The apostles expected and taught that these gifts would continue among the early church (1 Cor. 12: 11). They exhorted others to pray expectantly for healing, because 'the Lord will raise him up' (Jas. 5: 14).

As we review this short theology of healing in the Bible, the testimony stands that God is a healing God and his son, Jesus, as well as his first disciples, practised a ministry of healing among ordinary people. In Mark's Gospel, the healing ministry is a means to affirm or prove that Jesus is the son of God, that he is 'the Holy One of God'. In John's Gospel, he recounts *some* of the signs and wonders that Jesus did, 'so that you may believe that Jesus is the Christ, the son of God, and that by believing you may have life in his name.' (Jn 20: 31). On the day of Pentecost, the crowd heard testimony to 'the mighty works of God' carried out by Jesus and undoubtedly consummated in his own resurrection from the dead! The works of healing continue in the ministries of Peter and John (Acts 3: 1–16), but by the authority (name) of Jesus Christ. They are attested in the life of Paul and James. They continue to be available to the body of Christ in the power of the Spirit as he distributes gifts to people at his own discretion. To some 'the working of miracles' to another 'gifts of healing'. This language of the New Testament encourages us to be expectant, but also to be humble and dependent upon the God who heals 'as he wills' (1 Cor. 12: 4–11).

Practising healing in today's world

As disciples of the Lord Jesus Christ, are there ways in which we can practise healing and/or deliverance ministry in our world today? Are there biblical reasons for us to practise such a ministry among ordinary people? I am convinced through an examination of the biblical evidence, practical experience, certain church traditions, sound reason and the testimony of the wider community of God's people, that both these questions should be answered positively. Here is how I would recommend our practice in today's world.

1. **Expect the gifts of healing to be a witness to the deity of the Lord Jesus Christ.**

We should not be ashamed of the good news because it is the power of God for the salvation of everyone who believes. We live in a society that is marked by scepticism and unbelief, and the exercise of faith in asking for and expecting God's intervention in restoring health, well-being and peace to broken lives is still part of the good news. This ranges from restored physical well-being (and the healing of all other human hurts and pain) to a spiritual well-being that knows true peace with God through our Lord Jesus Christ. The risen and living Lord Jesus is still able to save to the uttermost all who will come to him. Invite and encourage people to have this expectancy of God in the privacy of their hearts before God, but also publicly before the congregation (Mk. 5: 25–34).

2. **Exercise faith that the gifts of healing may be given so that we can serve one another.**

All spiritual gifts given are for the common good, so that church might be built up, and the name of the Lord Jesus Christ be glorified. This is their purpose. The common good includes bringing us to maturity—we are to 'grow up in every way' into Christ. The practical task of exercising our faith helps us grow and be built up in love the one for another. We need to do it, not simply believe it. Our faith is made complete by what we do.

3. **Engage actively with the Spirit of God by choosing to walk in his power daily.**

The gifts that the Spirit gives are not demanded, or commanded, but offered at his discretion. The servant of the Lord has an ear inclined to God as he wakens him morning by morning (Is. 50: 4ff). We must learn to cultivate sensitive hearing that allows us to discern the mind of the Spirit. Living in this close communion with the Spirit allows us to be expectant and to exercise any gifts of healing or miracles that he may prompt us towards.

4. **Submit to the will of God in healing and deliverance ministry.**

This is true of all ministry but perhaps especially here in the area of spiritual gifts. This is not a 'get out clause', but it is an honest and open admission that God alone is God and we are not! It is a recognition that our human pride easily gets in the way in the exercise of 'the sign gifts'. God must be honoured, and his name given primacy in all these activities. We expect great things from God, we exercise our faith in a God who is able, we engage with the Spirit deliberately and actively, so that God's will might be done on earth as it is in heaven.

Help for devastated people

The need for healing and full deliverance in our world today is obvious. The ruins of people's lives need to be rebuilt, the brokenness of personal conflicts need to be renewed, the fragmentation of family relations need to be restored, the wanderer and the lost need to be returned. This is the language of Isaiah 61 which describes the servant of the Lord and the ministers of our God who proclaim the year of the Lord's favour for the display of God's splendour. There is in my mind and heart a relevant ministry described for us to practise today. A ministry that offers healing and restoration to a people who have been 'devastated for generations' (Is. 61: 4). Let's believe the Lord that he will do it.

For discussion

1. Having reflected on this chapter, what more can you church do for the 'sick' and what could that look like?
2. How could applying this help your church to grow?

A personal addendum and application

Martin Erwin

This chapter helpfully and biblically challenges us to raise our expectations in light of Scripture, to deepen our knowledge of God, and to expect growth in faith through the exercising it.

Some years ago, I had a conversation with a church elder and friend about the place and nature of healing today. He told me a story about a family of unbelievers who were connected to their church. The fellowship had prayed for a sick child in that family in a simple way at their weekly prayer meeting. The church prayed for healing, and that such healing would be a sign pointing to the power of the gospel and the person, work, and authority of the Lord Jesus. The child prayed for was healed, and it led to some of the family coming to faith in Christ. My friend said, "I think healing is more connected to the gospel that we realise." He added, with a twinkle in his eye, "I'm never too worried about praying for healing for some of our frail folks in the church, death for them is a doorway to glory and heaven, so they'll be better off going!"

That conversation led me to reconsider healing in the Scriptures, and particularly in the Gospels and in relation to the growth of the Church in the book of Acts. My friend was onto something. The prophecy of Joel, quoted by Peter in Acts 2 on the day of Pentecost, says

> Even on my servants, both men and women,
> I will pour out my Spirit in those days,
> and they will prophesy.
> I will show wonders in the heavens above
> and signs on the earth below.
>
> Acts 2: 18, 19

The Lord promised his disciples that signs would accompany their preaching of the gospel (Mk. 16: 15ff), and that is exactly what they experienced. Indeed, the final words of the Gospel of Mark read, 'Then the disciples went out and preached everywhere, and the Lord worked with them and **confirmed his word by the signs that accompanied it**.' (Mk. 16: 20)

Many hold a cessationist view regarding certain gifts (including healing), and even if we shift our view, we remain deeply uneasy when we see some of the 'grandstanding' of prosperity-style preachers who claim healings and miracles as part of their menu.

Let me offer an alternative understanding and experience of how such signs might work out in our evangelistic ministry.

I was invited by a close friend and pastor from a church in Hereford to attend a day conference for evangelists. His church 'stream' had its roots in the charismatic House Church movement, and the conference had a different feel to others that I had attended from my own background. The day was good, the teaching was encouraging, and the passion for reaching lost people with the gospel was tangible. At the end of the day, a group of visiting African evangelists were asked to pray for the gathering. We were encouraged to lift our hands as they prayed for God's Holy Spirit to bring a fresh anointing of power in our preaching AND to accompany the preaching with signs. I felt my hands gently warmed, and I asked that God would fill me again that day. But, strangely, only my hands were warmed and felt touched by the Lord.

As we travelled home, I said nothing of my unusual experience.

Perhaps a year later I was chatting with the pastor, stacking chairs after a joint evening Celebration. I told him of the weird occurrence that day, of my hands being warmed, but 'nothing else!' I confessed that I was left a little disappointed, that perhaps I had hoped for something different. Wisely, he smiled and asked, "Did you ever think that maybe God simply wanted to touch your hands? Martin, you are an evangelist, and I have been praying that God might give you boldness to lay hands on folk as you share the Good News, and where appropriate, pray for healing and deliverance."

I was stunned. How simple that perhaps indeed the Lord might do such a thing.

At our outreach tent that summer at the Three Counties Show in Malvern, we encouraged those on our team who felt so led, to offer to pray with visitors in the tent, gently and boldly interceding on their behalf. One of our evangel-ists prayed for a man with a painful knee dating from a war wound from the

Falklands war. He (an unbeliever, sitting next to his wife who described herself as a clairvoyant) immediately stood up and loudly declared "I can't believe it, the pain is gone!" He described a gentle warmth that had enveloped him as he was prayed for. The incident led to a deep engagement, sharing the gospel, and taking of Christian literature.

The following week, my wife and I were relating the story from Malvern to our house group. We met each week in the home of an elderly couple—she was a believer, and he was not. That week Edna had taken a tumble at the top of her stairs and her back had frozen solid. As we told the story, she cried out in her charming Lancashire accent, "Well, can't you and Rachel pray for me like that?" "Oh boy, here goes," I thought to myself. We sat either side of her on the arms of her old velvet covered armchair. With her permission, as the group watched on, we gently placed our hands on her back and began to pray. As we prayed, and much to our surprise, she began to groan and say things like 'Oh my,' and 'Oh boy!' To be honest, it was all a little awkward.

As we finished, she explained that a warmth had flowed through her back, she could feel the pain leaving, and right enough, she was up and about in no time!

Did it lead to her partner trusting Jesus? Sadly no. In fact, he put it down to 'coincidence,' though he was always asking for signs and proofs of God.

Healing in the context of evangelism seems wholly biblical, and gently we have seen God at work in this area. Maybe the Lord is encouraging you to step out in faith as you share the Good News, so that, like Paul, as we too come in weakness, we might say, "My message and my preaching were not with wise and persuasive words, but with a demonstration of the Spirit's power, so that your faith might not rest on human wisdom, but on God's power." (1 Cor. 2: 4, 5)

Conclusion

Martin Erwin

Well, that's it! Or is it or should it be?

Not too far from where I live is the Haynes motor museum, a veritable display of all things 'car.' When I was growing up, Haynes manuals were all the rage. Every new make or model of car had a Haynes manual, produced so the home mechanic or boy racer could discover all there was to know about his car. (I say 'his' as back then, it did seem to be a very male-oriented pastime to own and devour car manuals!)

The truth, of course, is that owning and reading a manual could teach me a lot about my car, but the real joy was not in owning or reading the book, but in having and driving the car. I bought the book on the Vauxhall Chevette that I shared with my older brother, but, I must say, the book is long forgotten. The sheer joy came in getting behind the wheel, driving that metallic blue saloon, and discovering the thrill and freedom of having a car.

Reading a book on evangelism has, I hope, been a blessing and an encouragement for you. However, the reason surely for owning and reading this book is that you have a sense that you want to get out and 'drive'. The discussion or reflection questions at the end of each chapter are there because we would love you to put the book down and pick up the opportunities that God will give you to make Jesus known where you are. Not all, of course, are called or gifted to be an evangelist, but each of us are called to be a witness. "You will be my witnesses," said the Lord Jesus to his disciples in Acts 1: 8, and this statement is still true for each of us.

Often, when a Counties evangelist shares the gospel, or works with a team of volunteers, some will say, 'I can't do what you do.' Others might think, 'I wish I could do as you do!'

Those two thoughts remind me again of my first car. You see, the only way to gain experience in driving was to grab the keys of my old Chevette and get out on the road. As a young lad, the Lord preserved me from many mistakes and near-mishaps. I remember telling my older brother that I had accidentally spun the car, thankfully causing no damage or harm to myself or others. My brother smiled: "I did the same thing last week, and dad spun it in Belfast a month ago!" he chuckled. Apparently, this was an easy error to make in handling this particular model.

Only two things would have been able to help me not to make this error. First, it would have helped if my dad and brother had told me what they had done, how the mistake happened, and how to avoid it myself. Secondly, the surefire way never to do it again was to get behind the wheel and experience it for myself.

This book fulfils the first part of 'how to learn.' The second and most thrilling part requires getting out there and giving it a go. Taking evangelism 'for a spin'!

"I can't do what you do!"

The great nineteenth-century evangelist, D. L. Moody, was once challenged by a woman who said, "Mr Moody, I don't like your way of doing evangelism!" After a brief conversation, Moody asked the woman, "how do you do evangelism?"

"I don't," she responded.

"It is clear you don't like my way of doing evangelism. You raise some good points. Frankly, I sometimes do not like my way of doing evangelism. But I like my way of doing it better than your way of not doing it."[1]

This book has been full of testimonies, ideas, methods and principles for sharing the gospel of Jesus. Our heart in writing this book is simply that you,

1. The Best Method for Sharing the Gospel | U.S. News (christianpost.com)

and many others, might be inspired to step out and share the good news of Jesus.

Another Evangelist, Billy Sunday, received advice that he was told would keep him from backsliding as a young believer. "Take 15 minutes each day to listen to God talking to you; take 15 minutes each day to talk to God; take 15 minutes each day to talk to others about God."[2]

That would be a great place to start!

"I wish I could do as you do!"

Maybe the second of these two thoughts has been stirring in your heart? As a teenager, I wanted to tell everyone about Christ. The gospel was not just powerful; it was simple, it was glorious, and it was for everyone! I gave out tracts, went preaching with church leaders who were keen to give me opportunities, led a Sunday school class, and joined GLO summer teams.[3]

Start where you are, pray for opportunities, and take the opportunities that the Lord gives you. And if you believe that the Lord may be gifting and calling you to serve him as an evangelist, speak to your church leaders and get in touch with us at Counties to see how we might be able to help you, train you, and support you in doing the work of an evangelist.

People are lost and broken, sin is still destroying lives, and our world STILL needs Jesus. Thank you for reading this book. Now, may the Lord help you as you step out to make Jesus known, where you are, today and tomorrow.

2. How to Not Backslide | Ministry127
3. GLO Europe Mission | Gospel Literature Outreach (glo-europe.org)

Learning more about evangelism

THE GOSPEL COMES WITH A HOUSE KEY

(The Good Book Company)

Rosario Butterfield

This is simply the best book that you can get on using your home for evangelism. It shows how the most challenging of people can be reached through Christian love.

TACTICS: A GAME PLAN FOR DISCUSSING YOUR CHRISTIAN CONVICTIONS

(Zondervan)

Greg Koukl

This is as much a book on apologetics as it is on evangelism, and all the better for it. Koukl demonstrates how to control a gospel conversation and graciously steer it towards a point of decision.

WITNESSING: HOW TO GIVE AWAY YOUR FAITH

(IVP)

Paul E. Little

Some books never grow old and this is one of them. Little gives some down-to-earth and practical advice on how to share faith with friends and acquaintances.

LEARNING TO SHARE THE GOOD NEWS: EVANGELISM AND THE LOCAL CHURCH

(Partnership)

Stephen McQuoid

A textbook on evangelism and the local church. It covers the challenges to evangelism as well as methods, both of church-based evangelism and personal evangelism.

QUESTIONING EVANGELISM: ENGAGING PEOPLE'S HEARTS THE WAY JESUS DID

(Kregal Publications (Third Edition, 2023))

Randy Newman

Newman copies Jesus' style in evangelism by asking questions of the enquirer. He draws on years of experience as a university evangelist, showing how to handle even the most delicate of gospel conversations.

EVANGELISM AND THE SOVEREIGNTY OF GOD

(IVP)

J. I. Packer

This book is somewhat of a classic. It argues that God's sovereignty is not a discouragement to evangelism, but actually an incentive to support it.

EVANGELISM IN THE EARLY CHURCH: HOW THE FIRST CHRISTIANS SPREAD THE GOOD NEWS

(Eerdmans (rev. ed. 2023))

Michael Green

Another classic, which roots understanding of evangelism in the New Testament and shows how the early Christians related the process to the society of their day.

EVANGELISM THROUGH THE LOCAL CHURCH: A COMPREHENSIVE GUIDE TO ALL ASPECTS OF EVANGELISM

Eerdmans (rev. ed. 2023))

Michael Green

This book is both scholarly and practical. Green brings together his knowledge of the Bible, church history and practical experience to provide us with a complete guide to evangelism.

THE ART OF NEIGHBOURING: BUILDING GENUINE RELATIONSHIPS RIGHT OUTSIDE YOUR DOOR

(Baker Books)

Jay Pathak & Dave Runyon

The authors argue that life has changed and now we tend not to know much about our neighbours. This book appeals to and encourages Christians to develop really good relationships with people in their street and neighbourhood so that they can share the gospel.

OUT OF THE SALTSHAKER AND INTO THE WORLD

(IVP)

Rebecca Manley Pippert

Pippert argues that evangelism is not just something you do, but rather it is a whole way of life. Evangelism is not just what we say, but our whole lifestyle.

EVANGELISM: HOW THE WHOLE CHURCH SPEAKS OF JESUS

(Crossway)

J. Mack Stiles

Evangelism should not be programme-driven because it is then too routine and scripted. Rather everyone in church should be talking to their friends about Jesus and he shows us how.

HONEST EVANGELISM

(The Good Book Company)

Rico Tice

Tice could not be boring if he tried. This wonderful little book encourages us to keep going in evangelism even when it is tough, and it does so with humour and compassion.

KNOW AND TELL THE GOSPEL

(Matthias Media)

John C. Chapman

This book is a simple and straightforward guide to how to share the gospel. It is easily accessible and very practical. It is also confidence building.

THE GOSPEL—WHAT IS IT?

(Partnership)

Alistair Hornal

This is a workbook written to help Christians properly to understand what the gospel is. It is well written, very accessible, and excellent in a house group context to prepare Christians for evangelism.